Precious *and* Adored

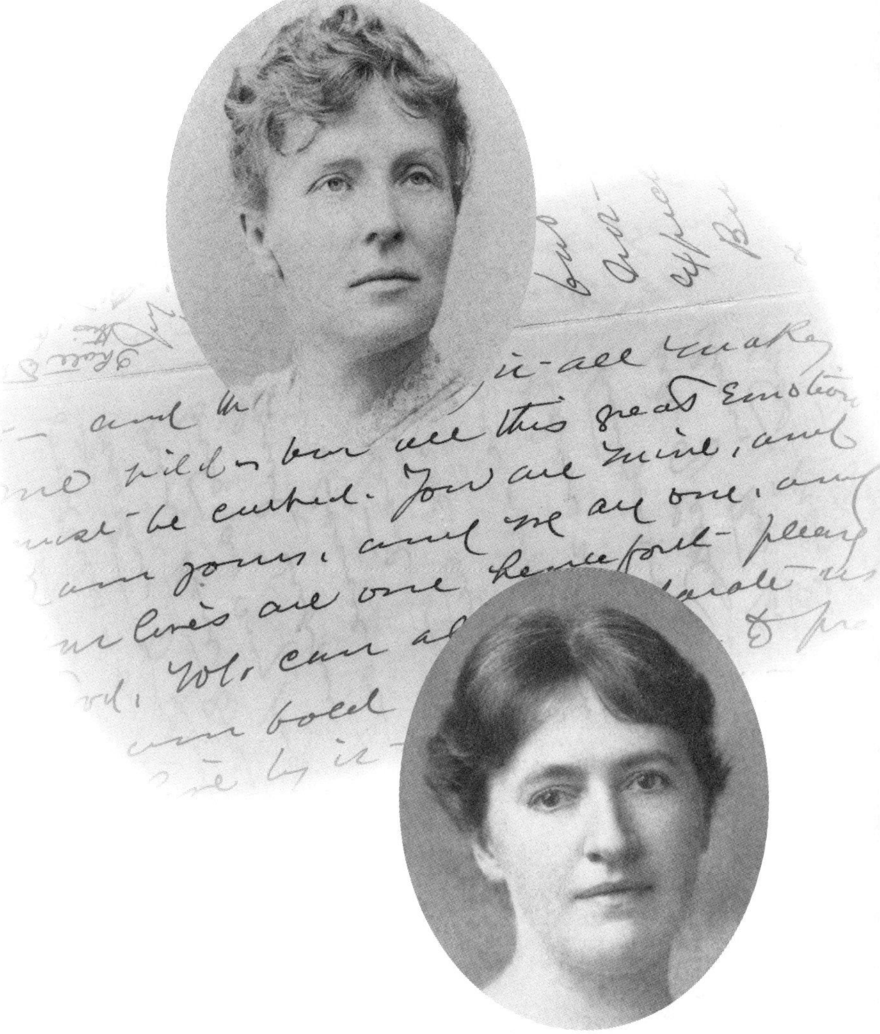

Precious and Adored

The Love Letters *of*
Rose Cleveland
and
Evangeline Simpson Whipple,
1890–1918

EDITED BY
Lizzie Ehrenhalt *and* Tilly Laskey

MINNESOTA
HISTORICAL
SOCIETY PRESS

The publication of this book was supported though a generous grant from the June D. Holmquist Publications and Research Fund.

The publication of this book was also supported, in part, with a gift from an anonymous donor.

mnhspress.org

The Minnesota Historical Society Press is a member of the Association of University Presses.

Manufactured in the United States of America

10 9 8 7 6 5 4 3 2 1

♾ The paper used in this publication meets the minimum requirements of the American National Standard for Information Sciences—Permanence for Printed Library Materials, ANSI Z39.48–1984.

International Standard Book Number
ISBN: 978-1-68134-129-3 (paper)
ISBN: 978-1-68134-130-9 (e-book)

Library of Congress Cataloging-in-Publication Data
Names: Cleveland, Rose Elizabeth, 1846–1918, correspondent. | Ehrenhalt, Lizzie, 1982– editor. | Laskey, Tilly, 1966– editor. | Whipple, Evangeline Simpson, 1857–1930, correspondent.
Title: Precious and adored : the love letters of Rose Cleveland and Evangeline Simpson Whipple, 1890–1918 / edited by Lizzie Ehrenhalt and Tilly Laskey.
Description: St. Paul, MN : Minnesota Historical Society Press, [2019] | Includes bibliographical references and index.
Identifiers: LCCN 2018060568 | ISBN 9781681341293 (pbk. : alk. paper) | ISBN 9781681341309 (ebook)
Subjects: LCSH: Cleveland, Rose Elizabeth, 1846–1918—Correspondence. | Whipple, Evangeline Simpson, 1857–1930—Correspondence. | Lesbians—United States—Correspondence. | Lesbians—United States—Biography.
Classification: LCC HQ75.3 .C54 2019 | DDC 306.76/630973—dc23
LC record available at https://lccn.loc.gov/2018060568

This and other Minnesota Historical Society Press books are available from popular e-book vendors.

Book design and typesetting by Judy Gilats

Contents

Foreword

Lillian Faderman

IN SPRING 1890, Rose Cleveland, sister of US President Grover Cleveland, wrote in a letter to Evangeline Marrs Simpson, a wealthy widow whom she had come to know that winter, "My Eve—! Ah, how I love you. It paralyzes me. . . . You are mine by every sign in Earth & Heaven, by every sign in soul & spirit & body." "Sweet, Sweet," Rose declared in another letter, "I dare not think of your arms—but I am coming to them." The sexual intensity in her letters to Evangeline is a humanizing revelation about the possibilities of women's lives in her day. They belie the image her contemporaries cherished of unmarried upper-class ladies as decorously and tranquilly nonsexual. In one sexually playful letter, for instance, Rose poignantly laments the passing spring and her passing youth, and she implores Evangeline to restore them both to her through their erotic intimacy: "Will it come again, Eve? Is it keeping for me? Are you keeping it for me, wrapped up warm and sweet, fresh and deep, all in a closed bud that will open—*when*? Make me believe it, Eve—give me a *writing*—sign or seal and deliver it to me as your bond or your pound of flesh—and I will *have both*." That Evangeline reciprocated Rose's sexual intensity we can glimpse through the occasional bits of her letters that are preserved by Rose's quoting them. "Oh, darling, come to me this night," Evangeline wrote, "my Clevy, *my Viking*, My—Everything, Come!"

Rose's love for Evangeline continued for almost three decades—through their erotic passion; through the shock, six years into their relationship, of the forty-year-old Evangeline's marriage to Minnesota's seventy-four-year-old Episcopal bishop Henry Whipple; and through Rose and Evangeline's gradually renewed intimacy after the bishop's death five years later. Evangeline and Rose finally left America permanently and settled together in Italy, where they lived until Rose's death in 1918. Evangeline, who died in 1930, chose to be buried in Italy, too, beside the woman she loved. The letters in *Precious and Adored* re-create this story of one of the most remarkable love relationships between women in American history. Lizzie Ehrenhalt and Tilly Laskey have done scholars as well as general readers a great service in gathering these letters and providing indispensable context for them through thoughtful and informative introductions and skillful annotations.

The Victorian era, when Rose and Evangeline came of age, assumed that proper women were passionless, that they would perform their conjugal duties if married because that was obligatory—but left to their own devices they were devoid of desire. Rose and Evangeline are not the only stunning proofs of that fallacy. There are numerous extant examples of women among their contemporaries who penned similarly fervid letters to another. For example, Mamie Gwinn, future professor at Bryn Mawr College, wrote to M. Carey Thomas, Bryn Mawr's future president, "My love, my little big love—'tis 11:30 but I am awake and longing for you. . . . I lie on the sofa and don't undress because I am a coward and miserable undressing without you." Mary Woolley, the president of

Mount Holyoke College, wrote to professor Jeannette Marks, "I love you so, I love you so, sings itself over and over again in my heart. . . . [I long] to lavish my love upon you, to let eyes and lips and hands tell you that I love you." Carrie Chapman Catt, last president of the National American Woman Suffrage Association, wrote to suffrage leader Mollie Hay on her birthday of Carrie's desire to "give you 69 kisses, one for each year"—though as she knew, it was Mollie's fifty-fourth birthday.[1]

Rose Cleveland never put a name to her love for Evangeline in her letters. If they had been a middle-class professional couple like the women mentioned above, their relationship might have been described as a "Boston marriage." The term signified a committed long-term domestic relationship between two career women, though the erotic possibilities generally went undiscussed by the outside world, the word *marriage* notwithstanding.[2]

But wealthy women of leisure such as Rose and Evangeline could not be seen as having chosen a Boston marriage over wifehood for the reason that they wished to be engaged in a profession. Though Rose and Evangeline were deeply involved in social betterment activities, they never concerned themselves with working for their livelihood. Nor could they claim, as many middle-class professional women in same-sex relationships did, that shared quarters were a practical convenience for them. Rose and Evangeline each owned several homes and often lived separately. *Boston marriage* could not describe their commitment to one another, nor did they need

1. Mamie Gwinn to M. Carey Thomas, March [?], 1882, reel 53, M. Carey Thomas papers, Bryn Mawr College; Mary Woolley to Jeannette Marks, August 20, 1900, Mary Woolley papers, Mount Holyoke College; Carrie Chapman Catt to Mary Garrett Hay, August 27, 1911, reel 3, Carrie Chapman Catt papers, Library of Congress.

2. I discuss numerous late-nineteenth/early-twentieth-century Boston marriages in my book *To Believe in Women: What Lesbians Have Done for America—A History*.

to explain away their relationship by that term: their class and wealth shielded them from the vulnerabilities of prejudice that middle-class professional women might have feared.

In earlier centuries, those observing these upper-class ladies from the outside might have dubbed Rose and Evangeline "romantic friends," as they did Lady Eleanor Butler and Sarah Ponsonby, the eighteenth-century Ladies of Llangollen, who famously ran away from their families and lived together for fifty years. But by Rose and Evangeline's day, the sentimental term *romantic friendship* had long fallen out of use. There were, in fact, many unsentimental terms that were current in their time to describe female same-sex relationships and those who engaged in them—but none would have been acceptable to Rose and Evangeline.[3]

The term *lesbian* came into popular American English in the nineteenth century with the translation of Baudelaire's *Les Lesbiennes* from his poetry volume *Flowers of Evil*. But in Baudelaire's poems, lesbians are "*femmes damnees*": characterized by their decadence and doomed to exotic destruction. The term *gay*, which came into use in the early twentieth century by those who loved the same sex, had a similar troubling history: it had been a term for prostitutes in the late nineteenth century. Rose and Evangeline would not have recognized themselves in words such as *lesbian* or *gay*.

There were other words, too—all of them equally objectionable. *Homosexual* had been coined in the 1860s, but that word emphasized *sexual* and elided love and devotion and all else that went into a relationship. *Queer* was used pejoratively to describe homosexuals in the late nineteenth century, and that vulgar, alienating term would have been repugnant to Rose and Evangeline, as would *dyke*, which came into use later in the twentieth century.

Late-nineteenth-century sexologists such as Dr. Richard

---

3. While the term *romantic friendship* was no longer used as a label, romantic friendships themselves were still thriving.

von Krafft-Ebing and Dr. Havelock Ellis used other words to describe women who loved women, particularly *female sexual invert*. But that was a medical term and associated with pathology. "Female sexual inverts" in the psychiatric texts of Krafft-Ebing and Ellis were often criminal and insane.

Rose and Evangeline could have found no comfortable terms to describe what they were and were to each other. What we see in these letters is that they were, for a time, passionate lovers, who became strained though devoted friends during Evangeline's short marriage to Bishop Whipple. Then they loved again, till death did them part. Despite the lack of a shared vocabulary to describe who they were to themselves and to one another, today's "lesbians," "queers," "dykes," "gays," "bisexuals," and all others will have no trouble recognizing the powerful ardor in Rose Cleveland's letters to the woman she loved.

Preface

Tilly Laskey

JUST AS IT CAPTIVATED people during her lifetime, Evangeline Whipple's charisma caught me. We have at least three points of connection: an East Coast heritage, a sojourn in Minnesota, and a love of Italy. I first encountered her in 2004 during my work as curator of ethnology at the Science Museum of Minnesota, where I cared for the collection of Indigenous objects amassed by Evangeline and her second husband, Bishop Henry Whipple, and his family. As is typical for many women in history, the information I found about Evangeline Whipple defined her in terms of the men she married and relegated her story to single lines of text and insinuating remarks about her "close friendship" with Rose Cleveland, a former White House hostess and President Grover Cleveland's sister.

I am a curator specializing in Indigenous art and culture, and my initial interest in Evangeline was in her role as a collector and supporter of Native arts. A research project with Marcia Anderson, a colleague and curator at the Minnesota Historical Society, led to a 2008 exhibition about the Whipples'

Native collections at the Minnesota History Center and an online reunification of the pieces held at the Science Museum of Minnesota and the Minnesota Historical Society. At that time, my focus did not include the love letters Rose Cleveland wrote to Evangeline Whipple, housed in the archives of the Minnesota Historical Society.

Evangeline Whipple left Minnesota in 1910 and moved to Italy with Rose Cleveland. Whipple departed See House, her Faribault home, abruptly and never returned, leaving intact her entire household, including hundreds of Native objects, antiques, books, furniture, paintings, photographs—and the love letters Rose Cleveland had written to her. After Whipple's death in 1930, the Cathedral of Our Merciful Saviour in Faribault inherited See House along with most of its contents. Minneapolis antiques dealer Alice Best Rogers managed a months-long sale in 1933, liquidating the contents of Evangeline's house. Eventually, the town of Faribault claimed the property for back taxes and razed the house. Some of the Whipples' personal collections made their way to the Minnesota Historical Society, the Rice County Historical Society, Shattuck–St. Mary's School, and the Science Museum of Minnesota.

During a 2009 trip to Italy, I found myself with a free day. I knew Evangeline Whipple and Rose Cleveland were buried in Bagni di Lucca, and I hastily booked a seven-hour train trip to visit their graves, leaving my very concerned friend, Francesca Piccinini, waving goodbye on the platform in Ancona. On that long train ride, I wondered what kept Whipple away from America so long, and why she settled in a small Tuscan village. My train arrived late on a drizzling Sunday evening in November at the rural mountain *comune*, and I was unprepared for the lack of public transportation and taxi stands. After hitchhiking to my hotel, I understood Francesca's concern and opted to hire a driver the next day.

Though I spoke no Italian and my taxi driver spoke very little English, he understood my quest. He drove me to the

English Cemetery, but it was locked and in disrepair. He then took me to numerous houses and buildings, all the while pointing and speaking rapidly in Italian, pulling me out of the car and insisting I take photos of each spot. The only words I comprehended, because of my art history training, were "Della Robbia"—a ceramic art form for which the region is famous. My inability to understand him was frustrating for both of us. Years later, I realized he took me to every house, church, road, and historic site in Bagni di Lucca that was related to Evangeline Whipple and Rose Cleveland.

I returned to Bagni di Lucca two years later, armed with conversational Italian language skills, a rental car, and connections at the Biblioteca Bagni di Lucca, the public library that administers and cares for the English Cemetery where Rose and Evangeline are buried through the Fondazione Michel de Montaigne. Professor Marcello Cherubini and Dottoressa Angela Amadei unlocked the cemetery and generously shared their knowledge with me. High on the side of a steep hill above the Lima River, I finally paid my respects at the graves of Evangeline Whipple, Rose Cleveland, and Nelly Erichsen—the first of many visits I would make to their final resting place. The next morning, I packed up my rented Peugeot to head east over the Apennines. When I turned on the car, an error message appeared: "Rear passenger's seatbelt not fastened." Thinking the weight of my bags had caused the warning, I removed them from the back seat, but the error remained. I clicked the seat belt, and the display read, "Rear passenger properly belted." I released the seat belt and got the original error. Since I was late getting on the road, I embraced the situation. Occasionally I would call out to the ghosts in the back seat, which I assumed were Whipple and Cleveland, asking directions or telling them to hold on while crossing dodgy mountain passes.

The error remained on the car's screen during my two-month stay in Italy. Evangeline and Rose became my imaginary and constant companions (along with the nineteenth-century

explorer Giacomo Costantino Beltrami, whom I was researching in Ancona and Bergamo). I envisioned them gleefully
"unbelted" in my back seat, happy to be on a road trip and
keeping me on task. When I returned the rental car, I pointed
out the message to the clerk. Perplexed, he checked the back
seat for an uneven load, tried clipping and unclipping the seat
belts, all to no avail. Finally he shrugged and said, "Perhaps
you have a phantom"—to which I replied, "or three!"

The Fondazione Michel de Montaigne invited me to present a paper on Evangeline Whipple in Bagni di Lucca, and I
became further entrenched in her life in Italy and her relationship with Rose Cleveland. Upon returning to the United
States in 2012, I decided I needed to know everything about
Evangeline Whipple and began a years-long collaboration
with Susan Garwood, executive director of the Rice County
Historical Society in Faribault, Minnesota. With support from
the Arts and Cultural Heritage Fund through the Minnesota
Historical Society, I inventoried Minnesota collections relat-
ing to Evangeline, searching for clues about her existence. In
2013, I traveled to the Minnesota Historical Society and began
reading the entire correspondence from Rose Cleveland to
Evangeline Whipple—hundreds of pages written in Cleveland's cursive scrawl.

I am from a generation that writes letters. Like Rose Cleveland, I had scripted long notes to my beloved—my heart
poured out on paper, sent via the US Postal Service. I, too, had
a long-distance relationship that experienced a separation
and ended in heartache. It seemed that Rose and I also shared
a connection, and because of this, her love letters to Evangeline Whipple made me wince. Reading the joyful, passionate
love letters from 1890, only to find evidence of betrayal and
separation following a few folders later felt too close, too voy-
euristic, and initially I turned away from their story. It was
impossible not to well with tears, to feel a sucker punch to the
stomach, to become overwhelmed with sadness for Cleveland
and Whipple—and to mourn my own lost love while reading

Cleveland's words: "I cannot speak nor write of my love. You *know*"; "I will give up *all* to you if you will try once more to be satisfied with *me*"; and, "I know you suffer—but because you are so sorry does not make it love."

While painful, my reaction to Cleveland's letters demonstrates their power and universality. I leaned into my discomfort and started phase two of the project, transcribing the correspondence between Rose Cleveland and Evangeline Whipple. The cap of the project included submitting an article about Evangeline Whipple to MNopedia, the Minnesota Historical Society's digital encyclopedia. I started working with editor Lizzie Ehrenhalt, who was also interested in the Cleveland-Whipple dynamic. Initially, I had no desire to delve into the letters on an intellectual level, but Lizzie suggested they warranted documentation and proposed we write a book together.

Our primary goal was to dispel myths and misinformation that surrounded Whipple and Cleveland, and to work beyond the sexy tagline of "the president's sister and the bishop's wife." Initially conceived as a publication that would briefly introduce the letters and present the transcriptions, this book evolved into a deep dive into the history of the twenty-eight years that Evangeline Whipple and Rose Cleveland shared.

Lizzie and I made a few discoveries. In addition to doing research on-site at cultural institutions, we used digitized archives and newspapers to search a worldwide dataset, allowing us to make detailed accountings for Rose's and Evangeline's movements and the events and people they encountered. After scouring the Boston city directories, I put a last name—Ames—to the previously mysterious "Evelyn," who was a subject and participant in the letters for fifteen years. Similarly, documents and photographs deposited at the Massachusetts Historical Society by Laura Norcross Marrs, Evangeline's sister-in-law, filled out genealogical information and yielded the only known photograph to date—previously unidentified—of Rose Cleveland and Evangeline Whipple together.

Careful reading of the original documents, however, provided two of the most important revelations. Lizzie's keen eyes detected that a series of letters stored in a folder with letters from 1893 was actually written in 1896. This cleared up decades' worth of conjecture about Cleveland and Whipple's separation, placing the "breakup" letters in 1896, just prior to Evangeline's marriage to Bishop Henry Whipple.

Another unexpected clue provided context for the motivations behind the creation of one of the most famous beaded bandolier bags in existence. The bag, made by Anishinaabe artist Sophia Smith, is preserved within the Bishop Whipple collection at the Minnesota Historical Society and was twice photographed with the artist—unusual (but very welcome) documentation. Evidence in Cleveland's and Ames's letters to Whipple indicate it was likely commissioned by Evelyn Ames, who was traveling with Rose Cleveland in Europe at the time. Back in Minnesota, Evangeline Whipple facilitated getting the gift to Bishop Henry Whipple.

This book provides a space where Cleveland's and Whipple's stories exist and expand, where the words they recorded are preserved in totality, where their love is celebrated. Wherever their "phantoms" settled, I hope they are satisfied.

Lizzie Ehrenhalt

IT'S HARD TO OVERSTATE the emotional impact of first-person narratives—the immediacy of opening up a letter or diary and seeing your own experience reflected back at you. For queer readers, especially young ones who feel alone in their otherness, that moment can be lifesaving. It disproves the idea that queer people have no history, no network of predecessors that stretches back before the invention of sexual orientation. Late-nineteenth-century sexology did change how we thought about ourselves, creating new identities and ways of thinking. But there are life stories from the dawn of sexology, and before, that still resonate powerfully with people who today call themselves something other than straight. Rose Cleveland's is one of those stories.

When I was a young adult, I found comfort in the letters of Violet Trefusis to Vita Sackville-West; the memoirs of Derek Jarman; the diaries of Joe Orton; and the autobiographical work, in various genres, of Natalie Barney and Renée Vivien. As I started working on *Precious and Adored*, I realized that the project offered a chance to pay forward the debt I owed to those writers—and to the editors who helped bring their words to the public. In that spirit, I hope this book gives a new generation of readers the same validation that I felt as an eighteen-year-old.

The Minnesota Historical Society, which preserves most of the letters in this volume, works to fulfill a mission of "using the power of history to transform lives." I can think of no fuller realization of that goal than showing queer youth, through the history of Rose Cleveland and Evangeline Whipple, that they are not alone.

Acknowledgments

FOREMOST, WE COMMEND the descendants of Bishop Henry Whipple for collecting and saving the family's correspondence. We give thanks to the Minnesota Historical Society for preserving and making the documents available and accessible for future generations, and to the staff at the Minnesota Historical Society Press, particularly Ann Regan, editor in chief, for having faith in our subject and publishing this book. Lillian Faderman examined Rose and Evangeline's love in her seminal book *Odd Girls and Twilight Lovers* in 1991, and we are honored she agreed to write a foreword.

Special thanks to Minnesota cultural institutions and people who supported this work: Jim Fairman, Ed Fleming, Jackie Hoff, Jill Rudnitski, and Scott Shoemaker, former and current staff of the Science Museum of Minnesota, St. Paul; Missy Donkers and former Very Reverend Jim Zotalis from the Cathedral of Our Merciful Saviour, Faribault; Fritz Knaak of Holstad and Knaak PLC; the librarians, archivists, and reference assistants and Jerry Jackson (retired) and Marcia Anderson (retired) at the Minnesota Historical Society, St. Paul;

Linda Schelin at St. Mark's Cathedral, Minneapolis; Susan Garwood at the Rice County Historical Society, Faribault; and Lonnie Schroeder (retired), the late Bob Neslund, Kimberly Bakken, and Amy Wolf at Shattuck–St. Mary's School, Faribault.

Special thanks to US cultural institutions and people who supported this work: Rangsook Yoon, Art & History Museums, Maitland, Florida; George T. Comeau, Canton Historical Society, Massachusetts; Terri Simms, Church of the Good Shepherd, Maitland, Florida; Carolyn Roberts, Holland Patent Public Library, New York; Patrick O'Bannon, Islesboro Historical Society, Maine; William David Barry, Maine Historical Society, Portland; the librarians, archivists, and reference assistants at the Massachusetts Historical Society, Boston; Professor Etta Madden, Missouri State University; Lila Zuck, Naples Historical Society, Florida; Joanne M. Nestor, New Jersey State Archives, Trenton; Nicole Casper, Stonehill College, Massachusetts; and Jonathan R. Stayer, supervisor of reference at the Pennsylvania State Archives, Harrisburg.

Special thanks to Italian institutions and people who supported this work: the late Mario Curreli, University of Pisa; Professor Marcello Cherubini, chairman of the Fondazione Michel de Montaigne, Bagni di Lucca; Dottoressa Angela Amadei, Biblioteca Bagni di Lucca; Maria Campo, Turin; Carla Piccinini and Francesca Piccinini, Ancona; Laura Reina, Vigevano; and colleagues at the Museo Civico di Scienze Naturali, Bergamo.

Tilly Laskey

I want to thank Lizzie Ehrenhalt for asking me to write this book. Without her expertise in queer literature and history, I would not have tackled this subject. As a straight woman, I was not comfortable writing about a community where I lack competency; Lizzie's guidance, generosity, experiences,

and knowledge were critical. This book would not have come
to being without the sponsorship and camaraderie of Susan
Garwood, executive director of the Rice County Historical
Society, and support from the Arts and Cultural Heritage
Fund through the Minnesota Historical Society. A number
of others deserve special thanks. To Marcia Anderson, my
champion and co-conspirator on all things Whipple, as well
as the definitive expert on Minnesota history. To my writing
mentor, inspiration, and taskmaster, Biloine (Billie) Young,
for demanding that I write every day, and for urging me to
tell Cleveland's and Whipple's story in the truest and most
respectful way possible, without losing sight of their love.

To my family, whose love and support provided a base for
this work. To my late mother, Susan Laskey, and my Laskey
siblings (especially Naomi and Michael), their spouses, and my
nephews and nieces who held down the home front in Maine
and allowed me to travel for research, and to the Grahams of
South Dakota for their heartfelt encouragement. Peggy Bros-
nan, Beth McLaughlin and Benjamin McLaughlin, and Nico-
lette Meister have fed and housed me and listened (probably
more than they wanted to) and provided feedback for decades.

I dedicate this book to my most ardent supporter, and the
subject of my long-ago love letters, James Graham, who, in
marrying me—coincidently around the same time Lizzie and
I started talking about a book—gave me the courage to re-
examine Cleveland's and Whipple's letters, free of heartache.

Lizzie Ehrenhalt

This is Rose Cleveland's book, but it's also Tilly's. It grew
out of more than fourteen years of her research and labor—
intellectual, emotional, and otherwise. I'm deeply grateful
that she let me join her for the last few years of that ride, and
for her consistent generosity, patience, and insight throughout the process.

ACKNOWLEDGMENTS

I owe thanks to Duane Swanson and Lydia Lucas, the manuscripts curator and former library processing manager, respectively, of the Minnesota Historical Society, for sharing with me their memories about the acquisition of the Whipple-Scandrett papers. Mark Rusch, Sarah Barsness, and Lori Williamson provided crucial help in confirming transcriptions and translations. My personal thanks are due to my parents, Alan and Suzanne; my wise and compassionate sibling, Jey; and my wife, Anjanette—my own Wingie.

Precious *and* Adored

Rose Cleveland (left) and Evangeline Whipple holding her Yorkshire Terrier, Dainty, at Whipple's estate, South Park, in Wayland, Massachusetts, circa 1893. This is the only known photograph of Cleveland and Whipple together. *Kingsmill Marrs Photographs, Collection of the Massachusetts Historical Society.*

Introduction

WHEN ROSE CLEVELAND DIED of influenza on November 22, 1918, Evangeline Whipple eulogized her in a letter as her "precious & adored" friend. Cleveland's death marked the end of a twenty-eight-year relationship—encompassing friendship, romance, sexual attraction, and partnership—that is partially documented by letters in the manuscripts collection of the Minnesota Historical Society. Part travelogue, part love story, the letters track Cleveland and Whipple's long-term love affair in Cleveland's words, revealing a layered, complicated, and enduring bond that survived the transition from the Victorian era to World War I.[1]

1. Unless otherwise noted, all letters are in the Whipple-Scandrett Family papers, Minnesota Historical Society, St. Paul (hereafter, MNHS). *Precious and Adored* is based on approximately 101 of them—470 handwritten pages that Tilly Laskey examined, transcribed, and digitized with the assistance of Minnesota Legacy Amendment funds during 2012–15. Lizzie Ehrenhalt contributed additional transcriptions of thirty-two letters between 2017 and 2018.

Evangeline Whipple and Rose Cleveland were wealthy women who traveled in privileged social circles. Whipple was from Massachusetts and married first into fortune, later into fame as the wife of Episcopal bishop Henry Whipple of Minnesota. Cleveland, a New Yorker, earned her wealth through teaching and writing and her notoriety as the official hostess of the White House during her brother Grover Cleveland's first presidential term. Both traveled regularly in the United States and Europe, but their paths did not cross until the winter of 1889 in Florida, where they first met.

That initial meeting sparked a lifelong romance and decades of correspondence between Evangeline Whipple and Rose Cleveland. Debates about the nature of these letters and Cleveland and Whipple's union have surfaced over the past forty years, raising questions about what constitutes a "love letter." Does it have to be happy to be romantic? Should it be devoted and painful? Can it be outwardly mundane, containing practical notes about train schedules and the mail?[2]

From a broad perspective, *all* of Cleveland's letters to Whipple are love letters. The first are classic examples of the genre: anxious, urgent, impassioned—florid, even by Victorian standards. But for twenty years, Cleveland continued to write to Whipple to show her devotion. Through periods of illness, boredom, and mania, she kept up a consistent stream of words to prove that her love persisted as the world evolved. Even as her subjects veered from house repair to the price of oranges to the Venezuelan crisis of 1895, Cleveland's message to Whipple remained the same: I'm still here, and I still love you.

The Minnesota Historical Society (MNHS) holds the correspondence that Cleveland sent to Whipple between 1890 and 1910—a one-way conversation, but a remarkable example of nineteenth-century queer history nonetheless. It reveals the

2. Many of Cleveland's more routine letters meet the four love-letter criteria identified by Elizabeth Hewitt: confession of hesitancy and reticence; appeal to unilateral attraction; insistence on ineffability; and speculation on non-reciprocation (Hewitt, "Prologue." 7).

most intimate details of Cleveland's love for Whipple—likely nothing she intended to publish or donate to an archive. The whereabouts of Whipple's letters to Cleveland are not known, leaving Evangeline the seemingly passive and mostly silent object of Cleveland's desire. However, Whipple's role as the recipient and keeper of Cleveland's letters is significant.

The Whipple-Scandrett papers are four and a half cubic feet of correspondence of Bishop Henry B. Whipple, the first Episcopal bishop of Minnesota; his son-in-law, Henry A. Scandrett; and their mutual family members of various generations. The collection arrived at MNHS in 1969 via a donation made by Betty Scandrett Oehler, Henry Whipple's great-granddaughter, and her husband, Cole Oehler. The documents' path to public use took an unexpected turn after accession, when the processing archivist arranging the collection found the letters from Cleveland to Evangeline Whipple, the bishop's second wife, in a binder saved alongside family notes and documents. The Oehlers, it seemed, had not known about them.[3]

At a subsequent meeting, curatorial and reference staff decided that Cleveland's letters "were sufficiently sexually suggestive" to "make [MNHS], the associated families, and the letters themselves the focus of titillation." They agreed to remove the letters from the rest of the collection, sequester them in a box closed to the public, and "review their status

3. Only a few letters exist that document Cleveland and Whipple's relationship between 1906 and 1910. The increasing availability of telephones may have made logistical letters—those sent to confirm visit dates, train arrival times, etc.—less necessary in this period. Whipple's letters about Cleveland extend the correspondence to 1918. When Whipple traveled to Italy in 1910, she left her house in Faribault, Minnesota, in the hands of Major William Milligan, who had been the caretaker for the Whipple family for more than sixty-eight years. She gave Milligan the directive not to move anything. Thinking she would eventually return, Whipple left her entire household and personal mementos there—including her letters from Rose Cleveland. But Whipple's house stood unopened for twenty years, until after her death in 1930. It was likely Whipple's stepdaughter, Jane, who retrieved and preserved the letters.

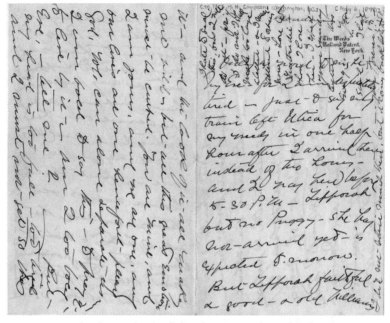

An example of Rose Cleveland's handwriting in a letter dated May 6, 1890. Cleveland's handwriting is challenging to read, and she often switched without warning from English to French, German, or Italian. *Whipple-Scandrett Papers, Minnesota Historical Society.*

in 1980." A memo documenting the closure offered little explanation beyond the fact that the manuscripts "strongly suggest that a lesbian relationship existed between the two women."[4]

The letters remained isolated in the collection's sealed tenth box until March of 1978, when a researcher—through either a hunch or a tip from MNHS staff—learned of their (unpublicized) existence. The researcher, who preferred to remain anonymous, alerted the Gay Task Force of the

4. Lucas and Swanson interview, 2017; MNHS, internal memo, December 23, 1969.

American Library Association, which in turn notified historian Jonathan Ned Katz. After Katz wrote to MNHS asking for an explanation, staff reconsidered the issue. Citing "recent scholarly interest," they removed the letters from box ten, interfiled them chronologically with the rest of the Whipple-Scandrett papers, and lifted the use restriction.[5]

The unsealing of the Cleveland-Whipple letters led to the first scholarly consideration of the relationship: a term paper, completed in December 1978 by SUNY–Binghamton graduate student Paula Petrik. In the paper, which sent selected transcriptions of the correspondence into circulation among historians for the first time, Petrik foregrounded the eroticism of the early correspondence between Cleveland and Whipple and laid out a timeline for the women's relationship. She also placed it within a historical context shaped by, among other things, feminism, sexology, the trials of Oscar Wilde, the second Great Awakening, and the Victorian separation of spheres.[6]

Petrik's paper remained the only source of letter transcriptions until 1988, when a handful of Cleveland's lines appeared in *Intimate Matters: A History of Sexuality in America* by John D'Emilio and Estelle B. Freedman. Building on

5. The reference to "recent scholarly interest" is curious, since the last documented use of the papers by library patrons prior to Katz's request occurred two years earlier, in 1976 (MNHS, internal memo, March 24, 1978). Though MNHS lifted the use restriction in March 1978, it did not revise the collection's finding aid to mention the Cleveland-Whipple letters until 1998. Lucas maintains that box ten was not "kept secret," as lore about the collection grew to allege; it was "closed to the public." Moreover, in Lucas's words, after the lifting of the use restriction, "Box ten did not disappear. Its contents were incorporated into their original folders."

6. Petrik, "Into the Open." Petrik is a graduate of St. Mary's School in Faribault, Minnesota, founded by Bishop Henry Whipple and heavily endowed by Evangeline Whipple. Evangeline's approximately seven-by-five-foot portrait hangs in the school's dining hall and, according to Katz, influenced Petrik, who later became a history and art history professor at George Mason University and the associate director of the school's Center for History and New Media (Katz, "President's Sister," 35).

Petrik's research, Jonathan Ned Katz published selected letter excerpts in a 1989 article for the *Advocate*. Lillian Faderman then included Cleveland and Whipple's relationship as a case study in *Odd Girls and Twilight Lovers* (1991).

After a lull, excerpts appeared in Rob Hardy's "The Passion of Rose Elizabeth Cleveland" (2007) as well as two full-length books: a biography of Grover Cleveland (2013) and one of Rose herself (2014). Publications after 1991 heavily relied on Faderman's transcriptions, and subsequent authors did not physically examine the letters at MNHS, resulting in a singular vision of the letters and the relationship between Cleveland and Whipple.[7]

Even the most recent of these works focused on Cleveland and Whipple's initial romance. They valued the letters primarily as sources of almost forensic information about sites of implied rendezvous, dates of separations and reunions, and intimations of sexual intimacy. As a result, they missed two dimensions of the complete collection's value: its evidence of late Victorian social history and its contribution to Cleveland's literary corpus. The original reception of the Cleveland letters relied on what Liz Stanley, expanding on a term coined by Janet Altman, has called the epistolary pact. That is, they rest on an implicit condition— a pact—of reciprocity, an understanding that Whipple would not just respond to the words in the letters but share their values and social context. As twenty-first-century readers, we stand outside Cleveland's epistolary pact with Whipple, and in the ensuing distance our reception of the letters shifts. Descriptions of expensive gifts, insulting references to African Americans, and patronizing notes about servants are laid bare, sometimes starkly, as evidence of late Victorian racism and classism. The complete transcriptions also demonstrate Cleveland's rhetorical skill in starker relief than out-of-context excerpts. The letters are sophisticated pieces

---

7. Lachman, *Secret Life*, and Salenius, *Cleveland*.

of writing, with recurring themes, humor, and diction that reveal as much about Cleveland's feelings for Whipple as any strict accounting of facts.[8]

To recapture these elements, this volume contains transcriptions of all the extant letters Rose Cleveland wrote to Evangeline Whipple from the collections of the Minnesota Historical Society, including fragments, along with selected letters written by Evangeline Whipple and their intimate friends, and it incorporates annotations from primary and secondary sources and newspaper articles from the time period. Most important, the letters demonstrate Cleveland's and Whipple's humanity and offer glimpses of their personalities and lives.[9]

Evangeline Whipple

Evangeline Marrs Simpson Whipple (1856–1930) experienced dramatic social change during her lifetime. Despite rumors of the Marrs family's grandeur, census records confirm that she came from humble beginnings in the western outskirts of Boston, Massachusetts. Her father, Dana F. Marrs (1825–92), was an Irish immigrant who worked as a machinist and farmer, and her mother, Jane Knaggs Marrs (1829–1906), was a first-generation American with English heritage. The family reportedly ran a boardinghouse in Roxbury before moving to a small farm in Wayland. The couple reared Evangeline and her older brother, William Kingsmill Marrs (1847–1912),

8. Stanley, "The Epistolarium" and "The Epistolary Pact"; Altman, *Epistolarity*.

9. Since Cleveland stated on two occasions that newspapers had not reported personal facts correctly, the editors have used these publications critically. The annotations, however, may inadvertently reflect the rumors and errors spread in newspaper reports. Cleveland's and Whipple's voices and observations about the events they experienced—so evident in the letters—allow readers to make their own deductions.

Evangeline Whipple by Roseti, New York, circa 1890–96, inscribed, "Faithfully yours, Evangeline Simpson." *Whipple-Scandrett Papers, Minnesota Historical Society.*

according to a progressive New England philosophy based in the teachings of the Episcopal Church.[10]

Although her writing was not widely distributed, Whipple published two books. In 1883, she wrote a romance novel under the pseudonym Van Saxon called *Marplot Cupid*, which was published by her uncle William Bense, a printer in Boston. In 1928, Jarrolds of London published Whipple's *A Famous Corner of Tuscany*, which detailed the history of her adopted home, Bagni di Lucca, Italy. The book's dedication reads: "To the memory of my beloved friend of many years, Rose Elizabeth Cleveland, who first encouraged me to write this book."[11]

Whipple's first marriage, in 1882, was to Michael Hodge Simpson (1809–84), who acquired his fortune from merchant shipping, inventing a wool carding machine, and producing textiles—especially the blue wool kersey used for making Union uniforms and blankets during the American Civil War. Simpson was a businessman and philanthropist, and employed many of the citizens of Framingham, Massachusetts, in his mills. He built homes for his workers, donated land and money for parks and public projects like installing running water and building a city library, and established the Simpson Block of businesses. Simpson was forty-eight years Evangeline's senior and died just two years after their wedding, leaving her a $2.5 million estate (equal to about

10. Evangeline Whipple self-reported her birth date as January 15, 1862, on passport applications. Her age varies on census records: 1870, fourteen years old (birth in 1856); 1880, twenty-three (birth in 1857); 1900, thirty-nine (birth in 1861); 1905, forty-two (birth in 1862). The record of her marriage to Michael Simpson listed her age as twenty-six (birth in 1856). On rumors, see "Dr. Francis Marrs and His Wife, Jane Van Poelien Marrs, of Distinguished English and Dutch Ancestry," Ancestry.com, *North America, Family Histories, 1500–2000*; for occupations, see US censuses for 1860, 1870, and 1880; on boardinghouse and farm, see "Her Two Romances—Bishop Whipple's Bride Widow of Famous Old Man," *Repository* (Canton, OH), November 8, 1896.

11. The introduction states: "This book, begun years ago, would have come to light in the Great War period, had not the call to join the multitudes of relief workers made its more urgent appeal" (Whipple, *Famous Corner of Tuscany*, 11).

$64 million in 2018), including the recently finished mansion "South Park," at the age of twenty-eight. His surviving children—Evangeline's stepson, Frank Ernest Simpson, and stepdaughters, Grace Simpson and Helen Seely—had already reached adulthood.[12]

After Simpson's death, Whipple led an independent life, supported her parents and brother, traveled, and assumed ownership and management of several large estates. Although Whipple inherited her wealth, she was an active manager of business, building, and philanthropic ventures. She bought, sold, and financed Boston-area real estate—a situation unattainable for most women of the time.

Financial security gave Whipple freedom, including the ability to choose between sustaining a same-sex relationship with Cleveland or entering, once again, into a conventional marriage. In October 1896, after twelve years as a widow—at least six of them spent attached to Rose Cleveland—she married seventy-four-year-old Episcopal bishop Henry Whipple and moved to Minnesota.

Whipple's charisma seems to have been irresistible. Letters sent to her from friends and lovers indicate she was personable, entertaining, and a constant center of attention; many of them gushed about her. Rose Cleveland passed on to her the response of a woman named Annie in New York: "*She raves over you*—says any one must fall in love with you *at once,* etc."

12. Hurd, *History of Essex County*; Emery, *The Puritan Village Evolves*, 134, 186. Michael Simpson owned Saxonville Mills and Roxbury Carpet Company in Massachusetts. South Park, located in the Cochituate area of Wayland, Massachusetts, and also called "Saxonville," was valued at more than $500,000 ("Her Two Romances"). Whipple retained ownership of South Park after her move to Minnesota, when Jane, Kingsmill, and Laura Marrs took up residence. The home became a roadhouse and restaurant called the "Mansion Inn" sometime in the 1920s and burned to the ground in 1956 ("Fire Destroys Mansion Inn," *Framingham Times*, March 26, 1956). Multiple scholarly articles written about the Cleveland-Whipple romance repeated the story that Michael Simpson died "at sea"; in fact, he had died of heart failure ("Death of Michael H. Simpson, the Boston Millionaire Carpet Manufacturer," *Milan [TN] Exchange*, December 27, 1884).

Correspondents and friends Evelyn Ames and Amelia Candler were equally enamored with Evangeline's charm. In 1895, Ames wrote to Whipple, "You came upon me like a spell, and I felt shut in your sphere as if in a crystal filled with all sorts of whirling colors and beauty." In a love letter to Evangeline, Henry Whipple confided, "If I were to die today, I should thank God for all this love which has made my heart young as a boy." Perhaps the most vivid portrayal of Evangeline came from Cleveland: "My Eve is all light and joy and triumph, like a red rose just open on a June morning, with the look of one who has found, not lost—one who has *reached* and no longer seeks and searches earth and air for resting place."[13]

Rose Cleveland

Rose Cleveland (1846–1918) was reared in upstate New York, the youngest of nine children born to Richard and Ann Cleveland. Her father was a Presbyterian minister who died when Cleveland was seven years old. She attended Houghton Seminary in Clinton, New York, and taught school afterward to support herself.[14]

In 1882, Ann Cleveland died, and Rose took ownership of "The Weeds," the Cleveland family home in Holland Patent, near Utica, New York. At thirty-six, Cleveland was the head of her household and wholly independent. Educated in Latin and Greek, she worked as an editor of literary journals to

13. Rose Cleveland to Evangeline Simpson, December 17, 1895 ("she raves"; possibly Annie Van Vechten [1856–1925], a close friend of Rose Cleveland); Evelyn Ames to Evangeline Simpson, November 19, 1895; Henry Whipple to Evangeline Simpson, August 16, 1896; Rose Cleveland to Evangeline Simpson, May 9, 1890.

14. The *Duluth (MN) Weekly Tribune* reported on May 27, 1887, that "The president doesn't like it because Miss Rose Cleveland has decided to teach school and earn her own living. He advised against it, but she has a mind of her own, and carried out her intention. It is to be hoped the president won't cut her dead."

Rose Cleveland by Roseti, New York, circa 1890–96. In 1896, Cleveland wrote to Whipple: "I did not mean to speak of the 'Roseti smile' on *your* picture [a portrait of Evangeline and Bishop Whipple], but the Roseti smile in general, and perhaps because I recall so vividly the method of its manufacture in my own case." *New Jersey State Archives: Department of State.*

supplement her teaching and writing career. She authored four books: *George Eliot's Poetry, and Other Studies* (1885); *The Long Run*, a novel (1886); *You and I: Or Moral, Intellectual and Social Culture* (1886); and a translation of *The Soliloquies of St. Augustine* (1910). She wrote introductions for temperance reformer Frances Willard's *How to Win: A Book for Girls* (1887) and *Social Mirror: A Complete Treatise on the Laws, Rules and Usages that Govern our Most Refined Homes and Social Circles* (1889).[15]

In March 1885, Cleveland's life changed when her brother Grover was sworn into office as president. Since he was unmarried, she was appointed official hostess of the White House and assumed the duties of the First Lady of the United States. Rose Cleveland was an intellectual, and while she was reported to have felt restricted by her social obligations in the White House, she concurrently used her position to advance conversations about reform movements such as women's suffrage, temperance, abolitionism, and Indigenous sovereignty, as well as matters of state. Although the public greatly admired Rose Cleveland for her upstanding moral stature, she readily relinquished her post on June 2, 1886, after her brother married Frances Folsom.[16]

15. Cleveland also published a short story in two parts in *Godey's Lady's Book* (January and February 1887). The story, "Robin Adair," returned to the theme of gender ambiguity implicit in her essays on George Eliot and Joan of Arc. Even in this later work, in which a woman marries a man who bears an uncanny resemblance to her "very, very dear" female friend, Cleveland's hints at same-sex love are fleeting. Compare to Hardy, "Passion of Rose Elizabeth Cleveland," 184–89, and Salenius, *Cleveland*, 75–80.

16. The editors use *Indigenous* and *Native* as preferred terms for *American Indian* and *Native American*.

Cleveland signed the national suffrage petition in 1909 ("Miss Cleveland a Signer," *Washington Post*, October 31, 1909, quoted in Salenius, *Cleveland*, 57), and her published works contain a feminist slant. For examples of her involvement in matters of state, see letters to Cleveland from reformers and politicians, including Susan B. Anthony, Sarah Winnemucca Hopkins, Elizabeth Palmer Peabody, Sarah Butler Wister, Elizabeth Cady Stanton, Harriet Beecher Stowe, Morrison Waite (chief justice of the US Supreme Court), George Hoar (US senator from Massachusetts), and John Griffin Carlisle

Though the Cleveland family was not wealthy, the siblings had entered profitable professions and businesses, and Rose's work was lucrative. In 1885, largely due to her notoriety as official hostess of the White House, her book *George Eliot's Poetry* became a runaway best seller. It was released simultaneously in London and New York by Funk & Wagnalls, and advance sales necessitated a third edition upon release. By August 1885, ten editions numbering between twelve hundred and five thousand copies had sold out, and an eleventh was in process; translations were sold in Russia, Italy, France, and Germany. Cleveland's publisher, Dr. I. K. Funk, commented, "No book of its kind has ever sold so well in this country." Reports speculated Cleveland earned anywhere from $15,000 to $100,000 in royalties (about $428,000 to $2.8 million in 2018), but her publisher refused to comment, stating it would be a "breach of confidence."[17]

(speaker of the House of Representatives), all in the Allyn Kellogg Ford Collection of Historical Manuscripts, at the MNHS. Cleveland was also a charter honorary member of the Women's Anthropological Society of America, formed by "ten intellectual women of Washington" on June 8, 1885. Although she corresponded and collaborated with reform leaders of the time, Cleveland's language in her letters to Whipple often describes African American people in derogatory terms that clearly demonstrate her racism.

During his first presidential campaign, Grover Cleveland had acknowledged responsibility for an illegitimate child. "His sister's austere probity . . . helped to allay the public's fears, his marriage completed the process" (Edward T. James, Janet Wilson James, and Paul S. Boyer, eds., *Notable American Women, 1607–1950* [Cambridge, MA: Belknap, 1971], 351, as quoted in Petrik, "Into the Open," 4). On her relinquishment, see "Miss Cleveland Quite Willing," *The Comet* (Johnson City, TN), April 29, 1886. The May 9, 1886, *Reading (PA) Eagle* quoted Cleveland: "[I]t will greatly please me to be relieved from the duties of hostess at the president's house, which I have felt were imposed upon me and which have interfered with my pleasures and pursuits."

17. Grover Cleveland was active in the law and politics, serving as governor of New York and two terms as president of the United States; William Neal was a minister, and Anna Neal Hastings married a minister; Susan Sophia Yeomans married a Republican state assemblyman and owned a plant nursery and fruit business.

Cleveland's wealth was discussed regularly in the newspapers; in 1887 the *Lewiston Saturday Journal* reported that "People are making a good deal of unnecessary fuss over the assertion that Miss Rose Cleveland received $400 more for her recent poem than Milton got for 'Paradise Lost.' There is nothing strange, in all this. Milton never advertised." In April 1888, while teaching at Mrs. Sylvanus Reed's School for Girls in New York City, Cleveland's daily schedule and affluence were recorded:

> Miss Rose Cleveland does not regularly teach in Mrs. Reed's school; she talks and lectures on history. She is a very busy woman, and finds very little time for reading, except in the line of her studies and researches. She reads a morning paper while a maid dresses her hair, and gets all that is necessary for the news of the day at that time. She goes into society a good deal, and has been seen at a number of dinner parties and receptions this past winter. Cleveland keeps a stylish brougham, and her high stepping horse is driven by a colored coachman. She is fond of luxuries and she earns all the money she spends for them.

In August 1888, Cleveland reportedly earned $10,000, equal to about $300,000 in 2018, for ten months of work at Mrs. Reed's School.[18]

As the official hostess at the White House and the president's sister, Cleveland became a scrutinized public figure and a subject of gossip; stories about her were transmitted over

---

18. "Miss Cleveland, Her Book," *Evening Telegram* (Providence, RI), July 7, 1885 (third edition); "Miss Cleveland's Book," *St. Louis Dispatch*, August 14, 1885 (ten editions, translations, and Funk quotes); "Society's Doings," *Star Tribune* (Minneapolis), July 26, 1885; *Lewiston (ME) Saturday Journal*, January 1, 1887. Funk went on to comment that sales of *George Eliot* were outpacing "Queen Victoria's recent book" and that Cleveland "may need the money for some private purpose."

"Rose Cleveland a Busy Woman," *Lewiston (ME) Wednesday Journal*, April 23, 1888 (daily schedule); "She Can Afford to Be Joked At," *Post Express* (Rochester, NY), August 9, 1888 (Reed's School).

telegraph wires and republished in newspapers nationwide. In 1886, the *Comet,* a newspaper in Tennessee, reported that she and Congressman Benjamin Le Fevre of Ohio were engaged. In 1887, a New York newspaper suggested Cleveland would marry a clergyman. From 1886 to 1887, newspapers tracked Cleveland's every move and her traveling companions. Annie C. Van Vechten of Albany, New York, was one such companion and a frequent long-term guest at the White House—so much that reporters suggested that Miss Van Vechten, rather than Frances Folsom, was Rose's pick for Grover's wife. Similarly, newspapers placed Cleveland with a "Miss Nelson" and a "Miss Hamilton," both from Albany, during 1886 and 1887. Starting in 1895, Evelyn Ames of Boston became Cleveland's constant companion.[19]

Laura C. Holloway was another woman linked with Cleveland. She wrote *Ladies of the White House* in 1870, and its sales made her wealthy enough to live independently with her young son. She worked for the *Brooklyn Daily Eagle* newspaper and later edited Cleveland's book *George Eliot's Poetry, and Other Studies* in 1885. In August of 1886, newspapers reported that Cleveland and Holloway were working together on the "editorial management of the magazine at Chicago,

19. On June 10, 1886, in "The President's Sister Next," *The Comet* (Johnson City, TN) reported, "To-day gossip says that the handsome congressman Lefevre [*sic*], of Ohio, had captured the heart of Miss Rose Elizabeth Cleveland. The report spread like wildfire. Mr. Lefevre blushed like a schoolgirl when the matter was mentioned. He looked guilty, but declared that he wasn't. He says he has only a pleasant acquaintance with the lady." On clergyman, see *Troy (NY) Northern Budget,* February 20, 1887. Annie Cuyler Van Vechten (1856–1925; no relation to photographer Carl Van Vechten) married Dr. George Lefferts in 1891. The *Palatka (FL) Daily News* ("Candidates of Other Sex for the White House," April 8, 1885) and the *Reading (PA) Eagle* (May 9, 1886) quoted a letter Cleveland wrote to an acquaintance of Folsom who had asked about her brother's plans: "I certainly would not interfere with the matrimonial choice of my brother. I am a very warm friend of Miss Van Vechten, and although I am not an intimate with Miss Folsom, I esteem both as true types of American womanhood. I am pained to read the gossip in the newspapers about the marriage."

called *Literary Life*. Mrs. Holloway has long been the intimate friend of Miss Cleveland." In the summer of 1886, Holloway and Cleveland sailed together for Europe.[20] There is no evidence Cleveland had romantic relationships with any of the women or men noted in the newspaper articles. Perhaps in retaliation against, or possibly in support of, Cleveland, the *Daily Argus News* in Indiana printed "What Is a Flirt?" pulling direct quotations from Cleveland's writings: "A flirt is the most harmless person in the world, a genuine flirtation is the fairest bargain possible—nothing for nothing nihil ex nihilo. If one gets hurt he recovers immediately—for flirts are ethereal creatures; you can walk through them and not know there is anything there. It is all a matter of tenuous reciprocity."[21]

In May of 1890, another rumor must have surfaced—perhaps due to Cleveland's outward projection of herself as a person in a committed relationship. Cleveland wrote to Whipple: "There is an absurd rumor in New York that I am to be married—& people are writing & congratulating me conditionally. It's very awkward for me to deny these rumors, Eve—what shall I do about it?"[22]

Behind her public persona, Cleveland was an energetic, intellectual, independent, and ambitious writer and businesswoman. She loved fashion and relished wearing sometimes risqué and brightly colored dresses—pink was her favorite. She glowed at receiving gifts of "dainty gowns & slippers" from Whipple and, at age fifty-eight, wrote, "*Such* pink gowns . . . with their lovely ribbons, and underneath a *shawl* of deep pink

20. Holloway (1848–1930) married Julius Holloway and had one son before she left her husband and moved to New York to become a writer. Through her reform work, she met Susan B. Anthony, as well as her future husband, Edward L. Langford, whom she married in 1890 (Rutherford, *South in History and Literature*, 416). *Baltimore American and Commercial Advertiser*, August 22, 1886 (editorial management).

21. *Daily Argus News* (Crawfordsville, IN), June 3, 1886.

22. Rose Cleveland to Evangeline Simpson, May 9, 1890.

... and a pair of pink slippers!" Her taste elsewhere—like Whipple's gift giving—was amusingly broad: "I love everything so, I don't know what I love more: one minute it is my whip, which is here with me, and a great joy to flourish and crack from bed—and all my *furs,* and the gloves & fox to top with—then it is my handkerchiefs for the Sunday and evenday noses."[23]

Romance

Evangeline Whipple and Rose Cleveland met in the late 1880s. Records from 1889–90 place them in the same location in Florida, where both wintered. In 1882, Evangeline's nephew by marriage, Thomas C. Simpson, incorporated the Altamonte Land, Hotel and Navigation Company and established a hotel and spa catering to northerners in Altamonte Springs, with Michael and Evangeline Simpson as investors. Whipple purchased additional land by herself in Altamonte Springs from 1883 to 1895, and she bought and sold parcels in Maitland from 1895 to 1929. Cleveland, who had been making seasonal trips

23. The writer of an 1887 survey of Washington high society called Cleveland "a woman of individuality, force, and restless energy, with a radicalism of opinion backed by unbounded courage of utterance" (quoted in Keim, *Society in Washington,* 15). On March 4, 1885, the *New York Times* reported from Grover Cleveland's inauguration, "Miss Cleveland wore a dress of black satin, with an entire overdress of Spanish lace. The satin bodice was cut low and sleeveless, and the transparent lace revealed the shoulders and arms." From 1885 to 1889, Cleveland became the de facto authority on the proper neckline for evening dresses. On March 26, 1886, the *Biddeford (ME) Journal* quoted Cleveland, after receiving a public "reproof" from Elizabeth Cady Stanton, as stating, "I approve of evening dress which shows neck and arms. I do not approve of any dress which shows the bust. Between the neck and bust there is a line always to be drawn and it is as clear to the most frivolous society women as to the anatomists. This line need never be passed, and a fashionable woman's low-necked evening dress need never be immodest. If it is so, it is she prefers it to be so." For correspondence, see Rose Cleveland to Jane Van Poelien Marrs, November 22, 1896 ("dainty gowns"); Rose Cleveland to Evangeline Simpson, November 15, 1896 ("Such pink"); Rose Cleveland to Evangeline Simpson, December 25, 1895 ("I love everything"). A horse whip would have been a practical gift for Cleveland, who drove her own carriage.

to Florida since 1888, had fallen in love with the climate—
so much that she published an essay in *Lippincott's Monthly
Magazine* defending the state from its reputation as a malaria-
infested hinterland. In March 1890, Cleveland was reported as
earning a profit from her orange grove in Dunnellon, about a
hundred miles from Maitland. The Woman's Christian Temperance Union, an organization Cleveland supported, held
an annual meeting in Tampa on March 10, 1890, and publicly thanked a *Tampa Daily Journal* reporter, Lucie Vannevar,
for her assistance. It is possible that Cleveland and Whipple
attended the event, since they were noted as part of Vannevar's
party in Tampa on Valentine's Day, 1890.[24]

24. Thomas C. Simpson Jr. (1853–1923) was a businessman and politi-
cian from Newburyport, Massachusetts; the Pine Crest Inn was located in
Paola, Florida, about twelve miles north of Altamonte Springs, where the
Simpsons and Marrs families wintered, and fifteen miles north of Maitland,
where Henry Whipple's family wintered starting in 1877. (Maitland is three
miles south of Altamonte Springs.) On the Simpson investments, see Orange
County, Florida, Comptroller records, Orlando (http://www.occompt.com).
Cleveland's essay is titled "My Florida."
    Scholars have identified the 1889–90 date (Lachman, *Secret Life,* 401;
Hardy, "Passion of Rose Elizabeth Cleveland," 186; Salenius, *Cleveland,* 70)
through Vannevar's newspaper columns. One in the *West Coast Department*
(Tampa, FL), January 30, 1890, gives particularly telling details:
    "There is here too another family who have seen the world, and all the
glories of it, and who wear antiques as calmly as we would deck ourselves with
pebbles and stones. I never see Mrs. Simpson the daughter without being possessed with a frantic desire to demand her bracelets or well not exactly her life
but her necklace. Mr. Mars [sic] her brother kindly showed me glasses once the
property of King Louis of Bavaria and a bit of the True Cross, also his. How
some of you Catholics will envy me when I tell you I held it in my hand. It is
probably genuine as the Pope presented it to the poor mad king."
    "The circle at Pine Crest Inn has grown much larger since my former visit
but it is still a very pleasant one. Miss Mollie Hastings, niece of Miss Rose
Elizabeth Cleveland, is here for a brief stay. She is a very attractive young
woman resembling her aunt in many respects. . . ."
    ". . . Miss Cleveland and her niece are central figures [in a photo taken on
an outing]. Mrs. Mars, Mrs. Simpson, Dr. and Mrs. Turner, Mr. Mars and my
'guidemen' are in it."
    For Vannevar party and WCTU event, see *Inter Ocean* [Chicago, IL], Feb-
ruary 26, 1890, and *Tampa Daily Journal,* March 10, 1890.

The letters from Cleveland to Whipple commenced on April 13, 1890, in an explosion of anticipation, confusion, and passion. A secret vocabulary developed between them, complete with pet names. Cleveland called Whipple her "Wingie" (in the 1890s, "My Wing" and in 1895, "My Wing of Wings!" i.e., Rose's support system), "Yourself," her "Eva" and "Eve," and signed letters "Clevy," "Clevie," "C," "Viking," "Myself," and, simply, "Rose" or "R."

Though "Grandmother" and "Grandma," Cleveland's favorite pet names for Whipple, first enter the correspondence around 1895, Cleveland's reference to herself as Whipple's grandchild (elsewhere "gran chile" and "GC") appears earlier, around 1893. At first, it seems odd for Cleveland to compare their dynamic to any parental relationship, let alone one that crossed two generations. The name might have been a self-mocking hat tip to the couple's age difference (ten years), or a reference to the language Evangeline used in *Marplot Cupid* (e.g., "Bress yah honey-chile . . .") to mimic stereotyped African American speech. But the "grandmother" epithet also captures a familial intimacy that was denied to Cleveland and Whipple as a couple publicly recognized only as, at most, romantically bonded friends.[25]

Equally revealing are the words Cleveland avoided. Nowhere does she suggest that she, Whipple, or their friends belonged to something equivalent to a subculture—a group of women who shared an identity built on their same-sex attractions. In this, Cleveland was consistent with the ideology of the 1890s, when the concept of sexual orientation as a fixed psycho-biological trait was only beginning to filter into American popular consciousness through scientific writing. Richard von Krafft-Ebing's *Psychopathia Sexualis* (1886) was not available in English until 1894; Havelock Ellis published *Sexual Inversion*, the first English-language medical textbook on homosexuality, in 1897. Magnus Hirschfeld did not complete

25. Simpson, *Marplot Cupid*, 176.

his *Homosexuality of Men and Women* until 1914. The new and evolving concept of sexual orientation would have puzzled most Gilded Age Americans who were not doctors, including Cleveland and Whipple. Though assigning an orientation to either woman after the fact is anachronistic, it's still possible to recognize their relationship, and their letters, as queer.[26]

Cleveland's style in the earliest letters to Whipple (1890–93) is richly poetic, with passages built on extended metaphors, similes, and metonymy. In a Christmas letter, she transforms the message she sends into a personified voice that flies to Florida to greet Whipple. Eventually she admits, "it is really no other than the Voice of Clevie . . . full of Clevie's sighing and singing love for her darling, every day and every night."[27]

In a pair of letters from the spring of 1890, Cleveland described feeling paralyzed by her love for Whipple, a common move for elegiac and lyric poets trying to capture their physical response to their beloveds. In the poems, as in Cleveland's letters, love-paralysis is overwhelming but also something to be endured and chronicled in writing. The trope of arrested movement sometimes took an opposite form: shaking, fluttering, and trembling, perhaps most famously in Sappho 31 ("it makes my heart tremble within my chest . . . trembling seizes all of me"). As a student of ancient Greek with an abiding interest in classical literature, Cleveland would have been familiar with these lines. Her first-person declaration "Oh, Eve, I tremble at the thought of you" carries a Sapphic echo.[28]

Cleveland was fascinated by poetic forms. In 1885 she wrote an evaluation of the poetry of George Eliot; in 1887 she

26. In line with the evolution of LGBTQ-positive terminology since the 1980s, the editors use *queer* in its empowering, reclamatory sense throughout the text. Although labeling Whipple and Cleveland queer themselves is anachronistic, the term captures the transgressive nature of their mutual sexual attraction.

27. Rose Cleveland to Evangeline Simpson, December 1890.

28. Sappho 31.5–6 ("τό μ᾽ ἦ μὰν / καρδίαν ἐν στήθεσιν ἐπτόαισεν") and 31.13–14 ("τρόμος δὲ / παῖσαν ἄγρει"); Rose Cleveland to Evangeline Simpson, April 23, 1890.

published the metrically innovative, sonnet-like narrative "The Dilemma of the Nineteenth Century" in *Lippincott's Monthly Magazine*. One remarkable poem, unsigned but attributable to Cleveland, survives alongside the letters. Dated February 11, 1894, probably intended for Whipple on Valentine's Day, it bears the hallmarks of Cleveland's assurances of enduring love. The four stanzas of free verse rhyme in an ABAB pattern recalling a free-form sonnet and develop a striking, extended metaphor, in which Cleveland's passion is an ocean wave rushing to meet Whipple. It leaves the impression that her emotion is an unstoppable force of nature; barriers of space and time (or the US mail delivery schedule) cannot block its path. The last couplet puts to rest any remaining doubts: "no pale shore of the past, oh Sweet, / shall stand betwixt you and me!"[29]

Through these passages Cleveland reveals her belief in the power of language—particularly poetry. But she acknowledges its limits, describing her feelings by contrasting speech and silence, secrets and revelations, confession and disavowal. In the letters that mention speech and revelation, silence and secrecy are never far away. Cleveland often expresses the hope that though words fail her, her connection to Whipple transcends language. "I cannot speak nor write of my love," she disclosed in one letter, written just before Evangeline married Henry Whipple. "You *know*." In another, she asked, "If you knew all I could tell you—do you?"[30]

Cleveland's nerve sometimes weakened at the same moment she resolved to speak out: "Let me cry & shout it. Oh Eve, Eve, surely you cannot realize what you are to me. What you must be." Elsewhere: "I dare not go on—dare not say what I think or dream—but you know." After Evangeline's marriage to Bishop Whipple, Cleveland comforted herself with a belief in a love beyond words. "To know that each knows," she

29. Rose Cleveland to Evangeline Simpson, February 11, 1894.
30. Rose Cleveland to Evangeline Simpson, n.d., 1896 ("I cannot"); Rose Cleveland to Evangeline Simpson, April 13, 1890 ("If you").

wrote in 1896, "to *believe* that each knows is the only thing we can do, *now*. I lie back on this belief and *go on with my life*."[31] Cleveland's search for a same-sex romantic vernacular coincided with a broader turn in late Victorian social history. The concept of "the love that dare not speak its name" (coined by Lord Alfred Douglas in his 1894 poem "Two Loves") entered public conversation in England and America after it surfaced in the testimony of one of the trials of Oscar Wilde in 1895. Cleveland doesn't use the phrase word for word in her letters, but her language reveals a similar concern for the consequences of speaking, naming, and confessing. It reflects both skepticism that written or spoken language could fully express her love and anxiety about what might happen if she did express it. These themes appear throughout the correspondence, from the first letter in the collection, dated April 13, 1890, to the note of condolence Cleveland wrote to Evangeline after Bishop Whipple's death in September 1901:

APRIL 13, 1890: "I must not write all I would"; "If you knew all I could tell you—do you?"

SUMMER OR EARLY FALL, 1896: "The right word will not be spoken"; "I cannot speak nor write of my love. You *know*—"

NOVEMBER 15, 1896: "The fact is all I am equal to, and I cannot find the words to talk about it"; "To know that each knows— to *believe* that each knows is the only thing we can do, *now*."

[JUNE 21,] 1897: "The great thing is to be sure of what there is to see, or, perhaps, what cannot be *seen*, but only felt. It is not to be summed up in this . . ."

SEPTEMBER 1901: "[W]hen you read the words just written think also of all that the heart leaves unvoiced, unexpressed."[32]

---

31. Rose Cleveland to Evangeline Simpson, April 23, 1890 ("Let me cry"); Rose Cleveland to Evangeline Simpson, April 22, 1890 ("I dare not"); Rose Cleveland to Evangeline Simpson, November 15, 1896 ("to know").

32. This concern surfaced, in a conversational context, in *George Eliot's Poetry, and Other Studies,* when Cleveland wrote, "How encouraged [we felt] to utter that which we had not dared to speak when all utterance was so different from it!" (39). Cleveland also meditated on the unspeakable outside

Cleveland's themes of self-censorship and failed speech appear in other mid-to-late Victorian erotic and romantic letters between women, as well as in their autobiographical writing:

MARY WOOLLEY TO JEANNETTE MARKS, APRIL 10, 1900: "I cannot express it in words . . . I cannot tell you what you are to me, first a part of my life and a very *big* part . . . I have tried to make *writing* take the place of *being*—but it does not, does it, dear? I cannot say all that I wish."

ALICE MITCHELL TO FREDA WARD, 1891: "How I love thee, none can know."

MINNIE BENSON, RECALLING FALLING IN LOVE WITH A FRIEND IN 1876: "Then I began to love Miss Hall—no wrong surely there . . . gradually the bonds drew round—fascination possessed me . . . then—the other fault—Thou knowest—*I will not even write it*—but, O God, forgive—*how* near we were to that!"

CHARLOTTE CUSHMAN TO EMMA CROW, 1860: "There are people in this world who could not understand our love for each other, therefore it is necessary that we should keep our expression of it to ourselves."[33]

Writing to or about their beloveds, each of these women took the same rhetorical tack: an appeal to the unspeakable. It's crucial to resist the conclusion that they anticipated the late Victorian sexologists, who spread the idea that same-sex

of romantic contexts. She wrote to Evangeline's mother, Jane Marrs, in 1896, "[T]here are some things we both know and feel which we shall never, never say to each other. But I want to say that I shall never, never cease to be Eva's if she ever needs me again" (Rose Cleveland to Jane Van Poelien Marrs, postmarked November 22, 1896).

33. Woolley is in "Mary Woolley & Jeannette Marks: Life, Love, & Letters," Digital Exhibits of the Mount Holyoke College Archives and Special Collections, https://ascdc.mtholyoke.edu/exhibits/show/woolleymarks/item/557. Mitchell is quoted in Duggan, *Sapphic Slashers,* 119; Benson is in Benson Family papers, quoted in Goldhill, *A Very Queer Family Indeed,* 190; Cushman is quoted in Rupp, *Sapphistries,* 137.

love was something diseased that needed hiding. All of them, from Woolley to Cushman, lived in societies that encouraged women to cultivate intense romantic friendships that sometimes developed erotic components. But the women quoted do seem to have sensed, as Cleveland did, that their same-sex relationships set them in opposition to accepted norms, whether social, religious, sexual, or all three.[34]

These excerpts draw their power from ambiguity. They forbid the spoken and written expression of love while at the same time doubting that love can find true expression in the first place. When Alice Mitchell tells Freda Ward, "How I love thee, none can know"—as when Mary Woolley "cannot say all that I wish"—is she saying that no one can understand her love, or resolving that she must keep that love a secret? She may have meant both. The two feelings are not mutually exclusive; in fact, they are mutually reinforcing.

In spite of exclamations that she failed or declined to find the language to express her love for Whipple, Cleveland did, in fact, do exactly that. Falling back on the standard vocabulary of Victorian affection used by friends as well as lovers, she made Whipple her beloved; darling; everything; Love; Sweet; and Sweetheart. The combined impact of the epithets throughout Cleveland's letters suggests a longing that bordered on obsessiveness. The US Post Office delivered the

34. For explorations of same-sex desire and the unspeakable in the Victorian period, see McGuire, "Victorian Unspeakable," and Flint, "Unspeakable Desires." For some women, there were limits to this encouragement. In 1899, the family of Gertrude Tate reprimanded her "wrong devotion" to photographer Alice Austen, with whom she had fallen in love; the couple nevertheless sustained an intimate partnership until 1952 (quoted in Novotny, *Alice's World,* 60). The excerpts provide evidence of Harriette Andreadis's "erotics of unnaming" in action. Looking at women's same-sex relationships in the early modern period, Andreadis proposed that "without being named, *without being spoken,* certain otherwise transgressive acts might simply be understood by the individuals involved as physiological gestures embodying mutual feelings of friendship, love, and/or affection. . . . An 'erotics of unnaming' could thus serve as a socially strategic evasion of what would certainly have been a devastating social opprobrium" (Andreadis, *Sappho,* 131; italics hers).

mail twice a day during Whipple and Cleveland's courtship. Cleveland's rapid frequency of correspondence and demand of prompt replies from Whipple during this time of heightened emotions can appear, at times, oppressive: "Eva—Do you know in what distress I was? No word from you at all since you had my letter written after receipt of your telegram and in anticipation of what your letter (it promised) should contain. The letter came on Thursday by Orange Belt and another by regular evening mail. Then on Friday one in Orange Belt and one in evening mail . . . your happiness & mine, are floating somewhere—impossible to get hold of!"[35]

Cleveland's insistence on possession, however, nudged the relationship into erotic and even conjugal territory. Cleveland repeated the epithet "my Eve" fourteen times throughout the letters written between 1890 and 1893. During the same period, she announced, "I will not longer fear to claim you. You are mine."[36]

Legal language—references to oaths, contracts, and evidence—appear in many of Cleveland's letters. "You must swear, Eve," she insisted in the spring of 1890. "Take all the oaths you can to keep me easy: *until I have you.*" Around the same time, she begged Whipple to sign a written statement of commitment. She later referred, teasingly, to a similar promise: "Please remember, Madam, that I have a writing that can appear as evidence, if you do not fulfill your contract."[37]

In the most dramatic example of legalese, Cleveland invoked a marriage vow, telling Evangeline, "You are mine, and I am yours, and we are one, and our lives are one henceforth, please God, who can alone separate us." The officiant's blessing used

35. Rose Cleveland to Evangeline Simpson, April 13, 1890.

36. Rose Cleveland to Evangeline Simpson, May 6, 1890, and [postmarked] April 23, 1890 ("I will not longer").

37. Rose Cleveland to Evangeline Simpson, May 9, 1890 ("You must swear"); Rose Cleveland to Evangeline Simpson, postmarked April 23, 1890 (written statement); Rose Cleveland to Evangeline Simpson, postmarked May 9, 1890 ("Please remember").

at many Protestant weddings in Victorian America used similar language, adapted from Mark 10:8: "What therefore God has joined together let no man separate." Without a vocabulary to express the seriousness of her love for another woman, Cleveland turned to a traditional and legitimate institution—Christian marriage—to confirm her commitment.[38]

Whipple and Cleveland traveled together in America and Europe between 1891 and 1893. They cohabitated for short periods of time in New York, Florida, and Massachusetts, but mostly lived separate lives between 1893 and 1896. The Simpson and Marrs families wintered near Maitland, Florida, starting in 1882. Evangeline likely met Bishop Henry Whipple (1822–1901) and his wife, Cornelia Whipple (1816–90), at the Episcopalian Church of the Good Shepherd, which Henry Whipple founded. Henry Whipple was the first Episcopal bishop of Minnesota and had moved to the state in 1859. He became a tireless advocate for Native people, especially the Dakota and Anishinaabe tribes of the region. Later, Henry Whipple was appointed to federal positions, such as the Board of Indian Commissioners. Bishop Whipple is recognized primarily for his action with President Lincoln advocating on behalf of Dakota people after the US–Dakota War of 1862. The bishop purchased land, including a citrus farm in Florida, starting in 1877, and began visiting to alleviate chronic health issues and to escape the brutal midwestern winters.[39]

38. Rose Cleveland to Evangeline Simpson, [May 6, 1890]. Cleveland's choice of words is similar to Catherine of Aragon's in a 1530 letter to the pope about her marriage to Henry VIII: "[T]he marriage between the King, my Lord, and me is indissoluble, since God alone can separate us." The similarity is telling but probably coincidental. See also Rachel Hope Cleves's discussion of Charity Bryant's long-term romantic partnership and de facto marriage with Sylvia Drake in early 1800s Massachusetts: "By laying title to the tie that binds, Charity claimed the language of marriage for her and Sylvia's relationship and invested their union with Christian authority" (Cleves, *Charity and Sylvia*, 105).

39. The *Buffalo (NY) Morning Express* (May 22, 1893) stated that Cleveland and Whipple returned to America together, along with Jane Marrs, on the SS *Etruria* after traveling in England, Italy, Switzerland, Palestine, Rome, and

Whipple and Cleveland did not hide their relationship from friends or relatives. As early as 1890, Cleveland was considered part of the Marrs family. Cleveland corresponded with Whipple's mother, Jane Marrs, and Whipple's brother, Kingsmill Marrs. Cleveland called Jane Marrs "Motherdie," as her children referred to her, and they all traveled together to Florida, along the East Coast, and to Europe. The Cleveland family, too, accepted Whipple.

A month after Evangeline married Henry Whipple, Cleveland wrote to Jane Marrs for comfort, and for clarification of their former mother/child relationship: "[W]e have been together 'in health, in sickness, and in sorrow.' You must let me feel that I can still be something to you, as much, perhaps, as ever, because I *need* my Motherdie so much. Try and need me sometime, so that I can be your child again. I shall always be that—in whatever land."⁴⁰

When Cleveland's brother and former president Grover Cleveland died in 1908, Rose invited Whipple to the funeral, suggesting she was both family and an indispensable friend: "Dear Wingie, We are asking no one, and only our familys [*sic*] and the oldest friends come now. It is your time."⁴¹

Remarriage

By the summer of 1895, Bishop Henry Whipple had joined the Cleveland-Whipple entourage. Correspondence from Cleveland and Evelyn Ames to Evangeline regularly mentioned Henry Whipple. In fact, Henry Whipple—a widower since

Geneva. It is unclear if Cleveland and Whipple spent the entire time together. Evangeline's father, Dana Marrs, died in Italy during this trip. The *Repository* article, "Her Two Romances," stated that Evangeline Whipple "has been acquainted with Bishop Whipple for years and was an intimate friend of his first wife."

40. Rose Cleveland to Jane Van Poelien Marrs, November 22, 1896.
41. Rose Cleveland to Evangeline Whipple, July 16, 1908.

Jane Marrs in Egypt, possibly Evangeline Whipple in the shadow of the Sphinx, holding her dog, Dainty, circa 1887. An inscription on this photo indicates Mr. Dana Marrs, who died in 1892, took this photograph. *Kingsmill Marrs Photographs, Collection of the Massachusetts Historical Society.*

1890—was secretly writing love letters to Evangeline. Iron-
ically, many of the bishop's letters are posted care of Rose
Cleveland at the Weeds. Bishop Whipple's postscripts often
included "Give much love to Rose." Cleveland was less generous when she wrote to Henry Whipple in August 1895, pas-
sively disregarding Evangeline's feelings for him: "Evangeline
keeps somehow full in the faith that you love her, but is not
the less happy to hear it from my letter. Ah, how much we
need, all of us, all the love we can get!"[42]

There is evidence that while she was falling in love with the
bishop, Evangeline was also falling in love with God. Bishop
Whipple told Evangeline, "God has given me this joy of leading you to the Saviour & now he has unlocked your heart to
see the love of that God who is our Father."[43]

During 1896, Cleveland realized she was losing Evangeline
to Bishop Whipple. She wrote pleading, pain-filled letters trying to convince Evangeline not to "do this thing"—to marry
Henry Whipple—and to reconsider her decision: "I will give
up *all* to you if you will try once more to be satisfied with
me. Could you not take six months for that experiment? We
would go away from everyone." Cleveland accused Whipple
of betrayal while simultaneously defending her: "[H]owever
much I would blame another who to another did this—never,
when it is *you* to *me*. It is too deep for blame because it is all
too deep for comprehension. The pain, the strangeness, the
surprise, the wrench, the hurt, the wonder."[44]

42. Henry Whipple to Evangeline Simpson, May 2, 1895 ("Give much
love"); Rose Cleveland to Bishop Henry Whipple, August 26, 1895. For mentions of Whipple, see Evelyn Ames to Evangeline Simpson, January 1, 1896;
Evelyn Ames to Evangeline Simpson, February 7, 1896 ("Give my love to the
Bishop"), and Rose Cleveland to Evangeline Simpson, December 25, 1895
("Thank the Bishop for his letter & tell him if he can promise me some *Minnesota winter* weather I will go to Florida)."
43. Henry Whipple to Evangeline Simpson, May 2, 1895.
44. Quotations here and below are all from Rose Cleveland to Evangeline
Simpson [summer or early fall 1896]. The letters indicating a break between
Cleveland and Whipple are grouped together in a folder labeled "undated,

Even as she protested, Cleveland accepted Whipple's decision and pledged her loyalty: "I will not stand in the way. That means that I will study only for your comfort and pleasure and happiness," adding, "What is yet for us I cannot see. But I think you will need me yet—in a future, perhaps."

On October 22, 1896, Evangeline Simpson married Henry Whipple, thirty-four years her elder, in a simple ceremony at St. Bartholomew's Church in New York. The couple shocked friends and family, and congratulatory notes came from well-wishers around the world—many barely able to remain polite. That people were stunned indicated that the bishop's courtship was covert, that no one expected him to marry again—especially at age seventy-four—and that the choice of the much younger, wealthy, and wholly independent Evangeline as a bride was unexpected.[45]

Why Evangeline chose to marry Henry Whipple at age forty when she was financially independent and attached to Rose Cleveland is more mysterious. When she was a younger woman, selecting the seventy-two-year-old Michael Simpson as her first husband had provided stability, support, and social approval. It also might have decreased regular (hetero) sexual activity and childbearing demands. Locals in Framingham, Massachusetts, called millionaire Michael Simpson the "benevolent King of Saxonville." The *Repository* published an insider's view of Evangeline's relationship to Michael Simpson as it reported her marriage to Henry Whipple. While the

1893?" in box three of the Whipple-Scandrett family papers. Close examination of the postmark on an original mailing envelope included in the folder revealed that it had been sent in 1896 rather than in 1893. The grouping of these letters and the correlation of their content suggest that the others also date to 1896.

45. Susan Kimball wrote from the Copley Square Hotel on November 1, 1896: "My Dear Bishop, the announcement of your marriage has just reached me. . . . Allow me to congratulate you most heartily for this next step you have taken—of course it was a surprise—"; Francis Morgan observed on October 23, 1896: "We are all so surprised at the news of your marriage in this morning's paper"—both in Whipple-Scandrett papers.

pejorative headline ("Her Two Romances—Bishop Whipple's Bride Widow of Famous Old Man") suggested that Evangeline was a social climber, eventually it cast her in a kindly light. At the same time, it intimated that Jane Marrs had connived, like a character in a Dickens novel, to marry off Evangeline to the elderly Michael Simpson in order to save the family from financial ruin. According to the anonymous account, Evangeline "was fascinating enough to captivate any man who appreciates the finer traits of woman's character. Her face was not a pretty one, but it was finely chiseled and very *spirituelle* and womanly. Tall and stately, her bearing was that of a high born lady." Michael Simpson was hard of hearing, and the author of "Her Two Romances" recounted that while on carriage rides together Evangeline "would throw one arm around his neck and shout into his ear." The author added that married life for the couple, though brief, "was apparently a most blissful one."[46]

In an entry of her daybook, written in 1897, Evangeline made clear that she genuinely loved and was attracted to Bishop Whipple, claiming him as "her bishop" and noting, "[H]is face is both remarkable, rare, and beautiful." Whipple related an admirer's view of her husband: "[She] thought the Bishop of Minnesota was the handsomest man, that he had a moral mouth, ecclesiastical face and the best figure that she had ever seen." After his death in 1901, Evangeline proudly wore her status as the bishop's widow, using it as a marker in her published works, and had his name and affiliations (but not Michael Simpson's) engraved upon her own headstone. She also safeguarded the financial status of his legacy and remains, heavily endowing his crypt, his churches, and the schools he established in Minnesota.[47]

Evangeline's genuine devotion to Henry Whipple and her

---

46. "Her Two Romances."
47. Evangeline Whipple diary, June 27, 1897, box 44a, Whipple-Scandrett papers (both quotations); Laskey, "Famous Corner of Tuscany."

commitment to Rose Cleveland suggest she was sexually fluid. When Cleveland and Whipple met, they had deep financial resources and did not need to marry for security. While Boston marriages—women living together, pooling resources, and sharing company instead of marrying a man—were acceptable for women of their region and generation, Cleveland's and Whipple's wealth made such an arrangement unnecessary and outside the expectations of their class.

Some have suggested that Rose and Evangeline's relationship fractured after Evangeline's marriage to Bishop Whipple, but the women continued their correspondence and saw one another during those years on trips to New York, Massachusetts, and Florida. Cleveland appeared to feel stifled in the United States and planned an extended overseas trip. She cleaned out the Weeds—all rooms except for her library—for possible rental and prepared herself for the life of an expatriate. She wrote Whipple, "It seems impossible—as death does—that we have the Atlantic States between us, and soon the Atlantic Ocean; but all that cannot wake separation, and I can conceive how it may be that, all the while, the real distance between us may grow less." On December 5, 1896, Cleveland and Evelyn Ames boarded the USS *Normannia* for a trip that lasted two and a half years. Cleveland wrote a letter on board as a goodbye to Whipple, signing off, "All my heart is full for you. With kindest remembrances to the Bishop, I am always, unchangingly, Your Myself."[48]

Traveling healed Cleveland's broken heart. In 1896, she told Whipple she was dedicated to being her friend, no matter Whipple's choices. When plans fell through to visit with one another in Europe during a trip Evangeline and Bishop

48. Rose Cleveland to Evangeline Whipple, November 22, 1896 ("It seems impossible"); Rose Cleveland to Evangeline Whipple, postmarked December 7, 1896 ("All my heart"). For examples of those suggesting fracture, see Hardy, "Passion of Rose Elizabeth Cleveland," 192; Faderman, *Odd Girls and Twilight Lovers*, 33; Katz, "President's Sister," 35; Lachman, *Secret Life*, 404–5; Salenius, *Cleveland*, 84–86; and Sibley, *Companion to First Ladies*, 267.

Rose Cleveland by Schemboche, Rome, Italy, circa 1897.
The inscription on the back of this photo states it came
from 1905, but it was more likely created during Rose
Cleveland and Evelyn Ames's trip to Europe in 1896–98.
Schemboche was a major cabinet card photographer for
Americans and English people traveling in Italy, with
studios in Florence, Torino, and Rome. *Kingsmill Marrs
Photographs, Collection of the Massachusetts Historical
Society.*

Whipple took to England in 1897, Cleveland was supportive but reserved: "No matter about not *seeing* me—time enough for that. The great thing is to be sure of what there is to see, or, perhaps, what cannot be *seen,* but only felt. It is not to be summed up in this—that you may depend on me, for all that a true & tried friendship can ask? And *I* on *you.* . . . So be as easy and tranquil about me, as I am about you. As never before, we can afford to be."[49]

Evangeline Whipple made Minnesota her home, and her financial resources and emotional care buoyed the elderly bishop during the last five years of his life. Upon his death on September 16, 1901, Cleveland prophetically wrote to Whipple, "All the languages in the world, you *darling,* could not possibly express my sympathy—the *perfect* love which I feel for you. Always remember this, and when you read the words just written think also of all that the heart leaves unvoiced, unexpressed, except as you feel my thought and sympathy and unerring interest during *all* of these coming days."[50]

Evangeline did not succumb to Cleveland's persistent calls to return to her "*perfect* love," but rather remained in Faribault for nine years after Bishop Whipple's death—living in Minnesota a total of fourteen years, when realistically, with her fortune, she could have lived anywhere in the world. Whipple continued the bishop's church work, so diligently that Cleveland commented, "I *know* you are hurting yourself with all that ambitious 'feverish' activity of yours. It is your duty to stop and take breath. So much is this borne in upon me that I beg you to heed my words."[51]

Cleveland's and Whipple's lives were grounded in their faith and Christian principles. Cleveland's father, Richard Falley Cleveland, was a Presbyterian minister. Rose lectured in the Presbyterian church, and her published works, as well

---

49. Rose Cleveland to Evangeline Whipple, [June 21,] 1897.
50. Rose Cleveland to Evangeline Whipple, September 1901.
51. Rose Cleveland to Evangeline Whipple, October 8, 1905.

as her correspondence with Whipple, demonstrated her commitment to faith-based education and morality. In *George Eliot's Poetry, and Other Studies*, she described her belief system:

> [I believe in a] faith which looks into poorhouses, and idiot asylums, and penitentiaries—ay, and into the darkness of great cities by night, and still believes in humanity reclaimable, however marred or fallen, and infinitely worth saving. A faith which contemplates the catastrophe of moral obliquity and spiritual suicide; of the mole and the bat-life of thousands of us; of the leprous spawn of human beings that are constantly thrown upon the shores of life to contaminate and curse, and yet which says, with Longfellow, "I believe . . . [t]hat the feeble hands and helpless, groping blindly in the darkness, reach God's right hand in the darkness [*sic*], and are lifted up and strengthened."[52]

Cleveland was ecumenical and progressive in her religious philosophy, telling Whipple, "I am reading to-day *L'Homme* by *Pere Didon*, the great R. Catholic author of the *Life of Christ*, and am delighted to find an apparent breadth & depth, which gives one hope; though, alas, the bigotry & blindness, i.e. ignorance & prejudice, which make *his* Church the '*seule*' and makes

---

52. In *And the Wilderness Shall Blossom*, Anne Beiser Allen stated, "In the winter of 1895 Bishop Whipple baptized both Evangeline and Rose into the Episcopal Church of the Good Shepherd in Maitland, Florida" (243); other published works have cited this source. Because Evangeline Whipple was part of Episcopal congregations from an early age in Massachusetts (see "Her Two Romances"), it is unlikely she would have needed baptism. Evangeline attended the Episcopal church in Wayland/Canton, Massachusetts, which is where she met Michael Simpson. Terri Sims, clerk of the Church of the Good Shepherd, Maitland, Florida, confirmed that the baptism ledgers for the 1880s and 1890s do not contain the names of Evangeline Simpson or Rose Cleveland (Laskey, personal communication, June 28, 2018). *George Eliot's Poetry, and Other Studies*, 47–48. Cleveland slightly misquoted Longfellow. In "Song of Hiawatha," his "feeble hands and helpless" touch, rather than reach; "God's right hand in *that* darkness" (emphasis added) (http://www.hwlongfellow .org/poems_poem.php?pid=62). Cleveland's reference to "the mole and the bat life" comes from Isaiah 2:20 (English Standard Version): "In that day mankind will cast away their idols of silver and their idols of gold, which they made for themselves to worship, to the moles and to the bats . . ."

the rest of us but poor creatures, exists." And, "We went to church this morning. . . . The minister is a Scotchman—is one of those shrewd, canny Scots of the 'newer sort' who 'gongs over the fundamentals' in a clean, clear way, good to hear."[53] Evangeline Whipple was raised Episcopalian, but it was in Bishop Whipple's ministry that she found a philosophical home, a venue for humanitarian work, and a purpose for her wealth, which she used to improve the status of women, people of color, and the poor. Michael Simpson was generous with his factory workers and the people of Wayland. Evangeline did not continue funding all of his charities after his death, but later supported women's education and libraries in Massachusetts as well as charitable work in Minnesota, Florida, and Italy. She had an active interest in the Sherborn Reformatory for Women (now the Massachusetts Correctional Institution in Framingham, Massachusetts), and she supported church work and cottage industries in Native communities in Minnesota. Whipple funded women's education at St. Mary's School and chaired committees at the bishop's Cathedral of Our Merciful Saviour in Faribault. Though she was not Catholic, in Italy Evangeline supported hunger programs in the Catholic church as well as educational initiatives and Red Cross refugee relief. Her support extended to environmental concerns, too. Evangeline and Henry Whipple, Rose Cleveland, and Kingsmill and Laura Marrs were founding members of the Florida Audubon Society in 1900; Henry Whipple was its first president, and both Evangeline and Rose served terms as vice president.[54]

---

53. Rose Cleveland to Evangeline Whipple, June 21, 1897; Rose Cleveland to Evangeline Whipple, February 18, 1899.

54. While Whipple's social justice work and education programs were well intended, the repercussions of programs like the boarding school system Evangeline supported had deeply negative effects on Native communities through the nineteenth and twentieth centuries and up to today. On the Audubon Society, see Poole, "Women of the Early Florida Audubon Society," 306.

Evangeline Whipple with her dog, Dainty. Portrait painted by Ernst Erwin Oehme (1831–1907), circa 1887. Oehme was a German painter who worked and studied in Dresden and worked for a number of royal courts in Europe. This portrait measures approximately seven by five feet. *Courtesy of Shattuck–St. Mary's Schools.*

Whipple and Cleveland were both incredibly wealthy. Whipple became a multimillionaire and savvy real estate investor after she inherited Michael Simpson's estate, and although Cleveland sometimes acted like a poor relation, she had accumulated a large sum from the record-breaking sales of her book *George Eliot's Poetry,* which allowed her to support three homes and invest in two farms. Cleveland and Whipple's society included presidents, chiefs, governors, bishops, bohemians, and notable people like Howard Carter, Harriet Beecher Stowe, Edmund Tarbell, Winslow Homer, and Isabella Stewart Gardner. Evangeline and Henry Whipple widened the circle to royalty when they met Queen Victoria at her Diamond Jubilee in 1897. The letters offer intimate details of Rose's and Evangeline's privilege in travel choices, property ownership, and consumerism. Wading through references to their opulence is sometimes shocking, even when tempered by mentions of their humanitarian and philanthropic projects.[55]

Starting in 1902, Cleveland and Whipple were visiting one another up and down the East Coast. At the age of fifty-six, Rose had begun numerous business ventures in addition to her publishing career, including a farm on the island of Islesboro, Maine, which she co-owned and managed with Evelyn Ames, and a citrus orchard in Florida. Cleveland and Ames first visited Islesboro in 1898, staying in a town on the south island called Dark Harbor. Islesboro was an out-of-the-way haven for the East Coast elite. Ames's sister, Anna Ames Nowell, and her husband, George Nowell of Boston, were the first summer, or tourist, residents of Seven Hundred Acre Island, a three-mile-long, two-mile-wide island west of Islesboro—usually shortened to "Acre Island." George Nowell initially bought thirty acres in 1899 and purchased a house.[56]

---

55. Winslow Homer was cousin to Evangeline's sister-in-law, Laura Norcross Marrs.

56. Shettleworth, *Summer Cottages of Islesboro,* 84.

Cleveland and Ames eventually owned two houses and about 220 acres of farmland on Acre Island, where they grew buckwheat, corn, giant pumpkins, and hay and raised cows, sheep, and about eight hundred chickens. As women running the enterprise, Cleveland and Ames were judged by their appearance and gender. In 1902 the *Belfast Republican Journal* reported that Cleveland "handles the affairs herself and employs a big crew of men." In October 1905 Cleveland complained satirically to Whipple about the sexism of the times and her attempts to manage the farm's hired hands, who had little confidence in Cleveland's ability: "Evelyn and I are twisting along, I worrying seven men over impossible jobs, which, however, *get done,* by sole dint of my hypnotizing them to do it: and I come out of this effort as if from a knot hole or a needle's eye, have an hour or two of jaw aches, and then go for 'em again."[57]

In 1905, newspaper articles hailed Cleveland as an adept real estate broker, a mastermind behind the creation of a self-supporting summer resort, and the "Queen" of Seven Hundred Acre Island. The papers reported she had purchased land on the island "about twenty years ago . . . paid $4500 . . . Since then, Miss Cleveland has sold house lots enough on the island to yield her a sum which has been estimated as high as $200,000, and she has acres and acres still to sell to those who will accept her terms." Records in Waldo County, Maine, show that Cleveland and Ames purchased four of nine tracts of land on Seven Hundred Acre Island together. On June 10, 1910, a month prior to sailing to Italy with Whipple, Cleveland

---

57. "Rose Cleveland: The Sister of the Ex-President as a Farmer," *Cassville (MO) Republican*, December 4, 1902; *Belfast (ME) Republican Journal*, July 28, 1902; Rose Cleveland to Evangeline Whipple, October 8, 1905. Rather than discuss the farming enterprise, the Cassville paper's article focused on Cleveland's and Ames's fashion and appearance: "Miss Cleveland as she goes about the farm looks eminently business-like. She dresses in a rainy day skirt and a plain little packet, throwing a golf cape about her shoulders in the morning air. Miss Ames also dresses in the simple fashion suitable for out of door work."

filed a quitclaim deed transferring ownership of their shared property to Evelyn Ames. Upon Cleveland's death, however, Cleveland's sister, Susan Yeomans, inherited portions of the island property. Eventually, Yeomans deeded the land back to Ames. Cleveland was frenetic in her businesses dealings and told Whipple, "[B]eing the *Wind* I cannot tell where I will blow next—perhaps to Maine, perhaps to Florida."[58]

Whipple and Cleveland's relationship changed after Cleveland's multiyear absence abroad and Bishop Whipple's death. Cleveland became more emotionally independent, and her obsessive and insecure tendencies toward Whipple subsided: "It was lovely to have the *little* visit I had with you—so much better than nothing that I cannot complain that it was not more. But I feel pretty certain of the future."[59]

In 1907, the tone of Cleveland's letters shifted again as she began to run out of money and energy to sustain her three properties, two businesses, and writing projects. She asked for Whipple's help in selling her house and citrus grove in Florida: "I fairly choke over it, but I am not quite well enough to do *so much* planning for three places, and realize that I must give it up, if I ever amount to anything but an earth-worm, and I do want to." The inevitability of aging seemed to surprise sixty-one-year-old Cleveland. As she complained about arthritis in her hands and loss of strength, she admitted, "I'm too old, Wingie, and I wouldn't be so old if I did not have to tend things so hard. It dries up all the founts of fancy & fine frenzy in my head."[60]

Aging deepened Cleveland's desire to be with Whipple, and her fear of regret if they stayed apart:

58. "Islesboro Speculation," *Olympia (WA) Daily Recorder*, November 15, 1905. The income from the sale of lots would be equivalent to about $507,000 in 2018. The editors give special thanks to Patrick W. O'Bannon of the Islesboro Historical Society for sharing the court and probate citations. For "[B]eing the Wind," see Rose Cleveland to Evangeline Whipple, January 5, 1903.

59. Rose Cleveland to Evangeline Whipple, November 25, 1904.

60. Rose Cleveland to Evangeline Whipple, January 9, 1907.

MARCH 30, 1907: "Life is not long enough to miss each other always."

JANUARY 6, 1909: "Let's meet somehow somewhere before another year rolls round. I take it neither of us feels like wasting time or strength."

JUNE 24, 1909: "I need you and life is not long enough to always wait."

Cleveland and Whipple's Relationship in Historical Context

If Cleveland had met Whipple after 1920, their relationship would have unfolded in a radically different era in the history of sexuality in the United States. Although Faderman notes that same-sex relationships between women were "universally encouraged in centuries outside our own," during the 1920s (and, more comprehensively, in the 1930s) the theories and terminology of the sexologists seeped into American popular thinking. Nonmedical people began to see same-sex attraction as evidence of not only an identity but also a pathology—a classifiable disease that set its sufferers apart from "normal" people, now known as heterosexuals.[61]

Women like Cleveland and Whipple who lived after about 1920 found themselves compelled to name their sexual identities as their predecessors had not. In that new social climate, they encountered a new set of choices. They could deny that their desire for other women amounted to homosexuality or bisexuality (i.e., claim they were not queer); repress their desire; claim a queer identity privately while denouncing it in

61. Faderman, *Odd Girls and Twilight Lovers*, 1. The era of homosexual pathology arrived later for women than it did for men, whose same-sex romantic relationships came under sustained social scrutiny as early as the mid-nineteenth century. Legal scrutiny and criminal suspicion of men who had sex with men, moreover, had prevailed in the United States since the colonial period and in England since much earlier. See Eskridge, *Dishonorable Passions*, 16–20, and, for an English perspective, Goldhill, *A Very Queer Family Indeed*, 132–33.

public; or, finally, self-identify as queer both privately and in public.[62]

Cleveland and Whipple did not have to choose from among those options. Instead, they came of age in the 1860s and 1870s (respectively), fell in love in 1890, and eventually moved to Bagni di Lucca, Italy—a small Tuscan town that had supported alternative Anglican lifestyles for more than a century. (Lord Byron, Mary Shelley, Percy Shelley, Elizabeth Barrett Browning, and Robert Browning had lived there in the nineteenth century.) This timing encouraged Cleveland and Whipple to view their relationship in the context not of homosexual pathology but of New Womanhood, the late Victorian revisioning of ideal femininity as educated, assertive, and independent. Rather than aberrations, same-sex couples, households, and even erotics were the natural results of this way of thinking.

Evelyn Ames Hall (1863–1940), Amelia "Millie" Candler Gardiner (1869–1945), Katherine "Pussy" Willard Baldwin (1866–1932), and Adelaide "Fiori" Hamlin Thierry (1879–1961) formed the core of the close-knit network of women with whom Cleveland and Whipple traveled, conspired, and corresponded. Cleveland's life dates (1846–1918) place her at the vanguard of the first generation of New Women; Whipple's (1856–1930) in the middle. Ames-Hall, Candler-Gardiner, Willard-Baldwin, and Hamlin-Thierry followed slightly later. Whipple and Cleveland supported these younger peers through periods of life transition, acting as affectionate, informal mentors. In addition to their friends, Whipple's and Cleveland's primary companions included their mothers (while living) and close family members. Within this female network, the women benefited from a support system that fostered a sense of self-esteem, independence, and power.

---

62. On naming, see Goldhill, *A Very Queer Family Indeed*: "The 1920s are a turning point in the public recognition—and thus the social and psychological expectations—of lesbianism as a pathology" (184). On choices, see Faderman, *Odd Girls and Twilight Lovers*, 3.

Whipple and Cleveland seldom traveled solo, and they often had an entourage of companions in their homes. Two of them, Candler-Gardiner and Ames-Hall, appear in many of the letters included here.[63]

Ames, a Bostonian, was Cleveland's confidant, traveling companion, business partner, and possible lover throughout Cleveland and Whipple's correspondence. An accomplished amateur pianist, she was the daughter of Oliver Ames, the thirty-fifth governor of Massachusetts (1887–90), and a granddaughter of Union Pacific Railroad baron Oakes Ames, who owned the lucrative Ames Shovel Works. Lauded for her piano playing and sweet character, she moved in a circle that included Boston arts patron Isabella Stewart Gardner. She and Gardner collaborated in 1888 to create the Manuscript Club of Boston, which provided a space at Gardner's palatial home (later the Isabella Stewart Gardner Museum) for composers to play original compositions.[64]

Ames began corresponding with Whipple in June 1895. It's unclear if Whipple met her through Boston society, or if Cleveland and Ames knew one another first. The consistency and longevity of Cleveland and Ames's friendship, their cohabitation, and their business partnerships suggest an intimate relationship. Was Evelyn Ames Rose's equivalent of Evangeline's Henry Whipple—a steady partner or placeholder whom she cultivated after a dramatic romance? While

63. Esther Newton granted New Woman status to "[those] who were born in the 1850s and 1860s, educated in the 1870s and 1880s, and flourished from the 1890s through the First World War" ("Mythic Mannish Lesbian," 561). She also identified an echo generation—a second wave "of New Women [who] were born in the 1870s and came of age during the opening decades of the twentieth century." This group included Margaret Sanger, Isadora Duncan, Gertrude Stein, Willa Cather, and Natalie Barney, all of whom had same-sex relationships.

64. *Town Topics: The Journal of Society* 29, no. 15 (1893): 8 (lauded); Tawa, *From Psalm to Symphony*, 124 (Manuscript Club). A newspaper article ("Former First Lady Summering in Maine," *Denver Post*, April 1, 1901) stated that Evelyn Ames was Rose Cleveland's niece. No genealogical evidence, however, supports this claim.

it's impossible to draw a conclusion from Evelyn's letters to Evangeline, or from Rose's repartees about Evelyn, it's clear that the three women were comfortable with each other and spent considerable time together over two decades.

In 1909, Ames married Harvard graduate Frederick Garrison Hall (1879–1946), an architect who gained renown as an artist who specialized in etchings. According to the June 18, 1909, *Boston Journal*, Cleveland planned to attend the Ames-Hall wedding. The Halls spent 1909 to 1912 in Paris, where Frederick studied at the Académie Julian, and took side trips to Italy, Holland, and England. Presumably, the Halls could have visited with Cleveland and Whipple during this span. Frederick Hall remarried in 1943, after Ames-Hall's death; his second wife, Ariel Hall, recalled her predecessor as a "rare personality—vivid, warm, generous, and inspiring," with "tremendous mental vitality, enthusiasm, and magnetism. Much of the social life of Boston and the North Shore during those years revolved around this couple and the brilliant atmosphere they provided."[65]

Amelia Candler, a close friend of Ames, was a graduate of Radcliffe College and the daughter of John Candler, a US senator from Massachusetts. New Yorker Katherine Willard was Frances Folsom's roommate at Wells College and the niece of temperance reformer (and Cleveland's colleague) Frances Willard. Adelaide Hamlin, another Radcliffe College graduate, traveled with Cleveland in Florida and eventually published two books in the 1950s. Ames, Willard, and Hamlin all married, later in life, men younger than themselves.

The cult of New Womanhood through which these women lived crested alongside what might be called the era of romantic friendship. As early as the seventeenth century, middle- and upper-class women (as well as some men) had cultivated intimate, sometimes erotic relationships with one another and documented them in poems, letters, and other

---

65. Hall and Hall, *Etchings, Bookplates, Designs*, 10.

writing. While social approval of such friendships between men declined during the nineteenth century, the social infrastructure supporting women who intensely loved their friends strengthened. Women's colleges, which were founded throughout New England in this period, brought together like-minded, independent young women in a same-sex environment that encouraged paired bonding. The first uses of the word *crush* to mean a romantic infatuation date to this time, when female students openly courted one another and fused into couples. Even after their school days, women continued to form intimate, same-sex partnerships—some that lasted for decades and supported them throughout their adult lives.[66]

The many-sidedness of late Victorian romantic friendship makes it a hard concept for twenty-first-century readers to grasp. The version that survives in the 2000s, moreover, bears only a passing resemblance to its ancestor. Today, romantic friendship is considered emotional but not physical; caring but not obsessive; loving but not sexual. The late Victorian version was based on platonic devotion but could also involve physical attraction, passion, obsession, eroticism, and sometimes sexual contact—traits that push it past the modern definition of romantic friendship. But for many women, it also

66. The scholarly literature on romantic friendships between American women is vast. In addition to Smith-Rosenberg's trailblazing "The Female World of Love and Ritual," key surveys focusing on nineteenth-century American (and English) women include, but are not limited to, Newton, "Mythic Mannish Lesbian"; Faderman, *Surpassing the Love of Men* and *Odd Girls and Twilight Lovers*; Stanley, "Romantic Friendship?"; Moore, "Something More Tender"; Martin, "These Walls of Flesh"; Vicinus, "Lesbian History"; and Rupp, *Sapphistries*. The founding of women's colleges influenced upper-middle-class sexual politics in the New England of Rose's and Evangeline's young adulthoods. Of the historically women-only Seven Sisters colleges, two (Vassar and Barnard) are in Rose's native New York; four (Mount Holyoke, Wellesley, Smith, and Radcliffe) are in Evangeline's native Massachusetts. All seven received their charters as colleges between 1861 and 1894. On "*crush*," see Inness, "Mashes, Smashes, Crushes, and Raves," 51, and Hunter, *How Young Ladies Became Girls*, 180.

involved a domestic partnership, a practical commitment, an emotional bond, and an intellectual understanding.[67]

Looking at the Cleveland-Whipple relationship alongside other late Victorian love partnerships leads to a more complete understanding of the letters. As Petrik pointed out in 1978, anticipating the lesson of the next two decades of academic research into romantic friendship, "Their correspondence is not unique." Faderman echoed her over a decade later, cautioning readers to realize that "Rose Elizabeth and Evangeline are not an isolated case." Indeed, many of their New England contemporaries lived in long-term partnerships of their own; several had personal and professional ties to Cleveland's native New York and Whipple's native Massachusetts. Mary Emma Woolley, the eleventh president of Mount Holyoke College, lived with professor Jeannette Marks in both states for more than four decades. Wellesley dean Katharine Coman maintained an intimate companionship with songwriter Katharine Lee Bates between 1890 and 1915. Carrie Chapman Catt, the founder of the League of Women Voters, lived with suffragist Mollie Hay from 1905 until 1928. The writers Sarah Orne Jewett and Annie Adams Fields lived more or less openly as a couple between 1881 and 1909. And M. Carey Thomas, the second president of Bryn Mawr, maintained overlapping romances with Mamie Gwinn and Mary Garrett between 1878 and 1915.[68]

67. Scholars writing after the 1980s pushed back against the assumption that Victorian romantic friendships never involved sex. See Rupp, *Sapphistries*, 133; Faderman, *Odd Girls and Twilight Lovers*, 31–36; Vicinus, "Lesbian History"; Stanley, "Romantic Friendship?"; Moore, "Something More Tender"; and Martin, "These Walls of Flesh." Partnership, commitment, and intellectual accord formed the basis of Boston marriages: long-term domestic partnerships between unmarried women who lived together independent of men. The name derives from the concentration of such couples in the Boston area as well as from the romantic friendship between Olive Chancellor and Verena Tarrant in Henry James's 1886 novel *The Bostonians*. See Faderman, *Surpassing the Love of Men*, 190, and Faderman, *Odd Girls and Twilight Lovers*, 15.

68. Petrik, "Into the Open," 12; Faderman, *Odd Girls and Twilight Lovers*, 33. Smith-Rosenberg names several couples who preceded them in "The Female World of Love and Ritual," 4.

Like Cleveland and Whipple, these women came from white, middle- and upper-middle-class families that gave them education, independent incomes, and racial privilege. Women of color of different classes, however, also shaped and responded to the cultural homoerotics of this period. Edmonia Lewis, an African American and Anishinaabe sculptor, formed part of the expatriate circle of same-sex female couples that revolved around Harriet Hosmer (also a sculptor) and the actress Charlotte Cushman in Rome during the 1860s. Addie Brown, an African American domestic servant, kept up an erotic correspondence with schoolteacher Rebecca Primus for more than thirty years. Another African American servant and cook, Emma Waite, developed a passionate infatuation with burlesque star Lydia Thompson in 1870 and recorded it in her diary. And in 1896, Angelina Weld Grimké (later to become a playwright during the Harlem Renaissance) wrote of her desire for her beloved, Mamie Burrill, to become her wife. Atlanta Baptist Female Academy, founded in 1881 (later renamed Spelman Seminary and finally, in 1927, Spelman College), brought together a generation of African American women in a sex-segregated environment, much as the Seven Sisters colleges united their white counterparts.[69]

Though Cleveland's letters to and relationship with Whipple were not unique, one element of the correspondence stands out as unusual: Cleveland's reference to sex in her letter dated May 9, 1890. Writing from New York and reflecting on a photograph, Cleveland observed that the image did not capture Whipple's expression—the true nature of "my Eve." The true Evangeline, Cleveland wrote, "looks into my eyes with brief bright glances, with long rapturous embraces,—where her sweet life breath and her warm enfolding arms appease my

69. For Lewis, see Buick, *Child of the Fire*; for Brown and Primus, see Rupp, *Sapphistries*, 133–34; for Waite and Thompson, see Lewis and Gwenwald, "Year of the British Blondes," 20–21; and for Grimké and Burrill, see Hull, *Color, Sex, & Poetry*, 139.

hunger and quiet my unrest, and carry us both in one to the summit of joy, the end of search, the goal of love!"[70]

It's not clear, in this passage, if Cleveland was recalling a past encounter, imagining a future one, or simply describing the way Whipple's gaze made her feel. The relatively unambiguous description of orgasm, however, leaves little doubt that the couple's dynamic was sexual as well as romantic.

Italy

In 1910, Whipple learned that her brother, Kingsmill, was seriously ill in Italy. Passport records confirm that Evangeline Whipple and Rose Cleveland left America for Italy on July 20, 1910, aboard the Cunard Line's SS *Saxonia*. Pamphlets and letters in the Minnesota Historical Society's collections indicate that although Whipple was living in Minnesota and Cleveland in New York, it was Cleveland—a member of the extended Marrs family who was likely as alarmed about Kingsmill's condition as Whipple—who arranged the trip. The two women shared a cabin during the voyage.

Whipple was fifty-four and Cleveland sixty-four years old when they finally began living together in Italy—for the first time as true partners. Cleveland's love letters to Whipple in the Minnesota Historical Society cease after 1909, but the story continued in Italy.

Cleveland and Whipple stayed in Florence with Kingsmill Marrs and his wife, Laura Norcross Marrs, for at least two years, until Kingsmill's death in 1912. It's unclear why

70. Katz ("President's Sister," 35) called this passage "one of the most explicit, unambiguous references in the nineteenth-century to two women's mutual orgasm with each other." Although Petrik, "Into the Open," transcribed it accurately, it has been widely misprinted as " . . . with long rapturous embraces, when her sweet life beneath and her warm enfolding arms appease my hunger and quiet my soul [also sometimes transcribed as "breast"]—and carry us both in one to the summit of joy, the end of search, the goal of love!"

Cleveland and Whipple chose to settle in Bagni di Lucca, a small mountain town in Tuscany. It did satisfy Cleveland's need for clean, cold air in mountain environments like upstate New York and Austria; health spas and sulfur springs; and an expatriate English enclave complete with an Anglican church. Bagni di Lucca may also have attracted Cleveland because her literary heroes, Elizabeth Barrett Browning and Robert Browning, had lived there in the 1850s. Even before their deaths, the Brownings came to symbolize for many readers an idealized romantic partnership nurtured in defiance of social expectations (the couple married in secret and left England to escape Barrett Browning's father's disapproval). That symbolism may have resonated with Cleveland in particular when she chose to settle in Italy with Whipple as her partner.[71]

The charm and romance of Bagni di Lucca's "atmosphere" fascinated Whipple, who noted, "the moment one enters her tree-arched roads, one feels an atmosphere of savoir-faire, if the term may be used in such a connection, as unmistakably as one feels the same quality in a fine old soul, whose long years of experience and contact have left him, or her, in the twilight of life, singularly wise and simple." Cleveland and Whipple integrated into the local community, and Whipple eventually owned three adjacent homes there: Casa Bernadini, Casa Burlamacchi, and Villa San Francesco. As they did in America, Whipple and Cleveland provided housing and support to a network of women.[72]

World War I began in July 1914, with Italy entering the fight in April 1915. Rather than trying to exit Europe and flee the dangers of war, Cleveland and Whipple instead petitioned the American consulate in Florence to stay in Italy, with permission to travel to the British Isles, France, and Switzerland.

71. On June 7, 1912, Cleveland wrote her niece, Clara Cleveland, from the Hotel Royal Continental de Parc in Bagni di Lucca, saying that she and Whipple had "settled in this charming place again after long and wide wandering" (quoted in Salenius, *Cleveland*, 87).

72. Whipple, *Famous Corner of Tuscany*, 20.

Whipple's paperwork reported, "Mrs. Whipple is collaborating with Miss Cleveland, ex-President Cleveland's sister, in some writing which will require their presence in Paris and London at some time in the near future."[73]

Nelly Erichsen (1862–1918), an English artist and writer, joined Cleveland and Whipple's circle in Bagni di Lucca sometime around 1914. The three women were deeply involved in Italy's World War I and Red Cross relief efforts in England, Belgium, and Italy. Although larger cities like Rome and Florence provided safety, and most wealthy people simply provided funding for projects, Whipple, Cleveland, and Erichsen chose to stay in Bagni di Lucca, and they worked directly with the war refugees. After the Italian defeat at the Battle of Caporetto in November 1917, refugees from Gorizia and Veneto flooded Tuscany. In her article "Debris of the War," Erichsen reported that the region's governor sent more than a thousand refugees to Bagni di Lucca, which had a population of just over two thousand people. In the war, the three foreigners, Whipple, Cleveland, and Erichsen, seemed to find purpose: "When once they [the refugees] had roughly shaken down, and one began to know them by sight, they ceased to be mere wreckage of the war and suddenly became intensely interesting human beings who were in bitter need of more things than it was possible for the overburdened government to provide. This fact gave us our opportunity. As *forestieri* [foreigners] we had held back, but we had longed to help. Now there was work for all, Italians and foreigners alike."[74]

Erichsen was in charge of organizing the male refugees; Cleveland and Whipple the women. Relying on her missionary

73. Evangeline Whipple US passport application dated October 27, 1916, and issued on December 3, 1916. National Archives, accessed via ancestry .com. In December 1916, Cleveland and Whipple applied for new US passports. Their 1910 passports had been extended twice and were expiring.

74. Erichsen, "Debris of the War," 167 ("When once"). The article offers Erichsen's first-person account of the local relief effort. Correspondence between Erichsen and Edward Hutton placed Erichsen in Bagni di Lucca in

experiences with Indigenous people in Minnesota, Whipple arranged for housing, food, and education for war orphans, in addition to her education efforts with Bagni di Lucca villagers, and employed about twenty women to manufacture clothing and bandages for soldiers on the front line.[75]

The worldwide influenza pandemic of 1918, known then as Spanish influenza, hit Bagni di Lucca hard. To combat it, Whipple and Cleveland worked with Bagni di Lucca's mayor, hired doctors and nurses from Livorno and Florence, set up makeshift hospitals in the churches, and isolated the sick to stop the spread of disease. Starting in 1917, Evangeline Whipple's voice enters the conversation through a letter she wrote to her friend Bishop Charles Slattery, asking—"for the first time in my life"—for help and indicating that her vast resources were running out: "If our friends at home can cable us money, we ourselves gladly take all risks; for unhappily it is a very contagious epidemic, and the air is heavy with germs. But thank God, we are not afraid, knowing that if we are meant to be of service to these poor sufferers, we shall be protected. If not—but that is in God's hands, and we are content."[76]

Nelly Erichsen caught influenza while tending sick patients in the hospital and died on November 15, 1918, four days after

1917. She discussed wanting to go "back to Bagni di Lucca to finish up my drawings" (Madden and Harkness, "Nelly Erichsen," 54), but it is not clear if she was living with Whipple and Cleveland at this time. Erichsen visited Bagni di Lucca in 1912 when she was working with coauthor Janet Ross on the book *The Story of Lucca*.

75. For work with refugees, see Evangeline Whipple to Charles Slattery, December 1, 1917, and "Mrs. Whipple Has Work Room for Refugees," *Grand Forks (ND) Herald*, May 20, 1918.

76. Evangeline Whipple to Charles Slattery, December 1, 1917. Whipple met Charles Lewis Slattery (1867–1930) in Faribault, Minnesota, where he served as the dean of the Cathedral of Our Merciful Saviour from 1896 to 1907. He was the rector of Grace Church, New York City, from 1910 to 1922, and he became the bishop of the Episcopal Diocese of Massachusetts in 1927. Whipple also wrote Slattery an account of the events leading up to Rose Cleveland's death, which he incorporated into a eulogy he delivered for

the signing of the armistice between the Allies and Germany. Cleveland became infected with the disease while nursing Erichsen and died on November 22. Whipple wrote her step-daughter, Jane Whipple Scandrett, in December 1918, calling Cleveland her "precious & adored life-long friend" and describing her grief over Cleveland's death, saying, "The light has gone out for me, but the work is too important for me to run away from" and "The loss . . . is a blow that I shall not recover from." Whipple told Bishop Slattery, "Miss Cleveland was one of the noblest, truest, and really greatest characters I have ever known. She was a passionate lover of her country, to which she has been an honor here. She was a true friend of Italy, an inspiration to us all."[77]

Whipple's letters from 1918 end the love letters between Rose and Evangeline and allow her intelligent and resilient voice to be heard loud and clear. Her strong words prove that although her responses are not represented in the love letters from 1890 to 1910, Whipple was never the silent or pliable pawn of Michael Simpson, Henry Whipple, or Rose Cleveland, but rather an independent, empathetic, and immensely capable woman. Just as she remained in Minnesota after the death of Bishop Whipple, Evangeline continued to live in Bagni di Lucca after Cleveland's death, serving the community for twelve more years. The mayor of Bagni di Lucca bestowed citizenship on Whipple in 1918, and a road, Via Evangeline Whipple, was named in her honor. She died of pneumonia and kidney failure in London on September 1, 1930.[78]

Whipple had planned her own burial in the English Cemetery in Bagni di Lucca. Her last wish was to be interred next

Cleveland on January 26, 1919, in New York, and later published (Slattery, *Rose Elizabeth Cleveland*).

77. Evangeline Whipple to Jane Whipple Scandrett, December 29, 1918; Slattery, *Rose Elizabeth Cleveland*, 12.

78. Whipple was rumored to be traveling home to Minnesota and was accompanied by Cleveland's niece, Carrie Hastings Lawrence. They were staying at the Burlington Hotel, Cork Street, London. "Reports of Deaths

to Rose Cleveland—as opposed to either of her husbands—with a matching headstone: "Two of the three burial places are now the resting places of Rose Elizabeth Cleveland, and Nelly Erichsen, my beloved friends who died while working for Italy in the World War. The third place is reserved for my own burial if I die in Italy or conveniently near . . . and [with funds] to pay for a stone, a Latin cross like the one marking the said grave of Rose Elizabeth Cleveland."[79]

Cleveland's and Whipple's histories are tied to their outward existence: social reform and humanitarian efforts. However, it is their intimate correspondence demonstrating their commitment to one another—which survived over twenty-eight years and a complete cultural revolution—that is their lasting legacy.

of American Citizens Abroad, 1835–1974," National Archives and Records Administration (NARA), Washington, DC; General Records of the Department of State, record group 59, entry 205, box 1404, 1930–39 England Si–Z.

79. Evangeline Whipple's American will, May 1, 1929, Whipple-Scandrett papers.

Notes on the Transcription

Proper names of people mentioned in the correspondence are not always identifiable. The editors have made every possible effort, given current resources, to reveal their identities. Many of the letters mention enclosures; no enclosures are archived with the letters, and the editors have not found evidence of them in the collection.

spaces between paragraphs	replace with paragraph indent
unintentionally misspelled words	represent as written; follow with "[sic]"
unnecessarily capitalized and/or uppercased words	retain
omitted final periods, commas, colons, and semicolons	insert as needed to improve reading ease
commas, em dashes, and swung dashes used as final periods	replace with periods
initial swung dashes	do not reproduce
ampersands	reproduce as written
tildes	do not reproduce
plus signs used as "and"	render as "and"
illegible words and phrases	render as "[illegible]"
page transitions	do not represent
underlined words	italicize
undated letters	add inferred date in *italic*
unclear abbreviations, e.g., "Vicks"	complete word in brackets, e.g., "Vicks[burg]"
quotation marks used as ordinal suffixes, e.g., September 23"	render as 23rd, 31st, 12th, etc.
times of day, e.g., "8.30 A.M."	render as "8:30 A.M."
letterhead printed on stationery (e.g., hotel names)	reproduce in *ITALIC SMALL CAP*
letter writers' signatures, when not written	add inferred writer's name in brackets, e.g., [Rose]
sender and recipient information	add inferences in boldface italic, e.g., ***Rose Cleveland to Evangeline Simpson***
crossed-out words, where legible	reproduce with strikethrough, e.g., ~~and King,~~
crossed-out words, where illegible	insert in brackets "[illegible crossed-out words]"
words written in languages other than English	italicize
processing archivist's notations	reproduce in brackets
editors' notations	reproduce in italic, e.g., *begins mid-letter*

List of Recurring Friends and Family

KATHERINE (PUSSY, PUSSIE) WILLARD BALDWIN (1866–1932). A New Yorker and Frances Folsom Cleveland's roommate at Wells College. A niece of Cleveland's colleague Frances Willard, "Pussy" was Rose Cleveland's travel companion and a frequent visitor to her home, the Weeds.

FRANCES FOLSOM CLEVELAND (1864–1947). Married President Grover Cleveland and was first lady from 1886 to 1889 and 1893 to 1897.

GROVER CLEVELAND (1837–1908). Rose Cleveland's eldest brother and the twenty-second and twenty-fourth president of the United States.

NELLY ERICHSEN (1862–1918). English painter and author; lived with Whipple and Cleveland in Bagni di Lucca, Italy.

CLARA C. FULLER (CIRCA 1853–CIRCA 1935). Principal of Ossining Seminary for Young Ladies, New York.

AMELIA (MILLIE) CANDLER GARDINER (1869–1945). Daughter of a prominent Boston family headed by a US senator from Massachusetts. Candler was a close friend and travel companion of Evelyn Ames.

EVELYN (ELOPHUN) AMES HALL (1863–1940). Pianist from a wealthy Boston family; daughter of Oliver Ames, the thirty-fifth governor of Massachusetts. She was a constant companion of Rose Cleveland from 1895 to 1909, when she married artist and architect Frederick Garrison Hall.

ELLEN MATILDA ORBISON HARRIS (AUNTIE HARRIS) (1816–1902). A member of Philadelphia's elite society who worked as an American Civil War nurse and later as an aid worker in Italy. Harris was related by marriage to James A. Beaver, governor of Pennsylvania between 1887 and 1891. The 1870 appointment of her husband, physician John Harris, to the US consulship to Venice transported her to Italy, where she lived until her death.

CAROLYN (CARRIE) HASTINGS LAWRENCE (1866–1939). Daughter of Anna Neal Cleveland and Eurotas Hastings, Rose Cleveland's niece. Married Robert Ashton Lawrence, was widowed in 1905, and lived in Florence, Italy.

LIPPORAH. Cleveland's maid.

JANE VAN POELIEN KNAGGS MARRS (1829–1906). Known as "Motherdie," she was mother to Evangeline Whipple and Kingsmill Marrs.

LAURA NORCROSS MARRS (1845–1926). A member of Boston's elite society and daughter to Otis Norcross, mayor of Boston from 1867 to 1868. She married Kingsmill Marrs in 1896.

WILLIAM D. KINGSMILL MARRS (1847–1912). Evangeline's brother and only sibling. Known as Kingsmill or King.

MARY (MAY) YEOMANS RODGER (1874–1968). Daughter of Susan and Lucien Yeomans; Rose Cleveland's niece.

JANE (JANEY, JENNIE) WHIPPLE SCANDRETT (1847–1932). Henry Whipple's daughter and Evangeline Whipple's friend and stepdaughter.

MICHAEL HODGE SIMPSON (1809–84). A wealthy merchant, industrialist, and philanthropist in Framingham, Massachusetts; Evangeline Whipple's first husband.

CHARLES LEWIS SLATTERY (1867–1930). A close friend of Evangeline and Bishop Whipple. He served as the dean of the Cathedral of Our Merciful Saviour in Faribault, Minnesota, from 1896 to 1907. He was the rector of Grace Church, New York, from 1910 to 1922, and he became the bishop of the Episcopal Diocese of Massachusetts in 1927.

ADELAIDE (FIORI) HAMLIN THIERRY (1879–1961). A Radcliffe College graduate who traveled with Cleveland and was a frequent visitor to the Weeds in Holland Patent, New York.

HENRY BENJAMIN WHIPPLE (1822–1901). The first Episcopal bishop of Minnesota and Evangeline Whipple's second husband.

FRANCES WILLARD (1846–98). A prominent suffragist and temperance reformer and the president of the Woman's Christian Temperance Union (WCTU) from 1879 until her death. Cleveland wrote the introduction to Willard's *How to Win: A Book for Girls* (1886).

WILLIAMS. Cleveland's maid.

SUSAN (SUE) CLEVELAND YEOMANS (1843–1938). One of Rose Cleveland's four sisters; wife of politician and fruit grower Lucien Theron Yeomans.

Letters

PART 1

1890–1896

Rose Cleveland sent her first extant letters to Evangeline Simpson (later Whipple) from Florida, where the couple had met in the late 1880s. Cleveland was finishing the winter season of 1889–90 there, and Simpson had traveled from central Florida to Luray, Virginia. At the time, their early romance was at its peak, and they were strategizing ways to see each other outside of family and business commitments. Staying in touch was a challenge; the frequency and reliability of mail delivery changed as they moved from place to place.

Rose Cleveland[1] to Evangeline Simpson,[2] Luray Inn, Luray,[3]
Virginia
PINE CREST INN, PAOLA, ORANGE COUNTY, FLORIDA
Sunday, April 13th [1890]

Eva[4]—

Do you know in what distress I was?

No word from you at all since you had my letter written after receipt of your telegram and in anticipation of what your letter (it promised) should contain. The letter came on Thursday by Orange Belt[5] and another by regular evening mail. Then on Friday one in Orange Belt and one in evening mail, I think, but all written before you had received my letter in explanation of why I could not go to you, and with the distracting little statements relative to my coming, in your ignorance of my situation. I confidently looked for a reply to my letter yesterday and certainly by the last mail, if not before, and I secretly hoped—not a wild hope of happiness yet—for the telegram which would justify my going to you on Monday.

But neither have come, and I have promised, if not prevailed (which I counted on), to go on to Naples[6] for a week with Mrs.

1. Rose Cleveland's siblings (Grover Cleveland in particular) called her "Libbie." She consistently signed off her correspondence with Evangeline, however, as "Rose."

2. Evangeline Whipple was born Evangeline Marrs. She became Evangeline Simpson after her marriage to Michael Simpson in 1882, and changed her name to Evangeline Whipple after her second marriage, to Henry Whipple in 1896. Most of the letters are addressed to Evangeline Simpson or Mrs. Simpson; she signed her letters "Evangeline" or "E."

3. Luray is in Virginia's Shenandoah Valley.

4. Cleveland referred to Whipple by various nicknames, including Eva, Eve, Evy, Evie, Grandmother, Gran, Second Mother, Wing, and Wingie.

5. The Orange Belt Railway, completed in 1888, connected the Florida cities of Sanford and St. Petersburg.

6. Naples, a resort town in Florida where Cleveland purchased a parcel of land in 1889 for $200 and commissioned the construction of a house that was finished in 1890.

Haldeman,[7] who has told me how Naples affairs stand, and I see that my interests there would be greatly served by my going now. But if I had had the courage to go to you, I should have gone and put Naples in later. Now how can I refuse to go to-morrow, feeling these letters, which would determine your happiness & mine, are floating somewhere—impossible to get hold of!—and I don't know where to send this letter—!

Well, if you received my other, which I sent to Sanford[8] to mail so that it surely would reach you that late Thursday ev'g, or early Friday A.M., you will know why I have waited to hear from you in reply before I risked another letter. It is useless to dwell on this. But I have not the least idea what to do with *this*; I think I will write it and take [it] with me; or send to the Cordova[9] to be returned to me at Punta Gorda,[10] unless forwarded to you. Yes, I will do that, and therefore I must not write all I would if I did not take these risks—for if I must be sure, for your sake, that only you will open the letter in which I am unreserved.

No mail has come for you at all.

Mrs. Haldeman arrived on Thursday, and we have managed to live. She is extremely delicate, and has a heartbreaking sorrow, but is as heroic and bright as she is slender. She has counted very much on the rest she would find in this change,[11] and I am much mortified that I am compelled to disappoint her: I can compromise for turning her out by going with her.

---

7. Elizabeth Metcalfe Haldeman, wife of Walter N. Haldeman, a white settler-colonist who founded Naples, Florida. Walter Haldeman built and owned the Naples Hotel; when it opened in 1889, Rose Cleveland was its first registered guest. Walter Haldeman also founded and published the *Louisville Courier-Journal* in his native Kentucky. See Kleber, *Encyclopedia of Louisville*, 365–66.

8. Sanford, Florida, was seven miles from the Pine Crest Inn, Paola.

9. The Hotel Cordova in St. Augustine.

10. A tourist town and the last stop on the Florida Southern Railroad.

11. Elizabeth Haldeman suffered from chronic health problems involving dizziness, lethargy, fainting spells, and menstrual pain. See Cusick, "Gentleman of the Press," 22.

But I shall return by Friday's steamer if there be one, so as to arrive here on Saturday evening and have your letters.

I have made up my mind to stay here two or three weeks unless you send for me. I will go anywhere to you, but otherwise I must stay here. Now that Mrs. Haldeman has come to me, I shall not go home by the Western route, but probably take a Clyde steamer fr[om] Jacksonville in May & accept chances as to comfort on sea, as against certain discomfort of, to me, the most trying sort in warm weather. Perhaps you can join me on my steamer when we touch a[t] Charlestown, or Old Point, if we touch there, wh[ich] I doubt. Can we not contrive something of that sort?

If you knew all I could tell you—do you?

[Rose]

Rose Cleveland to Evangeline Simpson, Luray Inn, Luray, Virginia
5 A.M., Tuesday, April 22 [1890]
Gulf of Mexico

The sun just above the horizon, and me just off a half hour from Naples. I in the boat, done up in a comfortable [chair], back against the main mast—my face set to the North, where all my hopes are centered. I slept almost none last night, and rose at half past three, and am off in this adventurous fashion because there is not other way to start. What will come of it, is a question.

Punta Gorda
Wednesday, 7 A.M.

On the train an hour. And I have just again read your last words—the last I can read until I reach our Pines[12]—

---

12. Pine Crest Inn at Paola, Orange County, Florida, near Orlando. An article by Lucie Vannevar published on January 30, 1890, in the *Tampa Journal*

"Oh darling, come to me this night—my Clevy, *my Viking,*
My—Everything, Come! God Bless Thee."

—and with them in my soul & blood, I have leaned heavily
(tho' I am very well & quite fresh this A.M.) against the window,
heavily, as if faint or very ill—suddenly paralyzed.

There are no words for this, my Eve, and I will not try, for
to tell you all in any connected way would be impossible. The
distress & shameful defeat of this last ten days is unsettling to
the mind, and I need my wits yet, for they are *all* I have.

You see, I have your letters. The one gleam in yesterday's
tragedy.[13] They were all waiting for me at Punta Gorda, & a
beaming Post Master, rejoicing in Grover C,[14] had guarded
them jealously & handed them over wit[h] delight. So I can
follow you now up to ten *days* ago, for your last [was] postmarked Monday, *Jacksonville,* April *14,* 11 A.M., and is dated
Sunday Evening. Then from St. Augustine written Saturday
the 12th, & one Friday the 11th. When the one written Friday
was written (in the eve'g) you had still had no *word* from me,
& my *first* reached you only on *Saturday* which makes me want
to *kill* somebody, for I certainly tho't & took comfort in the
thought that that first letter in reply to your telegram would
reach you Thursday night.

Oh, well. I thank God you have not been really able to know
all I have gone through in this last ten days, and you need not,
for I am preserved so far, and believe I shall come through and
reach you at last. Now, my one thought is to reach Pine Crest,
where I must find some other letters from you—and be able to
plan to meet you. From there I have up to the 14th. Know that
when you have changed your plans [and] *you* are at Luray, I

places Cleveland and Whipple at the Pine Crest Inn, along with Jane Marrs
and Kingsmill Marrs.

13. While sailing a chartered boat off the coast of Punta Gorda, Cleveland
and two others were nearly swept overboard in a violent storm. "They Clung
to the Sailboat—Narrow Escape of Miss Cleveland and Two Friends—A
Thrilling Trip," *Buffalo (NY) Courier,* May 1, 1890.

14. Grover Cleveland.

shall send this on to that address by friends, who will mail it at Jacksonville to morrow. No, I shall send it on by the train mail agent ~~when~~ on the JT & KW,[15] which will land me at Sanford at midnight to-night, and if it, this letter, goes on as it ought to, it ought to reach Luray by Friday. Then to-night at Sanford, as soon as I arrive, I *shall* send you a telegram saying, "I All Safe. ~~Letters~~ Expect letters. Will meet you in New York—R.E.C."

Then I shall see if I can be taken out to Pine Crest ~~to~~ at midnight (by Magruder, so don't worry), & if not I will go, I suppose, to the Sanford House,[16] & reach Pine Crest at 9 to morrow, Thursday A.M.—. Then I shall know where you are— and what you have planned, and if you have rec'd the letter I sent you on Monday the 14th from Sanford to the *Cordova,* St. Augustine, or the one I sent you on the eve'g of Monday the 14th, written on the train nearing Punta Gorda and sent to the St. James, and you ~~can~~ know *why* you have not heard from me.

Oh, the agony of the fear I have had that you did not know I could not understand all the awful baffling of this distance & no means of communication. —What have you thought?

Well, I shall send *all* these penciled, bound pages to you, with this, and just *wait.*

But I (just here I see on the floor behind me a paper dime novel entitled "Butterfly Billy's Man Hunt." Will you call me B. B. after this?!) But this is what, with my present light, I see ahead as a possibility for us. That you give yourself a little more time in New York, reaching there, say, on the 7th. Establish yourself in the hotel of your choice, & *I* will be at my brother's, or will be wherever it seems happiest for us. I can think of several things we could do which would provide us what we wish.

Another plan: what we might prefer. I conclude you will be

15. Jacksonville, Tampa, & Key West Railway.
16. Sanford House Hotel in Sanford, Florida, near Orlando, was built in 1876.

at Washington next week. Will you come from Washington to Savannah, & take the steamer for New York with me. *That* would be perfect. If you would & *will*, I will wait for you to name the steamer (I sh'd say the *City of Augusta*) and the *date*, & will *be* there, with Lippora,[17] to meet you, [and] have your state room & all arrangements made. Then we shall be *sure* of from two to four days together on *that* boat. At N. York, we will transfer (it is but a step from pier to pier) to the Albany boat (Hudson River) and spend more time on that, if you like, *or* will stop in New York. I should have to go to my brother's, but if you liked, I could spend most of the time at your hotel, in your room.

Another plan. I could come on to Washington, stay a day with Mrs. Laughton[18] & go on to New York with you. I do not think that would be nice, for I see how impossible it would be for me to see *you* alone. If you can meet me in Savannah, that would be best, but if you do not like to come back so far to join me, then we will arrange for New York, and I will leave all to you, promising only to *start* when I am bidden. I should go by Savannah steamer, if possible.

I have two weeks now, to the 7th of May, in which to hear from you, but your first letter in reply to this [had] better be final, as it is so unsafe to trust to any mail or telegraphic communications. *No* time is long enough for them.

Now I must pause. I have *lost* or *left* my eyeglasses and am reading & writing with less ease than I like, with several witnesses around holding me in full survey & frequent discourse. So I dare not go on—dare not say what I think or dream—but you know.

[*Rose*]

17. The name of Cleveland's housekeeper, often spelled with a final "h."
18. Possibly Flora Laughton, wife of Charles E. Laughton (first lieutenant governor of Washington, 1889–93).

Rose Cleveland to Evangeline Simpson, Luray, Virginia
postmarked April 23, 1890

Barton, 4:30 P.M.

And I have been in this little room for hours—dinner the only diversion, & a poor one, the witty and entertaining wife of the invalid man who came from Naples with me having just left, after a full hour of talk. I have sat nearly, or over, an hour, and now [she] comes again to my door. She is going to see the Jew doctor about her husband, who lies in pain all day & all night. Both so young it is sad to see them—he lying on a cot in the sail-boat yesterday with their faithful colored man, the three a sad picture. And they are going on to Jacksonville to night.

But no[w] I "have a letter to write," & so I lie here with my eyes a little off, & no glasses—dashing at these pages, because I *must* tell you—try to—*something*, yet it can be so little.

And just now a little Uncle Tom[19] comes with a flat, rather wet newspaper bundle, saying "someone sent you that." I tear off the old paper & behold a pillow of lovely roses, pink, white, yellow, fit to lay at your feet, in your lap.

My Eve—! Ah, how I love you! It paralyzes me. I have been going over & over your written words until the full message of them—*some* of them—has made me weary with emotion. This I must try and escape, for *your* sake. But let me cry & shout it. Oh Eve, Eve, surely you cannot realize what you are to me. What you must be. Yes, I dare it, now, I will not longer fear to claim you. You are mine by every sign in Earth & Heaven, by every sign in soul & spirit & body—and you cannot escape me. You must bear me all the way, Eve; clasp me in my despair of any other and give me every joy & all hope—this is yours to do.

And now, a little apparition in a white dress & flaxen hair curled at the ends, and pink cheeks & china blue eyes, stands

---

19. This derogatory term for an African American man originated in *Uncle Tom's Cabin*, by Harriet Beecher Stowe, first published in 1852.

before me looking in at the window, a gentle little girl, easy to be entreated—& now sitting calmly on the window seat! Conversing gently of the roses, of her chickens, of Mrs. Todd's rheumatism in her heel, of how long I have been in Barton &c &c—smiling a great deal & daring little.

And I write on, leaning my head in my hand, my cheek in the palm of my hand, as you have done often, looking at the blue of this sky over the handsome orange trees & the ugly place of houses & whitewashed fences & muricated sand, & hearing the sick man in the room cough, & talk freely. It is near time for us to move on, at 6 P.M., a *little* farther, where we wait three hours more, taking the train for Sanford at 9 P.M. But I bear it all, as I bear all things which take me on to you, for to you it shall be—sooner or later, somewhere.

I shall reach Sanford at I A.M. & sit in the station 2 hours, when it will be light enough to get Magruder & drive out to the [house], so reaching your letters four hours before the train *would* take me there.

I have been going over it all again, and, as I make it, these three letters (if you will permit such a name for these disgraceful scrawls, written on such paper, with such a pencil, & no eyes), will not reach you, at best time, before Saturday, & that would be your very latest [day] of leaving Luray. Ah, well, I can do *no* better!

And now the young wife coming back, saying I am to have *calls* and perhaps my time is short. Oh Eve, I tremble at the thought of you—you are ever before me, ever, ever, and my whole being leans out to you.

Here *Lucy* comes back, fluffy flax, china pink & all, with a wax doll, gorgeous in gauze & looking exactly like little Lucy herself. She holds it out to me in mute challenge of my admiration & ecstasy—the little woman with the baby, all over!

And there are signs in the ugly inn of approaching supper— my last word till to-morrow, Love! Ah, may this but reach you & carry to your rich red heart all mine cannot hold, cannot hold & live, unless it spills it over into yours. Sweetheart,

Sweetheart, let me once get you again & you shall not leave me. *Say you will not*—promise me! Write it & sign it. Do this for me.

Now Lucy returns & stands mute, heartbroken that I do not look at the uplifted doll—which I do—and send her to see what time it is. After all, *Dainty*[20] is the best one to have around—isn't he?

Sweet, Sweet, I dare not think of your arms—but I am coming to them. Nothing but *God* shall keep me from you. God & Yourself. Your Viking kisses you!

I *suppose* Luray is in Va—and I shall so risk it. But you do not mention it. My dear love to *Mütterchen*[21]—if only I could see [her]. She would be so sorry for her child[22] & would know why I needed her mother hands to comfort me for my sick heart!

[Rose]

Rose Cleveland to Evangeline Simpson, the Hamilton, Washington, DC
postmarked from Utica, New York
THE PARK HOTEL
Monday, May 5th, 1890

12 noon
And just on my train again for the home stretch, my Eve—and ready to report I did not write yesterday as I thought I would, as I reflected that I could carry my story closer by writing on the train. So I waited.

20. Dainty was Evangeline Whipple's Yorkshire Terrier.
21. German: little mother. The word recalls *Motherdie*, the Marrs family's pet name for Jane Van Poelien Knaggs Marrs, Evangeline's mother.
22. Early in their relationship, Cleveland and Whipple treated each other's extended families as their own. Cleveland consistently referred to Jane Marrs as her mother, and to herself as a child.

I arrived in Rochester[23] at 2:15 P.M. on Saturday after a comfortable ride from Williamsport. The dining room car conductor knew me, having often seen me in Washington, he said, & was very nice. In Rochester I had an hour to wait, but killed it by a lunch and a discussion of routes to New Orleans, through Vicks[burg], etc. It was only a half hour on the train and a half hour by carriage—instead of twice that, as I said in Saturday's letter—to my sister's home, where the time has gone as swiftly as any time in this next five months can go,[24] with very much talk, much laughter & sleep & eating. Sue[25] is very witty and keen, kind & generous to a fault, and drives four in hand in that little community, with her brisk husband and children at her side. It is a great diversion to be there, and I come away always with a *loaded* feeling—head, hands, & stomach full.

Just at this moment I am alone in the one parlor car of the train—the other three occupants, all men, having left, whether to return or not. The train is standing at this *Lyons,*[26] and I am writing more easily—but my eyes warn me that I must not try to keep it up. I am feeling very well, darling, with a sort of *Casabianca*[27] feeling, waking or sleeping, a sense of *holding out for life.*

We reach Utica at 4:40 P.M. and there I have, I find, nearly two hours, by a new arrangement of trains, but I do not object to it, for I shall do several errands for myself; and shall reach the Weeds[28] about 7 P.M. There I shall find letters from you,

23. Rochester, New York.

24. Cleveland and Simpson planned to reunite in October 1890.

25. Susan Cleveland Yeomans (1843–1938), one of Cleveland's four sisters, was living with her husband and children in Walworth, New York.

26. A town in Wayne County east of Rochester.

27. A reference to Felicia Dorothea Hemans's 1826 poem "Casabianca," which depicts a 1798 naval battle between the British and French off the coast of Egypt.

28. The Weeds, the Cleveland family estate and Rose's main home in New York, was in the town of Holland Patent, about fifty miles west of Syracuse. The nearest train station was at Utica, about eleven miles to the south.

which will make it seem warm and sweet to me, if all else fails me. And then I shall know how you got on.

Oh Eve, Eve, this Love is Life itself—or *death*. I love you, love you beyond belief—you are all the world to me. God bless you.

I have a box of hyacinths here which May,[29] my niece, put up for me. If I could only lay them in your lap . . . but I shall crowd them in this dear vase, and put them, as the first incense, before your picture on my desk this eve'g—and write you my first letter from the Weeds—& then dream of having you there in October!

[Rose]

Rose Cleveland to Evangeline Simpson, Washington, DC
THE WEEDS, HOLLAND PATENT, NEW YORK
May 6, 1890

Monday, 8 P.M.

Only a word tonight, My Eve, for I am desperately tired—just today my train left Utica for my Weeds in one half hour after I arrived there instead of two hours, and I was here before 5:50 P.M.—Lipporah but no Pussy.[30] She has not arrived yet—is expected to morrow. But Lipporah faithful and good, and old Williams,[31] with her curtseys & goodness, & Pussy's mother[32] to have me over there to supper, but as my people here had supper for me she came over here instead, and that is all the people—every one.

29. Mary "May" Yeomans Rodger (1874–1968).

30. A nickname for Katherine Willard, the roommate of Frances Folsom Cleveland at Wells College (Robar, *Frances Clara Folsom Cleveland*, 19). Katherine Willard's aunt Frances Willard was a prominent suffragist and the president of the Woman's Christian Temperance Union (WCTU) between 1879 and her death in 1898. Cleveland wrote the introduction to Frances Willard's *How to Win: A Book for Girls* (1886).

31. Cleveland's maid.

32. Mary Bannister Willard (1841–1912), an editor, teacher, and temperance activist.

But the little house with its old things, and the pile of letters with, oh dear, the [tie] from that May Day place with the violets, so blue and true—and the hearts are both here, and your first from Washington in the train on which I came, so sweet, oh so perfectly *My Eve,* to be here when I came. "Those violets she must pick"—now I understand! Well, I have you before me, and Dainty, & your picture[33] is resting against the dear vase, with hyacinths in it, and the look of it all makes me wild.

But all this great emotion must be curbed. You are mine, and I am yours, and we are one, and our lives are one henceforth, please God, who can alone separate us. I am bold to say this, to pray & to live by *it*. Am I too bold, Eve—*tell* me?

But my head is too full—too tired, and I must not get so that I will not sleep, as the confusion in my rooms will keep some clearness, & this letter to be written and all the getting settled into the rut for running again.

I shall go to bed, my Eve—with your letters under my pillow. I wonder if I will feel *alone*. God bless thee & keep thee safe!

Tuesday, 8 A.M.
And walking from my sleeping room, as I tie my necktie, across to my library, I drop down here at the table which stands as I left it last night to add a word to you before breakfast.

I slept, my Eve, [in] spite of the quite awful loneliness which almost submerges me when I come back here. Waking at midnight. Waked by the *stillness* and the heat and the little, very little cold I have taken, which goes the usual way. I made an excuse of the heat to call Lipporah, who pattered around and said things so that I heard the sound of a human voice. Then I felt for the letters and tried to feel your hand—but it

33. A photograph of Evangeline Whipple and her dog, Dainty, is preserved in the collections of the Cathedral of Our Merciful Saviour, Faribault, Minnesota. Shattuck-St. Mary's School in Faribault owns a painting of Evangeline Whipple, with Dainty at her feet, by Ernst Erwin Oehme (1831-1907).

Evangeline Whipple with her Yorkshire Terrier, Dainty, by J. Ludovici, circa 1890. Cleveland wrote to Whipple on May 6, 1890: "Well, I have you before me, and Dainty, & your picture is resting against the dear vase, with hyacinths in it, and the look of it all makes me wild." *Courtesy of the Cathedral of Our Merciful Saviour.*

is no use, Eve. I am sure of you but I do not see your delightful face, or feel your enfolding arms, and lose all else in the
shelter and happiness of that haven. It will be five months to
wait—that is all.

It is raining, the good old spring rains, and I am content
that it should while I settle myself inside and see the grass
grow out my windows. I feel very well, and wholly refreshed,
for I went to sleep again and slept until morning. Now Lipporah announces breakfast. She & Williams will look after me
for a while. Pussy is expected to night.

Later.

And now I am just up from breakfast, which, [in] spite of
all things, was good—Lipporah *had* one of her corn breads
of which I told you, which was better than any I ever ate. I
tho[ugh]t it a good time to break our plan to her, as she stood
behind my chair. She looked immensely pleased when I told
her you were going to be there with me—about *Lottie,* our
breakfasts, etc.—to which, *all,* she responded most loyally. So
now I must begin to walk around, and find the key to my *desk,*
the *other* one, for one which I carried with me does not now
appear, and to have my desk is the *first* thing.

Noon.

And now Lipporah has brought my milk, a *pint* in a glass
pitcher—very rich & sweet—and I have forbidden her to bring
anything else. I will have this for lunch & dinner at 5 P.M. as I
used to in the autumn, and see if I like it. I shall get fat on this
milk, and good porterhouse roasts for dinner, even if I miss
the oranges (which I do!) of Florida.

I have tinkered my desk open, and find the other key where
I left it. Now the other keys are missing—but I shall manage
them, too. Precious little I have accomplished, my Eve, this
A.M., with lounging and loafing to dream of October.

I am sorting the letters now. I have appropriated one

drawer in my desk to you alone, have spent a great while fumbling over those May Day violets,[34] trying to split a sheet of mica so they will go *inside,* but have to content myself with covering them with the mica over white paper,[35] on which I found myself writing—"[5].. [6] [L].. [frau + Mari][36]" and cast them at the bottom of the drawer.

The rain has stopped but the sky is steel & lead with a hint of silver now & then. The trees are only *hinting* their possibilities in green. Everything is soaked; it is the old-fashioned spring, slow but surer than last, & I am satisfied. You can scarcely imagine the quiet I am in, but I am very thankful for my Weeds, never so much so, for I am better here than elsewhere, while I *wait.* I did not notice much then, but it comes back like a sea tide.

Eve, new faith. You are my Paradise—my life.

I hate to seal this, but I will do it—for if I do not I shall make too large a letter & I must attend to other news. Love to Motherdie—How I love her. I expect your Sunday letter this ev'g. You said: "I love you Forever!"

[Rose]

34. Romantic friendships in this period, also called *smashes, crushes,* and *spoons,* involved courtship gestures like the exchange of flowers, notes, and packages. Often, the courting process took place on women's college campuses (Faderman, *Odd Girls and Twilight Lovers,* 19).

35. Cleveland was pressing the violets as a keepsake.

36. The note may be written in a personal shorthand recognizable only to Whipple and Cleveland. The ambiguous lettering of the final two words supports multiple transcriptions in languages other than English, including: *trans Mare* (Latin: across the sea); *frau + Mari* (German and French, respectively: wife and husband); and *braut Mari* (German and French, respectively: bride husband).

Rose Cleveland to Evangeline Simpson, Murray Hill Hotel,[37]
New York City
Friday morning, May 9, 1890

9:30 A.M.

And I sped down the village street [in] spite of Lipporah's astonished face to the post office to get—*no letter* from you! It seemed impossible and unbearable—but I live to record the fact.

Breakfast is over, and after a little strolling about with a feint of interest in household matters I am seated again at my desk—my ink and stationery replenished by the county store, and a fresh pile of letters before me to attack, [with] a dear generous letter from Mrs. Haldeman, who *missed me* when she came back from Naples and loitered a week in upper Florida but rejoiced in the *cause* of my absence. She says, "Even in my disappointment I was delighted to learn you were happy even then; I so rejoice in your happiness." There is not even one pang of jealousy, but an earnest prayer, "God bless her!"

Well, I don't know what is to become of all this trash I am writing you, but I don't seem to be able to settle down to my letters until I have written first a little to you. Don't be a dream, Eve—be my Vision!

10:30 A.M.

The freaks of mail are over—all the monopoly of our beloved Florida, my Eve! Behold—in an hour a transformation!—the train *direct* from the South, which brings the mail, brought no letter from you, but it meets a return train from the North somewhere up the road and this morning this south-bound brought the balance of my mail, with your two letters, of Tuesday & Wednesday, from Washington, with the photographs. I

37. The Murray Hill Hotel, built in 1884, stood at the corner of Park Avenue and Fortieth Street in Midtown Manhattan. It attracted a well-heeled clientele (including P. T. Barnum, Mark Twain, and Presidents Cleveland and McKinley) for decades but was demolished in 1947.

had gone dutifully to my letters and was hunting in Words-
worth for a line I carry near misquoting, when Lipporah
appeared at my library door with the dear pack of letters, all
valueless compared to the two from yourself. So now I sweep
away all that was engaging me, to record the joyful fact and
reply to their ten dear notes, [so] that the southward-bound
mail may take them to Murray Hill this ev'g. The explanation
of this occurrence is that the mail is sorted on the train, and
as my Weeds are the 2nd station from Utica, it sometimes, as
today, happens that the mail agent does not finish by the time
the train arrives & does finish by the time he meets the train
further up the country.

Both your letters are postmarked May 7, 10 P.M., but one is
written "*Wednesday* 9 o'clock"—and the other "Tuesday *nine*
o'clock." Well, no matter—all my migraines are over now.

Yes, I too woke before seven that Tuesday morning, and I
think my first consciousness was of your *absence*[38]—not presence. There is no such dear delusion possible to me, and it is
only by your constant coming by letter, and all the dear words
you can swear by, that I can be *sure* of you, Eve! A sad fact, darling, but a true thing. You must swear, Eve; take all the oaths
you can to keep me easy: *until I have you.*

The photographs are before me. I wish to keep *all* of them,
but not one of them shows me even your shadow, my Eve. My
Eve is all light and joy and triumph, like a red rose just open
on a June morning, with the look of one who has found, not
lost—one who has *reached* and no longer seeks and searches
earth and air for resting place. *All* these faces look other
ways—either of sad loss, or sad search, or hopeless indiffer-
ence, or dutiful effort, or proud acceptance of unlit days, all
something except what my Eve looks into my eyes with brief
bright glances, with long rapturous embraces,—where her
sweet life breath and her warm enfolding arms appease my

---

38. Cleveland's observation suggests that the two women regularly slept
in close quarters, if not in the same bed.

hunger and quiet my unrest, and carry us both in one to the summit of joy, the end of search, the goal of love! Here is no Beyond! Give me the looks of this Eve, and I will call it her shadow and it shall guide me to her, every inch of the long way, and keep me *safe* for her!

But this image will never get out of my brain; my Soul alone will give me back this reflection of the Woman who is my World—my Earth &—God forgive me—my Heaven!

Of all these pictures I like the Egypt[39] the best because it looks least like you, and least unlike the Thou I claim. But I love these shadows of your former self, Eve—they are all full of sweet or sad significance, and if I put them in a book with a name they would be a history which I would call *"The Makings of Eve."* But the last chapter would not be there. Well, send me another—that one I *want*—and let me keep what I have!

This Wednesday letter, with the yellow blossoms & the bit of flox from the old Washington garden, is in the same mail & records my first deliverance from our Weeds in awfully dear words of promise and love. Please remember, Madam, that I have a writing that can appear as evidence, if you do not fulfill your contract . . .

Ah, my Cleopatra here before me looks a very dangerous Queen—but I will look her straight in those wide open eyes that look so imperial, and will crush those Anthony-seeking [*sic*] lips with her army close over me (alas for my hair—not all those armlets) and she becomes my prisoner, because I am her captive![40]

And this will never do—it is now 11:30 and I must return to my mutton; a different creature, warm & full and ready for

---

39. The "Egypt" or "Cleopatra" photo could have shown Whipple dressed in costume. Victorian cabinet cards depicted women dressed as Cleopatra, especially after French actress Sarah Bernhardt's performances of the title role in *Cleopatre* in 1890.

40. Cleveland compares her bond with Whipple to Mark Antony's with Cleopatra—what Petrik calls "one of the celebrated erotic relationships of literature and history" (Petrik, "Into the Open," 14).

a host of enemies! I certainly cannot call the letters I propose to attack enemies, for they are of the friendliest—especially the new ones, which come daily, congratulation & condolence on the shipwreck & escape[41] which, going all over the country, reappear at every turn, and really gives me great annoyance. I enclose this[42] from Prof. Charlie in this mail, as it is so like him, the true dear old budgets of Goodness & Naughtiness! I have written to the editor of my Utica paper—a great friend—and given him facts about the case. Which he can publish if he likes. It is clear that the whole unnecessary sensation proceeds from my traveling companions[43] (with whom you observe I am in the closest bonds!) who thus achieve a Friday notoriety.

4 P.M.

And now I must halt in this writing again. The church here has just stopped tolling for the laying away of the worn-out body of my little busy sempstress,[44] and the farmer folk are passing in the[ir] Sunday clothes going home from her funeral. Yonder comes my good Old Williams, respectable in her long crêpe veil and speckled black with all the black silk I have given her & the cashmere her sons send her in decent piety and respect. School boys pass shouting to [a] big dog over there & swing their dinner pails, and a fat robin on the maple, which is getting covered with little ripped-looking green leaves [in] spite of these drear windy winds, is mournfully arguing to some disconsolate mate that spring *is* coming—is here. He does not believe it [is] warming, tho'—that is plain.

I have not been able to do a very driving business to-day, Eve. And only five letters beside yours show for my

41. See page 66, note 13.
42. The enclosure does not survive in the Whipple-Scandrett papers.
43. Cleveland was traveling with A. D. Milliken and his wife, a daughter of US representative Oscar Turner (1825–96). Turner represented the state of Kentucky between 1879 and 1886.
44. An alternative form of *seamstress*.

perseverance. I have had a rebellious "small of my back" which protests against such constant erection over this desk—and several times I have loafed off on this broad lounge, reading Browning's *Poems*[45] because they were in reach of my hand, & because you have them—or lying with my hands clasped under my head, as you do, thinking, oh, *of course,* of *you*—and seeing many visions of you in this room. Dear, dreamy, full-of-comfort Eve—will they come here?

I read your words over—for answer—"Yes, darling, I shall be with you, surely, in the autumn." But the days *will* be long, Eve. They cannot be short—only I shall have to work while I wait.

There is an absurd rumor in New York that I am to be married[46]—& people are writing & congratulating me conditionally. It's very awkward for me to deny these rumors, Eve— what shall I do about it?

Just here, one of the good old village men came in to tell me the villagers were raising a little fund to relieve the burden which the sickness & loss of the little sempstress has put upon her family, and to give me the pleasure of contributing. Good people these, Eve—with slow, sound hearts for each other when in trouble.

Tomorrow I shall send you, and your mama, ~~and King,~~ each a package of *tea.* You see I crossed out King,[47] but you can say I sent yours for him if you think he would like it. I am

45. Several editions of Elizabeth Barrett Browning's collected poetry were originally titled *Poems.* The 1850 collection, known as *Sonnets from the Portuguese,* contains some of the most popular love poems in the English language. Cleveland later wrote her own poem for Whipple in the style of *Sonnets* (see pages 86–87). Cleveland and Whipple followed in the footsteps of the poet and her husband, Robert, in 1912, when they moved to Bagni di Lucca, Italy.

46. An article printed in the *Nebraska State Journal* on December 8, 1887, had stated, "According to current rumor, Miss Rose Cleveland will marry a young clergyman whose name is withheld out of respect for his family." Even earlier, on February 20, 1887, the *Troy (NY) Northern Budget* had announced, "Rose Cleveland to Marry a Clergyman."

47. Evangeline Whipple's brother, William D. Kingsmill Marrs, known as Kingsmill and King.

not sure enough it is so very remarkable to make any great wonder of it—but all testimony goes that way.

I wrote very carefully about the grapefruit, darling, when on the train, calculating every day closely & giving all directions to Mr. Robinson.[48] But I hardly dare hope that he will be able to fill the order with nice fruit at this season. I gave him the steamer address— Steamship Allan—of North German Lloyd,[49] [leaving] May 1st and 2nd. Exactly how should it be written?

These are terribly long letters—I never dreamed I should wander on so, and still find so much to say—but I shall stop it after you sail, & only write, say, two sheets in a letter—to match "in a measure" yours. How much kissing can Cleopatra stand?

My love to Motherdie. I shall be so glad of King's picture.

[Rose]

Jane Marrs, Evangeline Whipple's mother, by Schemboche, Florence, Italy, circa 1897. *Kingsmill Marrs Photographs, Collection of the Massachusetts Historical Society.*

48. In the mid-1870s, Richard G. Robinson was one of the first white settler-colonists of Zellwood, Florida, in Orange County. He practiced law, was elected to the Florida legislature, and managed orange groves for northern investors (Cutler, *History of Florida*, 200). He likely managed Rose Cleveland's citrus crops.

49. The Allan Line Steamship Company Ltd., North German Lloyd (Norddeutscher Lloyd), provided transatlantic service for passengers and mail delivery.

Rose Cleveland to Evangeline Simpson
May 1890 Holland Patent
begins mid-letter

. . . promises yonder and the burly robins whose red breasts must keep them warm, [in] spite of the bleak May. "*Mir hat er abgeblüht*"[50]—my May has bloomed away! Will it come again, Eve? Is it keeping for me? Are you keeping it for me, wrapped up warm and sweet, fresh and deep, all in a closed bud that will open—*when?* Make me believe it, Eve—give me a *writing*—sign or seal and deliver it to me as your bond or your pound of flesh—and I will *have both*.[51]

Now the hills that rise up through the still, leafless branches of the maples are taking on cold, red last gleams, and Pussy comes in—and I must stop. Whatever comes I know *you* love me and are true to me and will never be the cause of any sorrow to me, and oh, it is only this cruel outrageous time and distance—that is all! "God bless thee and keep thee safe."

This cannot reach you at earliest now before Saturday A.M., for I cannot post it until I have your address, and which I cannot now have until tomorrow's morning mail. I shall have it then, for I shall [have] letters from you then. How shall I bear the weeks—O coaxer—if the days kill me so?

Good night, my Eve. I love you beyond belief.

Your C.

Since the period between June and December 1890 is not documented in the correspondence, Cleveland and Simpson probably

---

50. The phrase concludes a line from Schiller's 1786 poem "Resignation": "*Des lebens Mai bluht einmal und nicht wieder; / Mir hat er abgeblüht*" (Life's youthful May blooms once, and then no more; / for me its bloom has gone).

51. A reference to Shylock and *The Merchant of Venice*; surprisingly, the comparison aligns Cleveland with the villainized moneylender and Whipple with his debtor.

reunited in the autumn, as planned, or earlier. The following letter
suggests that they separated again before Christmas of that year. ∿

Rose Cleveland to Evangeline Simpson
REC [Rose Cleveland letterhead]
December 1890

Merry Christ-mass, Wingie!
The very night you reached Florida and I reached the Weeds, Wingie, this little voice arose and set out to follow you. I could not keep it back, for I knew it would follow, but I did not think it would go so close upon your heels. However, there was nothing for it. But I let it have its way, and so start it did, sighing and singing, and here it is Christmas morning, at your side. I wonder if it will find its voice at once or if you will have to rest and nurse it after its journey and coax it out of shyness with its new surroundings. I don't think it will take long to do the latter, for the home of soft, scented breezes, is its own. But if it should be mute, or rheumatic from fatigue, here is the prescription its doctor sends, which I copy for you.

"It should be tuned not higher than 7 in the major scale and each string should be tuned exactly in unison. By being particular in this you will get all the sweet tones and harmonious chords for which the harps are noted."

That is not the way to speak of it, my Wing, for it is really no other than the Voice of Clevie,[52] full of Christmas carols, whether it will give them out or not, for Christmas, and full of Clevie's sighing and singing love for her darling, every day and every night; and the rest It will tell you, *sometime*!

[Rose]

---

52. Clevie was a nickname for Rose Cleveland.

In early 1891, Whipple began traveling in Europe and the Middle East with her family; Cleveland may have gone with them or joined them at a later date. The Philadelphia Record *reported "Miss Cleveland Off for Egypt" on March 14, 1892. Evangeline's father, Dana Marrs, died in San Remo, Italy, on March 21, 1892. Cleveland's later letters indicate that Cleveland and Whipple traveled through Germany, Austria, Italy, and Egypt together, presumably during 1891–93. For at least part of this time they were accompanied by Whipple's mother (Jane Van Poelien Marrs, aka Motherdie). The three women returned via New York on May 22, 1893.*

While they were abroad, Grover Cleveland beat Republican Benjamin Harrison in the US presidential election of 1892, securing his second (but nonconsecutive) term in the White House. Soon after taking office, he found a lesion in his mouth. In June 1893 his doctor confirmed that it was malignant—perhaps the reason for Rose and Whipple's return to America. A secret (and successful) surgery to remove the tumor took place on a yacht outside of New York Harbor on July 1, 1893. Rose's subsequent duties as the president's sister were minimal—more personal than official—and she remained free to travel, socialize, and visit Evangeline. The gaps in correspondence during this time period could indicate Cleveland and Whipple were together, or that the letters are missing. ∿

Rose Cleveland to Evangeline Simpson
February 11, 1894[53]

And so, forsooth, I am told that in vain
I love you, because I have love[d] before?
Shall yesterday's ~~shower~~ drip of summer rain
beat back the sea from its shore?

---

53. The poem's date suggests that it was written for Valentine's Day. Its tone and register recall Browning's *Sonnets from the Portuguese.*

This, which has rolled through a hemisphere
gathering strength each league, each hour—
shall it recede, because last year,
the sandy wave wet not a stone?

Nay—though you fly, it shall follow swift.
Face it, Ah, face too proud for dismay!
~~But tho~~
Make me a sign:[54] ~~though~~ a finger left,
and the storm's high tide will obey.

Sign me down—it will rest at your feet.
Sign me back—it will sweep to sea.
But no pale ghost of the past, oh Sweet,
shall stand betwixt you and me!

Amelia Candler to Evangeline Simpson
High Street, Brookline. [Massachusetts]
postmarked June 18, 1895

My dear Mrs. Simpson,
May I have the great pleasure of seeing you at luncheon next
Thursday at half past one? Evelyn[55] and I are going to be much
disappointed if you do not come. I feel as though I quite know
you through Evelyn, and that, to me, is one of the beautiful

54. Several of Cleveland's letters mention making signs to prove devotion, including those dated April 23, 1890; April 16, 1896; November 15, 1896;
November 22, 1896; and August 7, 1897.

55. For more on Evelyn Ames Hall, see page 46. The *Journal of Society* (New
York) reported on the wedding of Lillian Ames on April 25, 1893, and described
her sister: "The eldest daughter, Miss Evelyn Ames, the most accomplished
and most sought after by society, is still fancy free. She is one of the most
brilliant amateur pianists in Boston, if not the leading one, and is universally
popular for her strength and sweetness of character."

things of friendship, that we may know and care for the friends of our friend in advance.

Cordially yours
Amelia B. Candler[56]
Sunday—

Amelia Candler to Evangeline Simpson, Saxonville,
   Massachusetts
postmarked August 12, 1895
Masconomo House,[57] Manchester, Mass[achusetts]

My Dear Mrs. Simpson,
My visit to you is still giving me happiness—as though it had not yet ended, for I live each moment over and over again in my mind. It stands quite by itself as a very precious experience because you and Rose are *dear* to me.

lovingly yours,
Millie Candler

Rose Cleveland to Bishop Henry Whipple
from South Park, Saxonville, Massachusetts
August 26, 1895

My dear Bishop,[58]
I take the ribbon for a sign of the blessedest of practical truths: that "giving doth not impoverish," and that obedience to a

56. For more on Amelia Candler Gardiner, see page 47. Her father was John Wilson Candler, US congressman for Massachusetts, 1881–83 and 1889–91.
57. A hotel in Manchester-by-the-Sea, Massachusetts. The town's name was changed from Manchester to Manchester-by-the-Sea in 1989.
58. Bishop Henry Benjamin Whipple, who had been part of Cleveland and Simpson's circle of friends since the early 1890s. While most of the Cleveland-Whipple correspondence is preserved in the Whipple-Scandrett papers, this letter is part of the Henry B. Whipple papers, also at MNHS.

right impulse, which involves seeming loss, results in a greater gain. But even were the sign, supplied by your letter and its contents, wanting, I should have been satisfied to know that your Dainty's bishop was represented at his burial.[59] I delight in all you say about our speechless friends. Brenner lies, at this moment, in his place at my fireplace, his head between his paws, a little on his cheek, sentimentally, unsleeping, tail rappings and mighty sighs testifying to his faithful companionship.

How we have missed you! You know all about this. And how we want to go into the Indian County [sic] with you. Already I am planning for the Seminole trip[60] when I join you next winter in Florida.[61]

Evangeline keeps somehow full in the faith that you love her, but is not the less happy to hear it from my letter. Ah, how much we need, all of us, all the love we can get!

Just reading Harold Frederic's letter from London in yesterday's *Times*, which ends with the enclosed paragraph.[62] How sad—and yet not so bad as it might be?

---

59. Dainty, Evangeline's dog, had died. Evangeline Whipple was devoted to her animals; in her Italian will she ensured that her Yorkshire terriers (Peter and Paul) and whippets (Duke and Prince) would be placed with caretakers who would provide for them after her death.

60. The ancestors of the Seminole people have lived in what is now the southeastern United States for more than twelve thousand years. The US government forcibly removed them to reservations in present-day Oklahoma after the Second Seminole War (1835–42). About five hundred people refused to leave, and today their descendants make up the Seminole Tribe of Florida and the Miccosukee Tribe of Indians of Florida. Bishop Henry Whipple encountered Seminole people during his first visit to Florida in 1843. He ministered to them in Tallahassee in 1853 and later at the Church of the Good Shepherd in Maitland (Whipple, *Lights and Shadows*, 13, 384).

61. Henry Whipple gained national prominence as an advocate for Indigenous people. As an advisor to four presidents over forty years, he wielded considerable influence. Elected to various government commissions for Indian affairs from the 1860s to 1901, Whipple fought for Indigenous peoples' rights during treaty negotiations.

62. *New York Times* London correspondent Harold Frederic ended his column for August 25, 1895, with the epitaph carved on the tombstone of

Have you read Nordau's book *Degeneration?*[63] Never seems to me were such sound principles applied in so wholesale a way; and so far as I have read, I feel very thankful for the book, but very anxious that some one shall separate its truth from its lie. If you could take the job! But you are about better business.

Love to dear Janey[64]—and Mrs. Bartlett—and Miss Whipple[65]—and, for proof, the unchanging love of

Your devoted friend,
Rose Cleveland

Amelia Candler to Evangeline Simpson, Saxonville, Massachusetts
postmarked September 4, 1895
Masconomo House, Manchester

My dear Mrs. Simpson,
The days are going by so quickly, and such beautiful days. The ocean like a great blue sapphire, and at night flooded with moonlight. There is a crisp freshness in the air [that] is exhilarating, and no description can do justice to the woods.

Darwinist agnostic Thomas Huxley, who had recently died: "And if there be no meeting past the grave, / if all is darkness, silence, yet 'tis rest. / Be not afraid, ye waiting hearts that weep! / For God still giveth His beloved sleep. / And if an endless sleep He wills, so best!" The lines are taken from a poem written by Huxley's sister, Henrietta Huxley, that reflects on the death of poet Robert Browning ("Browning's Funeral," 1889).

63. Social critic Max Nordau published his most famous work, *Degeneration*, in 1892. The inflammatory book—much of it based on racist and eugenicist science—called on Nordau's peers to reject what he claimed was the immoral influence of late Victorian *causes célèbre*, including Oscar Wilde and others connected with the Decadent and Aesthetic Movements.

64. Henry Whipple's daughter Jane (Jennie) Whipple Scandrett.

65. Possibly Mary Webster Whipple (1842-1916), first cousin to Bishop Henry Whipple.

All this makes me long for you and dear Rose to be in the midst of it and enjoy it as I do. I am sure you would forget the hotel and the dining room, with all there is outside.

I have been waiting for Evelyn to be able to leave home almost ever since I was at Saxonville, and now I must leave here, not to return on Friday, the thirteenth, till late the next day. It would be altogether too fatiguing to come, as Rose suggested, for the day only, and you would not want to miss the moonlight.

My thoughts have gone to you and Rose very often, and I feel to you both very lovingly.

Millie

[P.S.] I shall feel *horribly* disappointed if you do not come. With so little time left, I am growing quite anxious lest something will prevent you and Rose from coming. I cannot tell you what a disappointment that would be to me. If I send you a telegram that Evelyn will come either next Saturday or Tuesday, will you and Rose come for at least one afternoon[?]

Amelia Candler to Evangeline Simpson, Saxonville, Massachusetts postmarked September 18, 1895

My dear Evangeline,
Your letter meant so much to me. I treasure it and have read it over and over again. I would not write before because I wanted to be all thought for you when I did write, and during the last ten days, or since I left South Park,[66] there has been one steady perpetual motion on my part.

My illness did not last long, for I am quick to recuperate. Of course I felt your dear atmosphere constantly when I was at South Park, and more than I expressed to Rose. Though I do

---

66. Whipple's estate in Wayland, Massachusetts.

not see you, Evangeline, I feel nearer and nearer to you, and my feeling for you is growing all the time. But in the very beginning it did not seem like a new thing, but like a recognition, definite and strong. I had a place waiting for you, Evangeline.[67]

The next two weeks are unsettled with me and the house in Brookline half closed, and workmen will soon be in it, but *how* I wish I could see you there, notwithstanding! You will be constantly in my thoughts.

Lovingly
Millie
Tuesday

Amelia Candler to Evangeline Simpson
CORNER IRVING AND HIGH STREETS BROOKLINE
October 2, 1895

My dear Evangeline,
It is very hard to feel that you are so soon to go away, and without my seeing you again. I would feel quite sad if it were not that all my hopes are centered upon a visit from you after you have left the Mohonk House[68] and have been to New York with Mrs. Marrs. I have thought of having you all to myself with such delight. What long talks we would have in the fire light! Then Evelyn would come and we would all be so happy.

I do not want to feel doubtful about Rose's coming with

67. The affectionate, sometimes effusive language in this and the following letters is typical of the correspondence of American women cultivating romantic friendships in the 1890s.

68. A resort in New Paltz, New York, founded by Quaker brothers Albert and Alfred Smiley in 1869. From 1895 until 1916, Mohonk House held annual conferences for peace; from 1883 until 1916, politicians and religious leaders convened there to discuss improving the living standards of Indigenous people at what was called the "Lake Mohonk Conference, Friends of the Indian." Bishop Henry Whipple was a regular attendee but did not attend in 1895 (Barrows, *Proceedings*, 59).

you, but she spoke of some relatives that she would have to visit—but you will persuade her not to visit them just at that time, won't you? My father knows you and Rose through my affection for you both, and he is planning drives already and wondering which of his favorite drives you will like the best. If you would rather come to me from the Weeds, please come whenever it is easiest, and know that I am always ready and longing to have you.

Dear Evangeline, I love to think of you and remember you. Truly, that, even that, is not nearly enough. I long to be really with you again.

lovingly yours
Millie

Amelia Candler to Evangeline Simpson, Murray Hill Hotel, New York City
Oct. 17, 1895

My dear Evangeline,
It is such a disappointment to me, but then, you know that, so I am not going to say one word about it. The one comfort is that I feel all through [your] letter that you wanted to come, and that makes me happy. You need not fear, dear Evangeline, that I shall not ask you again. I was half amused when I came to that little sentence.

No, I have asked you for now and for always, for you have a real place in my heart, and my home must always be waiting for you to come when you can. I am so sorry for the cause that keeps you from me now and hope very earnestly that Mrs. Marrs may be entirely well again as soon as she reaches a warm climate.

I can easily imagine how wonderfully beautiful Lake Mohonk must be now, for I have been there and I shall never forget it. Evelyn and I were there all by ourselves and we were very, very happy together. It was before the autumn color was at it's [*sic*] height, but I can imagine it all.

I have thought of you and Rose so often and have loved to know that you were in the midst of such beauty. Indeed I do care for the Indians, and feel from what I have heard that our race must have disgraced itself everlastingly in its treatment of them.

If I should go to New York within a few weeks and could have a glimpse of you, how delighted I would be! I expected all summer to be in New York some time this fall, but I feel now that I must stay near Evelyn. Her father has grown rapidly much worse during the last few days, as you probably know. I shall therefore not expect to see you, but yet want to know where you are in case I should run on to New York suddenly for a few days. If Evelyn does not need me I must go to New York.

I know that the future holds some very precious experiences, companionship with you, and I cherish the thought. It will come, I know.

Hoping that the next months will pass pleasantly for you and Mrs. Marrs, and with so much thought and love to you, dear Evangeline,

Lovingly ever
Millie

Evelyn Ames to Evangeline Simpson
Care of Miss Cleveland, Holland Patent, New York. Postmarked
    November 19, 1895
Saturday night

Darling Evangeline,
It is so perfect, so cozy here, and I feel your dear spirit throughout the little house. I am needing this change and rest

so much as one can need, for since my father's death[69] I have worked night and day, literally, and have to hurry back next week to more work. I shall leave here on the morning train Tuesday, just missing you, you see.

Darling Evangeline, your loving words brought comfort to me in those days of pain. I know you will wish to hear all about me, but I do not seem to realize or know much about myself at present. Rose, bless her heart! will be able to tell you more than I can. She is better, she says—her cough seems to be passing, but it must have been severe. Here is Libbie for the letters & this must be finished now.

I love to think of you here in the red wrapper with lambswool. Oh, I *hope* you are going to be able to stay here a while. Goodnight! dear, wonderful Evangeline,

Evelyn

Tuesday night

Darling Evangeline,

I long to see you tonight. I have been with Anna Lee[70] all the afternoon while she chose photographs for her little house. We saw the *Paradise* of Fra Angelico,[71] and at once your beautiful blue room was before me. You came upon me like a spell, and I felt shut in your sphere as if in a crystal filled with all sorts of whirling colors and beauty. Precious Evangeline!

Tomorrow ev'g we (Anna Lee & Mr. Nowell,[72] Millie, Susie,[73] and I) are going to hear Paderewski.[74] He is going to play three

69. Evelyn Ames's father, Oliver Ames, had died on October 22, 1895.
70. Evelyn Ames's sister, Anna Lee Ames Nowell (1864–1934).
71. Fra Angelico's tempera-on-panel painting *The Last Judgment* (most often dated to between 1425 and 1431) includes a depiction of Paradise, as does his lesser known 1450 triptych of the same name.
72. Anna Lee Ames married George Manning Nowell (1862–1933) in 1891.
73. Evelyn Ames's sister, Susan Ames Taylor (1867–1949).
74. Ignacy Jan Paderewski (1860–1941), a Polish composer and concert pianist.

great concerts with the symphony orchestra. Have you heard him, or seen him? He leads all hearts to him like an Orpheus. With the love of his music, a mighty personal love rises from the audience—a wondrous tribute. Have you seen the Burne-Jones head of Paderewski?[75] It is he in his apotheosis.

Evangeline—what are the most beautiful photographs you know? I love the St. Helena of Veronese, several of the Botticelli Madonnas and many of his details. I love so *many,* and yet in my present mood, please call it what you will, I have not found quite what will most help me. Just tell me of one or two that flash into your mind and among them may be the very ones I am needing and searching for vainly. Anna Lee chose the St. Helena, Velazquez' little Don Carlos, two of Botticelli's, some cupids of Rubens, the beautiful Braun photograph of the Sistine Madonna—just the heads & shoulders of the Madonna & Child—and a Corot. You may know it: "La Matinee."

It is ten o'clock. The great clock in the hall is just striking! and I *promised* Millie to go to bed early. I must say goodnight at once, but there is so much in my heart for you that I am loath to say goodnight.

Lovingly, lovingly,
Evelyn.

Amelia Candler to Evangeline Simpson
Care of Miss Rose Cleveland, Holland Patent, Oneida County,
New York, December 6, 1895
CORNER IRVING AND HIGH STREETS BROOKLINE

There never were two dearer telegraphs than Evelyn and I received this morning, you sweet Evangeline. I cannot send you the pieces of that letter, for they have gone long ago. You

75. The British artist Edward Burne-Jones painted Paderewski in 1890. Burne-Jones (1833–98), a collaborator of William Morris, was influential in the late Pre-Raphaelite and Aesthetic Movements.

have had many loving thoughts sent you, and your sweet picture is looked at long and lovingly by me, though it is not altogether you—I do not think all that you are could be caught in a photograph. Oh, I want to see you so much! Can't you come to me, if for two days only, before you go South?

Leave naughty little Rose at the Weeds, and come to me without her. I call her naughty because if she thinks I am "mad," as she expressed it, why then she *must* have done something to make me so. I feel as though I had written you more of what I feel, not only of affection for your dear self, but other things too, in the letter Evelyn made me tear, than I can again.

Precious Evelyn has frightened me very much,[76] but now that I have her safe with me at last, where she thinks of nothing but happy, restful things, is fed with all the nourishing things she can hold, receives her massage twice a day, is in the bed at night by 8:30, has plenty of fresh air, and is all relaxed— Oh, how at last my fright is subsiding!

Some hours later.

The four hours since I wrote the last sentence have been passed with a girl on the verge of ruin—help has come to her and to her sister before it is too late and she has left the house sustained. Dear little Evelyn is restful—I mean, feeling so. And I am going to take her out for a gay sleigh ride, and bring some color into her cheeks. She has been laughing to herself all day over some of my foolish mistakes—she says that you and Rose shall hear about them. Naturally, Evelyn is more amused than I am. I do not speak to her of depressing things—like that girl, for instance. I kept running back & forth to see how Evelyn was getting on while I talked to the girl.

If I make six more blots I shall even then send this letter just the same. Evangeline, *will* you come to me before you go South? Won't you try? I live in a whirl all the time but now

76. Ames was physically and emotionally exhausted by her father's death.

that little Miss Wee[77] has come, I shall drop every thing. The "whirl" consists of things that are worth while. I shall write you about a little of it next time.

Dear Evangeline, I am very glad and grateful that *you* exist—and that we are friends. How much that means!

I am always lovingly
Millie

Dec. 6th
A very great deal of love to Rose. Ask her to write.

Evelyn Ames to Evangeline Simpson, Holland Patent, New York,
care of Miss Cleveland
postmarked from Back Bay, Boston
Dec. 11, 1895

My darling Evangeline,
I have wrested Millie's permission to write to you, breaking the rule of one letter a day. Rose has written so often, and so much about you—pages about you—that it has been like living with you. Some day you must read them and see how others see you. You have been like a radiant presence flitting in & out of every room, and dear Rose has learned to come, too, with all your Christmas feeling & hers warming my heart.

A year ago my little Missy died, my wonderful little Missy.[78] And although the date & time had left my mind, vivid dreams of her for two nights past have called for all my memory. I did not write you about Dainty's[79] going. I could not at the time. Now I am sorry that I did not, because I understand it all to[o] well & might after all have been able to speak to you.

77. A nickname for Ames.
78. Ames's dog.
79. Evangeline Whipple's dog, also deceased.

Night after night, that little heartful creation (I could not write creature) met me in my lonely room when I came home late, & all else about me seemed like a desert. She was wonderful! And, I believe, immortal. Perhaps she and Dainty have found each other out and are happy. I have been, and still am, very weary, but precious Millie is helping me along in every way, and by January I hope to be able to go to Rose. *Shall* be able, I mean. There is, *could* be, *no* doubt.

We realized yesterday that of course you could not come to us here, but we had one day of hope and anticipation. This is all so wonderful, this time at Millie's. It is helping so. You may not perhaps realize to what finality, almost, of exhaustion I had come. These days of utter quiet, of sinking into pillows, of regular routine, the little drive when I am up to it! All what I have needed & now have at last. Instead of going tense & nerved by exercise I am learning to be quiet & relaxed, trying not to think *ceaselessly,* ceaselessly, learning to sleep. In two weeks I hope to be far, far ahead, far better, and then the Weeds will come—& that certainly will cure. Goodnight! Too much writing & I feel worn.

Lovingly, lovingly,
Evelyn

Rose Cleveland to Evangeline Simpson, Park House, Maitland, Florida
postmarked December 17, 1895
GRAND UNION HOTEL OPPOSITE GRAND CENTRAL STATION,
  FORD & COMPANY, PROPRIETORS
New York
Tuesday night 1895

Half past ten, darling, & Will[80] just gone to his room after a long gossip over the ginger ale. I did just as you said—left

80. Possibly William Neal Cleveland (1832–1906), Rose's brother.

the car windows closed, & sat in my warm cloak—& reached 33 East 33rd at 5:30. Came over here with Will (there was no question of extra pay to the good old coachman, who was delighted with his fee) and got a nice *warm* room right next to Will's & supper a là carte in the gay dining room—then a fine walk (Will smoking his cigar) to Annie's,[81] where we stayed an hour. *She raves over you*—says any one must fall in love with you *at once,* etc. Then long walk back looking in windows and talking everything over. Then in my warm room with ginger ale & crackers—& now to bed. I take the 9:30 to-morrow A.M., get up at 8 with time enough for all, reach Utica at 3:14 & shall do all you said.

I could not be more comfortable than I am in this fancy hotel.

I cannot get over not having thought to pack you a basket of dainties, & keep seeing how the little good things would have looked. Oh, what torment! And I tried to say how I would spill all my blood for you, Wingie, Wingie—& could not—but you know it and how I cry & cry in my heart over the long, perfect loving kindness of Granny, who takes such care of me, and oh, how you are perhaps sleeping now—or waking—& now I must just pray God to bless, bless you—& heal my heart ache and ours for each other.

Oh, how I love you & want you to be *so happy* & will have you so. Oh, be happy, happy for Clevie's sake—whose happiness is to know you happy. My Wingie—my pet, whole world-y, my love, my petsy—petsy!

[Rose]

<hr/>

81. Possibly Annie Van Vechten (1856–1925).

Rose Cleveland to Evangeline Simpson, Park House, Maitland,
  Florida
postmarked December 18, 1895
7:30 P.M.
Weeds.

Here I am, Wingie—supper over & Pussy [spending] *the evening*
in the hall while I get this ready for Libbie to take. I slept well
in my fancy warm room next to Will at the "Second Union"
& got off at 9:30—reached Utica at 6:15 & had just [enough]
time to get the brushes & comb marked W. H. H. & S. C. Y.[82] as
fine as fiddles and order the "pure white velvet box" with the
greatest caution, nagging & repetition, so it is to be "as nice as
can be made," and for *$2.00!* Marking cost only 25.05[83] (Utica
for *me*, every time!). Then I got my train and Pussy was at the
station and lugged me home—Williams at the door & Libbie
in the rear. A letter from Evelyn very full of you!

Shall I give her the little scarab[84] as soon as she comes that
night? As it is to be Christmas—it ought to belong to the old
year. And why don't you send a note to go with it, *saying* those
things—if you send at once I will get it next week and then I
won't say anything. But if you don't want to then I will try and
remember everything you said and tell it all.

I will do everything as you said about everything, only now
I must stop up this joy to-night. I am awfully tired of course—
but glad to be here. Oh, I can't speak of you not being here,
& your red gown hangs there empty. I hope you have begun
before this reaches you.

---

82. The initials of Rose's sister, Susan Cleveland Yeomans. The identity of
W. H. H. is unknown.

83. In 1895, $2 was equivalent to about $60 and $25.05 to $758 in 2018.

84. Whipple's Christmas gift to Ames was a piece of amethyst jewelry
in the shape of a scarab, a type of beetle. Scarabs are common symbols in
ancient Egyptian art representing rebirth; Whipple's choice reflects a shared
interest in Egyptology.

My brother's wiring to England about Venezuela![85] The most perfect characteristic, this! & oh, I see him so—at his greatest in every line. It has set the world nagging, I tell you—& again Grover Cleveland is the watch-word. [illegible crossed-out words] *Get* all the papers—do. I send some with this—will send the *Times* tomorrow. But you must get them for *yourself* & read all. You will have all the big feeling you want to over the president's tone to Great Briton [*sic*]. It will tickle Motherdie!

Now I *must* stop. Pussy sends her love. Oh Wingie, Wingie! God Bless you!

[*Rose*]

Rose Cleveland to Evangeline Simpson, Lake Maitland,
   Orange County, Florida
postmarked December 25, 1895
Christmas Eve.
9 P.M.

Darling,
Yours of Saturday A.M. here tonight, and I want to begin a letter before I sleep. Pussie is here for the night but I shall give her her things in the morning. She has a great mysterious something hid behind the big chair in this room and I am devoured with curiosity but cannot see it until tomorrow morning. Pussie's packages are beautiful. I have made yours— the brush—*lovely*. Mine—the gloves—I put in the long Lord & Taylor glove box and tied it with green ribbon & put the Burns calendar on it. The *photos* have *not* come! Too bad. Evelyn's "pure white velvet box" is here & is *perfect*—really exquisite, &

85. President Cleveland had weighed in on the competing claims of Great Britain and Venezuela to the territories of Essequibo and Guayana Esequiba on December 3 and again on December 17, when he affirmed the right of the United States to intervene in the crisis on the basis of the Monroe Doctrine ("President Cleveland's Message on the Venezuelan Question," *New York Times*, December 18, 1895).

the scarab looks like a king's spirit—all everything else—in it. I sent off my little things yesterday & today.

My cold is about the same. The weather warmer & warmer—streets deep with *March* mud—no Florida marsh could exceed the situation. Of course I will never be well until this changes. I will go *nowhere* when I cannot get some clear, cold weather. Thank the bishop[86] for his letter & tell him if he can promise me some *Minnesota winter* weather I will go to Florida. If I go it will be in search of winter—not away from it. *This* will kill me, if it lasts much longer. "A green Christmas!"

Well, Darling, my heart is full! I go to bed because I must— but I shall *wake* early & begin to tip-toe & peer & peer. Oh, Wing & Granny! Christ-mass be with you! With us all!

[the next morning]
Merry Christmas! Now, my Granny of second mothers—my Wing of Wings! And I am writing with my miraculous new pen—"ideal" indeed![87] Its first mark is on the envelope in which I enclose this—and I shall send, as the worst it can do— because the first, and good enough for the best of any other! What a comfort!

Well, it is about *eleven.* I am in bed, where I solemnly promised Pussie I would stay today, and I think I can *afford* to with *such* a Christmas all around me!

Oh, Wingie, how you have saturated me with your love and thoughts this morning. If only you could look *in* & see! *First* came your telegram with Granny's blessing, then commenced the carnival! Until now all is around me, and I feel *spoiled*-er than ever! Everything is so lovely—where can I begin? The two wings[88] sit up here presiding, the dear message crying

86. Bishop Henry Benjamin Whipple, with whom Evangeline was spending Christmas.

87. The Waterman Company made an "Ideal Fountain Pen" starting in 1884. The self-filling pens did not begin gaining popularity until 1888, suggesting that Cleveland was an early adopter of the new technology.

88. The gift—possibly a pair of photographs—seems intended to bring a symbol of Whipple (Wingie) into Cleveland's home.

at their feet, as if it had just dropped from your lips. I have opened *every one* now—and *hid* some, so Pussy nor *no* one will see how my granny *spoils* me. But about *half* are on exhibition, to Pussy's wild delight—& Libbie & Williams wondering at me! I left the drawer & cupboard, *most* of them, until Pussy went to church, where I could not go, for the cold (the *warm* still outside!). Then I got slyly up and just *revelled*. But I can't yet discriminate. Each one is yet to be gone over separately and each one is perfect. Pussy led me triumphantly into the library to show me my splendid book stand! Enough for one Christmas & one grandchild!

I love everything so, I don't know what I love more: one minute it is my whip, which is here with me, and a great joy to flourish and crack from bed—and all my *furs* and the gloves & fox to top with—then it is my handkerchiefs for the Sunday and evenday noses—& now it is my pen—oh dear, I can so tell your faces in the charming frames—oh, how I like them! My photos only came this morning but I got them off to you by this noon mail. I can't write any more now—because I must be good and rest—and Clara Fuller[89] is coming—or Pussy. I have left the package of magazines & the box of *candy* (I *guess* it is) to be opened bye and bye [*sic*]—when Clara and Adelaide[90] are here.

Am going to stay in bed & try not to get tired. Tell Darling Motherdie (I cannot write today) I have on my exquisite light scarves—they other when it shed color all over the room— was ever any thing more *Motherdie-ly*! How I love and enjoy their amplitude—they make me willing to stay in bed—I am so much admired in them! Darling—Good bye for to-day!

[*Rose*]

89. Clara Fuller, principal of Ossining Seminary for Young Ladies, New York.

90. Probably Adelaide Hamlin Thierry (1880–1961), a poet, writer, and alumna of Radcliffe (class of 1901) who married Louis Thierry in 1905.

Evelyn Ames to Evangeline Simpson, Lake Maitland, Florida
New Year's Day, 1896

Blessed Evangeline,
I am writing from the Weeds to wish you a wonderful, happy New Year. All the bells of this little village lifted their voices this morning at midnight, or the second after, and rang so merrily, so jubilantly, that Rose had to get up and mingle her little sleigh bell chimes too.

This morning we reread your dear telegram, and I thought of the telegram my precious Millie sent to you the night before Christmas and which was brought back Christmas Day with the word that there was no office at Maitland. Christmas morning I held your little perfect gift in my hands and looked and *looked* and felt very happy in it and thought long messages to you, which perhaps you felt.

I could not write before now. That day, for the first time, I went to Boston and met all my brothers & sisters *en fête*[91] at home. It was very exhausting after so many days spent in bed, & I demeaned myself so hysterically that the next day my mother, panic-stricken, sent for me to come home. There the noisy city nights kept me awake again. Friday there came a strange neuralgia in two great nerves in my back, and that with enforced dentistry threatened to quite undo me. But the back grew well in two days, and yesterday I succeeded in making the long journey up here in the comfortable little state room and met Rose in Utica feeling better than when I left Boston.

Now that is all about myself, except this: that this is a haven of rest, that a great many distressing considerations had come upon me while ill (for decision) and there was so much fatiguing personal contact & friction that this seems to me salvation. And Millie was tired out, bless her heart! and so glad to send me, because she saw rest could not be had so near Boston.

91. French: having a party.

So here I am for Rose to cure me of all unnecessary depression. I found her better than when I left her, the cough not so violent, grown thinner and somewhat tired, but gathering new force from this sudden winter turn. She has been writing, all brown & quilted from head to foot, looking so sweet and concentrated at her desk—that I feared even my occasional glances from the hall when I am writing might be intrusions. She is very fierce for work on this New Year's Day, and is revolving à la little owl between desk & new reading table, where her Latin lexicon is spread open on the reading shelf with most scholarly air.[92]

Do not worry about Rose, Evangeline. Her cough is really better and if I think she ameliorates anything for your sake, I will let you know.

Evangeline, darling, Rose brought me your little white velvet box last night with the amethyst scarab in it. It is beautiful, so thrilling—it means so much to me that I think I cannot even try to tell you—Oh no, I *cannot*. And yet I want you to know. [illegible crossed-out words]

I cannot write more now. Will you give my love to your Motherdie?[93] And to the Bishop. God bless you, Evangeline. I wish you were here today. I long to see you. And it seems very far away.

Lovingly,
Evelyn

6:30 P.M.
We had a drive with May & then called on Pussy, who is housed by a cold, & then took a perfect walk, my first one for a month, in the pure, glacial air. I am wearing the scarab, but next to loving to wear it because you gave it to me, I like best to hold

---

92. Cleveland was already at work on her translation of Augustine's *Soliloquies*—a project that was to occupy her until its publication in 1910.

93. Ames's reference to Jane Marrs as "your Motherdie" contrasts with Cleveland's more direct and possessive "Motherdie."

it & look at its purple clouded depths & fancy that it has an infinite capacity of cloudy expansion, some kind of diffusion, as if it held a genie. (Do you remember reading of such things in the *Arabian Nights*?!)

Here comes Libby with pleasantly clinking implements for the little dining table. Rose, in that most delightful & appropriate of brown quilted gowns, your gown for her, is writing business letters in the library. It is so warm & comfortable, that I have put on my nice room gown, too, to bear her company.

Goodnight, Evangeline.

New Year's Day Evening
Darling Evangeline,
Your dear letter has just come, breathing of the South. Oh yes, the scarab spoke to me! & gave me such joy, such feeling, and so much of you, yourself, that I had to cry a little when Rose had put it into my hands. I could not find words to tell you of it that morning or now. This must go now.

Faithfully, lovingly,
Evelyn

Amelia Candler to Evangeline Simpson
postmarked January 6, 1896
CORNER IRVING AND HIGH STREETS, BROOKLINE

My dear Evangeline,
At last I have your address and can tell you of my delight in the exquisite book! It will mean so much to always associate you with those beautiful thoughts that I shall read, and to have a book that I shall always enjoy, from one I care so much for.

Dear Evangeline, it was very sweet of you to think of me, when you have so many to think for. I am very happy that you did; it has been very disappointing to have my long telegram to you returned from the office, because there was no telegraph office where you are. I had your Florida address then, and lost it afterwards, but Evelyn has now sent it to me.

I hope this new year will be a happy one for you, and the kind of a year that you want it to be. Evelyn and Rose begin it together and I wish so much happiness for them.[94] The last year was very eventful in bringing us four together. I wonder what this next year will bring, and if we are going to be together during any part of it. When are you going to return to the North? How I wish you were not so far away and were coming to me while Rose and Evelyn are together. Life is beginning to seem interesting again, but I have been so tired and anxious, while Evelyn was ill. I sent her to Rose a very different person from the one who came to me.

Are you having an interesting winter? I cannot imagine enjoying Florida. I feel too much activity in myself to enjoy the climate and surroundings. I want to hear of your life there. It would always be a beautiful one, wherever you are, dear Evangeline.

With love, I am always, yours faithfully,
Millie

Evelyn Ames to Evangeline Simpson, Lake Maitland, Florida
Jan. 12th [1896]

Dearest Evangeline,
It has been such a beautiful Sunday! and it is drawing to a sweet close while Rose writes to you at her desk & I write here between the table & the fire. Rose was very "low in her mind" last night because she had not heard from you since Monday, both anxious and sad & chafing at the distance that separates her from you, and repining at the ~~unknown~~ irregularity of the mails.

94. On January 31, 1896, Evelyn Ames stated she was assisting Cleveland with her manuscript work; the statement that "Evelyn and Rose begin it together" could refer to this academic arrangement.

We have been doing a great deal of work together. Rose is very exclusive in the mornings. I am practically shut out of the library, but in the afternoon we take her books & papers & by our mental vexations & compassion seem to stimulate her to satisfactory work, a sort of revision of the morning's accomplishments. There is so little to tell. It is just this dear, interesting routine and the delight of this incomparable little refuge! A beautiful upright piano came yesterday & tomorrow I shall begin to practice an hour, if I find myself strong enough for such concentration. I love the scarab more & more. It is like a living thing. I am so happy to have it!

Goodnight, dear Evangeline. By night I am so tired that I can only write you these few words. I have to be patient. With love to dear Motherdie, whom I can never forget, and to your own loved self.

Evelyn

Evelyn Ames to Evangeline Simpson, Lake Maitland, Florida
postmarked from Holland Patent, New York
Jan. 31st! [1896]

Dearest Evangeline,

Rose is sitting over the register, putting on shoes & moaning to herself and interrupting every sentence I have written in a half hour with the most pathetic plaints I have heard from her. She says "she wants to see Wingie," then she moans she is "getting homelier & homelier & will be a dreadfully ugly old woman," then she discovers that the tips of her brown quilted shoes are wearing shabby and puts them away for special occasions—although she says that when they wear out "Granny will get her another pair."[95] She is very "low in her

---

95. Suggesting that Evangeline Whipple will buy Rose another pair of shoes.

mind," but now she wends her murmuring way to her library, bright with sunlight & snow light, & she will soon be at work and engrossed. Her work is progressing well, and I am able to help her greatly, I really think, in the critical version, and in the tiresome copying of corrected manuscripts.[96]

I am troubled about little Haruko.[97] As soon as I hear from my mother I will write you about her interpretation of the little creature's condition. In the meantime, I enclose a little "bone food," a powdered preparation that I take myself at meals. My dentist, who invented it, calls it Nature's food for teeth and bones as well as for the brain & nerves. It certainly helps digestion. I once gave it to Missy—between a half & a whole teaspoonful mixed well with each meal. She was very weak at the time, and I think it helped her very much. It is used in the form of dog biscuit in some well-known kennels in Brookline & I wish Jeannie[98] [sic] would try it for "Ruko," giving it at her discretion. The poor little thing may not be having enough bone food for her system. Do they give her bones? What does she eat? I wish Jeannie would write me all about it. I am sorry she has so much care & worry for the little thing! Is it an affectionate dog?

Oh, the winter here has been so beautiful! Rose's little furry sleigh has done daily service. You did indeed wrap us up splendidly, once and for all, in the thick robes and the soft red rug, which is wide-spreadable, and we glide along so warm, so snug, with the soft little chimes ringing all about us. Yesterday we drove sixteen miles in a nice big "bob-sleigh" to & from

96. A reference to Cleveland's work on the *Soliloquies.*

97. A pet dog owned by the Scandrett family. At the time, the reigning empress of Japan (Empress Shōken, 1849–1914) was using Haruko as her personal name, which may account for the Scandretts' choice. As the wife of the reformer Emperor Meiji, the empress was relatively visible to Westerners (see, for example, "The First Lady of Japan: Empress Haruko Wears Parisian Gowns and Is a Very Busy Woman," *Harrisburg [PA] Telegraph*, September 13, 1894).

98. Either Jane (Jennie) Whiting Whipple Scandrett (1847–1932) or, less likely, her daughter, Jeanie Whipple Scandrett (1878–1970).

Whitesboro, where we took the electric car into Utica. We call ourselves *oxygenarians* and Rose uses up a great deal of energy in complaints that Wingie does not like the snow & the "cold blast," and that it is all because she doesn't know how to dress warmly enough, and that she does not believe the South is good for her, & *is* she getting enough to eat? and all in all bemoaning, and Rose is devising original and attractive & comfortable head gear for you, & I think now it is a slowly maturing plan to keep you North next winter.

And here I must stop! We are both doing well. Rose's cough is gone and she has improved greatly, looking better than last summer.

Love to your dear Motherdie & yourself.

Evelyn

Evelyn Ames to Evangeline Simpson, Lake Maitland, Florida
Friday, Feb. 7th, [1896]

Dearest Evangeline,
Here we are in a great white blur! Locked in the tumultuous privacy of storm. There is no going out today. It is the most beautiful storm I have ever beheld.

Later! I began to write at noon, quite in the mood to write of many things. An interruption came, however, and all the afternoon I had to rest, & now another hasty note must go to you.

You would be so glad to see Rose. Of course she has ups & downs physically, but for three days she has been so round, so fresh, so bright, with a little pink color, and such a cunning Shetland pony look! It would delight you to look upon her. And she works so faithfully, so trudgingly, so hopefully! I pray that all her earnest labor will be rewarded by a satisfactory conclusion. She is a brave, persevering little worker. I too am improving and hope soon to be "available" (Rose's word) and able-bodied. So, little as I may write, it is all good news.

I enclose a letter from my mother about the little dog. Will you read it to Jeannie [*sic*]? If you let her read it herself, hadn't you best cross out the line in which she says she is sorry she parted with it, as it really does not mean anything that could pain Jeannie. The homesickness theory can have no base of reality, either. The rest may interest Jeannie, however.

And now, dear Evangeline, goodnight. God bless you. Give my love to the Bishop, and to your Motherdie, who has made a long, enduring impression in my heart, and believe me,

Most lovingly yours,
Evelyn.

Evelyn Ames to Evangeline Simpson, Park House, Maitland, Florida
Wednesday, March 11, 1896

Dearest Evangeline,
Here we sit,[99] red flames dancing up the chimney place, broad, blackened, nice old chimney-place, quaint little black iron andirons, "weird" (in your and Rose's sense) little black ~~teapot~~ kettle standing in the hearth and boiling and purring away.

The gray afternoon is closing—a soft shower is falling over the grand bare oaks, and the red-berried holly trees, and the evergreens without our windows, and the wonderful little peach trees that stand in hovering, rosy bloom here and there over the dark soil just quickening into tender green. Oh, the spring! Do you know Millet's "Printemps"? I believe it is at the Louvre. I have a photograph of it in dark brown tints, and yet each time I look at it it seems on the point of breaking out in

99. Ames may have written this letter to Whipple while vacationing with Cleveland in South Carolina. Two weeks earlier, the *Baltimore Sun* reported that Cleveland was spending time in Summerville, close to Lakes Marion and Moultrie ("Ovation to Miss Mildred Lee," April 27, 1896). Ames's reference to peach trees corroborates a southern setting.

real, prismatic life, or bursting into color. It is strangely vital with the wondrous life of spring.

It is very cozy here this afternoon. There are dashes of vivid color about the room, a tall red and gold screen, red cushion, and a red leather portfolio, a splendid bunch of jonquils at the mirror, pansies and hyacinths contributed by Miss Perkins, our wise, distinguished "hostess," a spray of peach blossoms and two sprays of spirea [sic] in a little vase at the window, the mute Aeolian harp just below, and some red-berried holly branches over the fireplace, just where they catch the dancing firelight—Rose's last "effect." It is so easy that, notwithstanding my weakness consequent upon yesterday's severe illness (nausea and headaches), I am impelled to follow my invariable custom, i.e., that of replying to your "tomorrow's letter."

Rose says I must tell you about our afternoon yesterday on the ~~shore~~ banks of a big blue lake. We sat just over the millwheel in the niches of a great timber frame, with the rush and roar of waters in our ears. Most companionably near, in the sunny field below, we were aware of a family of coal-black pigs. Big mother pig, big father pig, diminutive, galloping litter of seven, four or five older brothers and sisters—the whole family disporting themselves in delightful fashion. An old negro but near us with his futile fishing rod, immovable like a bronze. Darky cabins all about at picturesque distance and the yellow dog much in "evidence." All rush and ripple of nature, the comfortable sympathy with happy animal life, and the feeling of a homely, happy humanity nigh.

Rose calls out, "Stop writing at once, Evelyn!" I long to expatiate. How you would have loved it! There is much I am glad you missed. A rabbit hunt across the open field, negro boy and the hound in pursuit. How it hurt to see it! Perhaps the brave, beautiful little creature escaped. Wingie, dear, I don't want you and Rose to eat squirrels. Rabbits and squirrels must be exceptions, but yet they are poor little destructive things.

[Evelyn]

Rose Cleveland to Evangeline Simpson
postmarked April 16, 1896
Easter Monday
11 P.M.

My Darling,
Your telegram came at 1 P.M. Of course I shall do as you say, and have to-day, this P.M., after your telegram came, telegraphed Mrs. Cleveland[100] that "I am detained."

So I shall do as you say. *Where* I shall spend the intervening time I cannot say—not at Asheville, for reasons I cannot now state—but as soon as I hear from you ~~I will~~ *when* you will be there, or where I shall join you, I will go.

You have treated me dreadfully, Wingie, but I shall act just as if you had not, and maybe you have not. You actually must *not* keep me waiting for you longer than next Monday the 13th. I will look up the route to-morrow and see where I can join you, hoping that you will do the same and I will have a letter from you telling *me*.

I am too wild over my beautiful, beautiful gifts to say more on above subject to-night. The darling box came to-day and just filled me with the precious sweetness of the dear love they represent, so I cannot even suffer at my own sense of poverty in being able to make no such sign to you. Oh, but my whole heart makes it to you, my beloved Wing, over and over and through and through, but all my soul.

Thank blessed Motherdie for her thought of her slave, Rose. How I would go on my knees to her! Never, never did I see anything that more melts me than this circle of orange blossoms—wonderful, thrilling Wingie! God bless you body and soul!

It is near 12 midnight, so I must not write more—shall write to-morrow definitely. ~~Of course you can go~~ What is your shortest way to Asheville? Or will you visit Charleston

---

100. First Lady Frances Folsom Cleveland.

en route? I rather hope to spend a day here. I shall love to see Charleston.

[Rose]

Rose Cleveland to Evangeline Simpson
postmarked April 25, 1896[101]
EXECUTIVE MANSION, WASHINGTON, DC

It is nearly dark—& I have come up for a letter while Mrs. C. is with the baby.[102] The President is off for the day, so I shall only see him this eve'g late & tomorrow morning. Long enough to talk a little politics, altho my duty is very clear. But just what I can do for my brother remains to be seen when I get home. In *any* case, there will be no disturbance of the upper floor. It will be just as it was—all *ours*. Evelyn telegraphs that she cannot arrange to take the sail up the river with me—so I shall have it all alone—for wh[ich] I am sorry.

I have been trying to think of other things or not think at all—talking with Mrs. C.[103]—driving—a nice man to lunch—callers at 5—(the Willie Endicotts[104] & Lawrences—Leiters[105]—Baron

101. Folder labeling provided by the collection's processing archivist indicates that this and three other undated letters (and letter fragments) were sent in "1893." The faint postmark on one of their envelopes, however, shows that it was in fact sent in 1896. A newspaper article ("Rose Cleveland Returns," *Buffalo [NY] Morning Express*, May 22, 1893) reported that Cleveland did not return from Europe until May 1893, making it impossible for her to have sent letters from Washington, DC, during April of that year. Because of this evidence and the letters' allusions to Simpson's engagement to Whipple, the editors have grouped them together in 1896.

102. The baby is probably Grover and Frances Cleveland's daughter Marion, who had been born in 1895.

103. Frances Folsom Cleveland.

104. William Crowninshield Endicott served as Grover Cleveland's secretary of war between 1885 and 1889.

105. Levi Leiter, founder of Chicago's Marshall Field & Company, and his wife, Mary Theresa Carver Leiter. The Leiters had built a mansion in DC's Dupont Circle neighborhood two years earlier, in 1891.

Sternberg[106] (of the German legation) and various others). But [on] my window the sober light falls where the sunset glow was—and the moon is brightening. The monument[107] *alone* puts in the human suggestion, for the soft mist obscures other signs of the distant city. This *Woodley*[108] is a dear old place. The children[109] are fine—clever and sunny and natural; altogether happy & right.

I have never been able to forget you or your affairs. Yet I dare say nothing—only the same prayer, pain, problem—is it safe—to do what you so much feel like doing? Is it right all around?

This is the last letter I can write you to Asheville as I shall have no opportunity to post anything again before Monday and that would be too late. My heart aches to say something just right. I think of Motherdie—of many things—but I can see your side of it. As for myself—I give you my best blessing whatever you do.[110] Try and feel what that means—as I shall strive to have it mean all that can give you joy and peace. *You can count on me.* God bless you!

I feel strange, and outside; a nightmare of feeling. But do not fear. I am going to think of myself. I love you enough for anything, and in time I shall fulfill all your wishes. Even to believe in your love for me, perhaps. I know you suffer—but because you are so sorry does not make it love. But we must do the best we can.

[Rose]

106. Hermann Speck von Sternburg, secretary of the German embassy in Washington, DC. Between 1903 and his death, in 1908, he served as ambassador to the United States.

107. The Washington Monument.

108. President Grover Cleveland's wife, Frances, and children often stayed at Woodley Mansion (3000 Cathedral Avenue NW), three miles from the White House, during the summer months.

109. In April 1896, Grover and Frances Cleveland had three children: Ruth, Esther, and Marion. Ruth died of diphtheria in 1904, at the age of twelve.

110. An apparent reference to Evangeline's consideration of marriage to Bishop Whipple.

Rose Cleveland to Evangeline Simpson
summer or early fall 1896
Station 3:30 P.M.

Wingie,

I have been trying to find just the right thing to say—but nothing comes. The right word will not be spoken. A frightful storm may just come—and in the greatest hurry I have got to this station an hour before the time, lest if I waited I could not come at all.

A newspaper reporter has followed me from the hotel, where he blocked my way & was repeatedly refused but waited hat in hand, following me, standing before me, though I say over and over that I will [111]

What is yet for us I cannot see. But I think you will need me yet—in a future, perhaps. I do not think you need me now. But I *plead* that you will consider what I said this morning. I will give up *all* to you if you will try once more to be satisfied with *me*. Could you not take six months for that experiment? We would go away from everyone.

I wish for your happiness and good. Think what I said this morning, and do not decide hastily that there is only this one way. Remember *our* Florida.

If—after all—there is but this way for you—if you *will* do this thing—then I will not stand in the way. That means that I will study only for your comfort and pleasure and happiness. That will mean to take myself out of your way—for awhile, at least—and to reappear only when I can act gracefully and well in my new role.

Do not dream that I blame you. Never—never. However, it should have been my due to at least have *known* the danger. I have guarded against it—however much I would blame

111. "Will" is the last word written on the page. The first sentence on the opposite side of the same piece of paper, "What is yet for us I cannot see," does not finish the thought. It is possible that additional pages are missing, or that Cleveland did not send all of what she wrote.

another who to another did this—never, when it is *you* to *me*. It is too deep for blame because it is all too deep for comprehension. The pain, the strangeness, the surprise, the wrench, the hurt, the wonder. There is no *fright* about it now.

I do not know whether it is I who understand or you. Perhaps we neither of us understand each other.

I cannot write. It is nearly time for me to leave. God bless you—you can depend on me.

-Rose

[written on back of last page:]
I cannot speak nor write of my love. You *know*— —.

In a move that surprised their families and friends, Evangeline Simpson married Bishop Henry Benjamin Whipple on October 22, 1896. By November 15, Cleveland had planned a transatlantic trip of indefinite length with Evelyn Ames, possibly to deal with the loss, and, as she had written in the previous letter, "to take myself out of your way—for a while, at least—and to reappear only when I can act gracefully and well in my new role." ∿

Rose Cleveland to Evangeline Whipple
Weeds – Nov. 15th, 1896
Sunday P.M.

One and only "Granny"—
I have, this morning, *gone through* that wonderful box and now I know each content by *heart*. Never was such a "setting out" for a vagrant grandchild—never such an apotheosis of rose-color. Each thing is so perfect. Those soft, fine sheets. The *marvelous* green wrapper, with their lovely slippers. The rose slips that I wish I had shown off along with their wrapper to the admiring crowd in Boston! *And* the hot-water bag that cures all chills in advance!

As for the photographs, I certainly *never* saw anything like them—did you? They are too extraordinary to talk about, and how you ever produced them or *got* them produced, I cannot conceive, and shall not try to. The fact is all I am equal to, and I cannot find the words to talk about it (as the darkies exhort each other in their revivals.) This box is only one more sign of your lavish, loving kindness, shown by the multitude of signs which have gone before, and which surround me everywhere in this house, and go with me wherever I go.

You have your own understanding of all these things, I mine. We cannot, *yet,* compare notes on these subjects; and we do not need to. As you say, in the ending of your note, each *"knows all, surely"*—all that need now be known, and when more need is, more knowing will be.

"Love and blessings and tears and smiles" are always passing in the still space between us—and to know that each knows—to *believe* that each knows is the only thing we can do, *now.* I lie back on this belief and *go on with my life.*[112] From this quartile[113] I would gladly eliminate the "tears"—and I know you would; and here again, the knowing each would if each could is the best comfort we can have.

This will not be the last letter I shall write you before I go if I receive your address, but I am afraid to send more letters to Faribault.[114] I sent one before this, and hope I can know you have received both. So if I do *not* hear from you, remember that I sail on Dec. 5,[115] three weeks from yesterday, in S.S. "Normannia," Hamburg American Line. Foot of First Street, Hoboken, New Jersey, at 10 o'c in the morning.

112. Cleveland indicated that she was resigned to Evangeline's decision to marry Henry Whipple.
113. The quartile of love, blessings, tears, and smiles.
114. Evangeline Whipple moved to Faribault, Minnesota, after her marriage to Bishop Whipple.
115. Cleveland traveled overseas with Evelyn Ames from December 1896 to at least the summer of 1899. Cleveland indicated in February 1899 that she and Ames intended to be back in the United States to attend Amelia Candler's marriage to William Gardiner, which occurred on June 15, 1899.

Pussy announces it as her settled belief that she will never see me again, and when pressed for her "foundation" of belief says that she thinks I will die over there. I argue the matter—but it does not swerve her; and, as I don't look upon getting out of this incarnation as the worst of evils by a long shot, I do not feel at all depressed by her persistence. It may not be so agreeable to all my friends, though I do not think that any wheels will stop if mine do. And I am not anxious to have mine stop; in truth I never was more willing—ready, perhaps—to live or more anxious and hopeful of doing something.

But it is a sane attitude of mind to feel that oneself or one's friends are likely to leave—that places that know us now, may know us no more. Death means only *change*—transition—and seems a much more natural thing to me than it used to. I hope you feel this way—so that if you should have to face this passing of any friend you would not feel it as much different from my sailing to Genoa.

Now I must take a little rest, as the tyranny of the after lunch hour is upon me, aggravated by a monstrous cold, so much approaching the one I had this time last year—but not yet as bad. I am fighting it my very best, but experience tells me that I shall not *lose* it as long as I stay *here,* and the weather keeps mild. I have fully determined that if I return next fall to this country I shall move to another climate, for it is folly for me to try to overcome the influence of this. I think it may be Northhampton [*sic*], for a while, at least—for several reasons that suit my fancy!

When you *know* your dates for *your* foreign visits[116]—to England &c—you will let me know, would you? I may spend some time next summer in Scotland. A letter from Mr.

---

116. Some scholars have suggested that communication between Whipple and Cleveland ceased after the former's marriage to Bishop Whipple. As this statement proves, however, it continued—and included plans for future contact.

Crosby[117] [is] coaxing me to go to Dresden, but when the Vienna episode is ended, *I* shall go to the nearest warm place and "sit down," as the president says. I have no desire to travel.[118]

I wrote Miss Andrews after you told me of the death of her mother, and she answers very satisfactorily. Perhaps you may *like* to see her letter. Do not trouble to return it. I will write her again.

Yesterday a big box came to me from Saxonville.[119] In it were the scrap books, *and* the miniature *but* main bulk was a box from Motherdie, *outdoing,* impossible as that may seem, that of past Xmases. *Such* pink gowns, folded so motherly, with their lovely ribbons, and underneath a *shawl* of deep pink such as she knit in Florence for me, and a pair of pink slippers! And a note so *wonderful,* so *Motherdie,* that I was all done up.

Pussie has just come in with her aching ears: she is having a good deal of trouble with them. I have been dropping boric acid into them—and now she is lying on the lounge. She wrote you the other eve'g, she says—rather the effort of her life. I think she loves you very much. Old Williams, too, is full of you. I have showed her some of the contents of the box, to her entire demolishment; she is more than ever overwhelmed with a sense of "how the folks does," "Mrs Simpson" in particular. So let me hear from you at once.

R.

---

117. Cleveland's friend Fanny Crosby was married to Reverend Dr. Howard Crosby, a Presbyterian minister and son of a prominent family with deep roots in Massachusetts and New York.

118. "I have no desire to travel" is a strange statement, considering Cleveland's plan to stay abroad for two years.

119. Saxonville is the local term for the area in Massachusetts where Whipple's home, South Park, was located.

Rose Cleveland to Evangeline Whipple, Piney Woods Hotel,
Thomasville, Georgia
Holland Patent, Nov. 22, 1896

Dear Granny—dear "Yourself"
Your good letter from Thomasville[120] came Friday night, and I
have been ever since waiting for the "good winter" in which I
could reply—but it hangs off, and now I shall write in the still-
bad winter, bad with the most persistent neuralgia I ever had,
which digs me with daggers that make me jump every minute.
I do things that do not require *behavior* or *words*, and let the
rest go. So excuse any lack in this.

You can imagine about how my days are passing now,
when I tell you that I am trying to do things *up* so that all will
take care of itself, in any event. That cannot quite be done,
but as near it as possible I want to accomplish. I am going to
leave this house so that all rooms I use, except library, can be
rented in the summer, or the cottage—*or* be sold, if (which
s'ever imminent) a good chance comes, for I see that I cannot live here prosperously until I am strong enough to snap
my fingers at climate and monotony. I swear to leave almost
all there and in this house which I value, in my library, and
reserve that as a store room—or for myself in case I should
wish it suddenly.

Now you will know how I am jobbing along, and wondering every day if the next day will show more progress than
this, and if *I*—or just a kind of grip-sack[121]—will really get off
next week Saturday. At present I do not feel very anticipa-
tory—but that is perhaps just as well. I am trying to find a
cloth that will go in the long cloak of yours, for new sleeves,
and if I can, I shall have sleeves made & wear it all the time it

120. Thomasville, Georgia.
121. A reference to her illness, with its symptoms similar to influenza
(grippe).

is cold—and feel more than ever like Granny's "child," or try to.[122] And that is all about me, I swear.

I am so glad you are *both* so well and happy. The pictures are great, & should make Roseti famous[123]—altho' I do not like his style; don't let him make any more of you. That Roseti smile is not quite human, as how can it be, with his big smacking lips before you, as a model for doing yours?

Before this you will have rec'd mine of last Sunday telling you how I *had* opened the box and trying to tell you how I felt about it. Of course send the president[124] the Infanta (you must call her that now she is your own horse) picture "with a note"—he will like it—but I warn you that *Mrs. C.*[125] may think it should have gone to *her*, as it was supposed to be *her* colt. However, that you need not care for.

My sister Sue has been here this last week, instead of coming on Saturday next—as her family engagements left her no choice. We have had a nice visit and talk, and now I am alone. Pussy, as usual, is in and out. Yes, I know no other peace for Pussy at Christmas, or any other time, but this. You will give her great comfort by simply showing her that you do not forget her.

No, my dear "Yourself"—I do not know of anything you can do for me—except to keep yourself.

~~The~~ It seems impossible—as death does—that we have the Atlantic States between us, and soon the Atlantic Ocean; but all that cannot wake separation, and I can conceive how it

122. Cleveland planned to tailor one of Whipple's cloaks to take on her voyage in order to feel, metaphorically, enveloped by Whipple.

123. Roseti ran a photography studio at 297 Fifth Avenue, New York (1890s–1900) according to www.langdonroad.com. Cleveland may have referred to a portrait of Evangeline (standing) and Bishop Whipple (seated) in the collections of the Cathedral of Our Merciful Saviour in Faribault, Minnesota. Roseti also took Evangeline's picture before 1896 (see page 10); this photograph is preserved in the collections of the MNHS.

124. Grover Cleveland.

125. Frances Folsom Cleveland.

may be that, all the while, the real distance between us may grow less. No matter about that, if we only *grow,* it will follow. There is but one goal for growth.

I suppose this time next Sunday King will be a married man[126]—good! But I think most of Motherdie.

Now I must stop, for reasons you had in the preamble. Will write again next Sunday.

"Myself-ie."

Rose Cleveland to Jane Van Poelien Marrs, Piney Woods Hotel,[127]
Thomasville, Georgia
postmarked November 22, 1896

My dearest and only Motherdie,
When I came in from my drive this afternoon I found a big box at the top of my stairs and lost no time in opening it. Oh, Motherdie, what shall I say of your love, your goodness, your thoughtfulness, your *motherliness!* It touches me beyond any words I can write or speak, and brings tears to my eyes! The dainty gowns & slippers, the wonderful shawl—what power they have, will always have to make me believe that *you,* at least, do not change. That you are "always Motherdie." It has always been so, Motherdie, from the time you laid your hand upon my head in Florida. It will always be so.

Oh, how I love you, and believe in you and shall always—whether any sign is made of it, or not. *Your* call will always

---

126. Evangeline Whipple's brother, Kingsmill Marrs (1847–1912), married Laura Norcross (1845–1946) on November 28, 1896. Laura Norcross descended from a prominent Boston family; her father, Otis C. Norcross (1811–82), was mayor of Boston from 1867 to 1868. The couple married quietly, perhaps because the Norcross family was not in favor of the marriage (see Rose Cleveland to Jane Van Poelien Marrs, November 22, 1896).

127. The Piney Woods luxury hotel, built in 1895, had three hundred rooms.

be the first to take me to your side, because we have been together "in health, in sickness, and in sorrow." You must let me feel that I can still be something to you, as much, perhaps, as ever, because I *need* my Motherdie so much. Try and need me sometime, so that I can be your child again. I shall always be that—in whatever land.

Of the beauty & charm and rose color of those Xmas things, my Motherdie, I can only say that they are as only you can make them; no one in the wide world ever made things look or feel as you do, and so charged them with the "warmth of your love enfolding."[128] They will be a panoply against the chills & damps I shall have to meet, as others have been. I have just now been warding off a *grip* [*sic*][129] by the sweet last year's pink gowns, and this minute the beloved pink shawl 1st hangs from my shoulder. There is no way of accounting for their virtue except by the truth: that you have put yourself into them.

Oh, Motherdie, there are some things we both know and feel which we shall never, never say to each other. But I want to say that I shall never, never cease to be Eva's if she ever needs me again; nothing can ever break my sense of loyalty to her; you know all about it.

I saw Miss Norcross[130] in Boston and she talked very frankly to me; a good and true soul she is, Motherdie, and a hard time she has had. I said you spoke of her so kindly and warmly, and that broke her down. I never saw her self-restraint give way before. It was most touching to see how her whole nature vibrates at kindness—"if people are good to me," as she said, she will be your adoring slave, I can say, and you will be what she has never known: a mother. She is very clear headed and positive, yet uncombative and gentle—and I love her! I was so impatient for her & King to get off—perfectly willing they

128. The phrase evokes language about God's love used in Christian sermons and prayers.

129. Grippe (influenza).

130. Laura Norcross Marrs. Cleveland wrote this letter prior to Laura Norcross and Kingsmill Marrs's wedding.

should run away—will meet Laura any dark night at the back door and put on her clothes & serve her mean Ma[131] in that disguise until she & King clear the coast (I should be a great success in that rôle—the thought of what a chance I'd have to pinch and pull the old lady gives me a rare relish for the position).

My own program moves on. I am picking over old papers & letters now & a great clearing out is going on. I think I shall have time enough, not too much.

I had nice visits with my sister and nieces and other old friends after I left you[132] and came home much satisfied. The little call at South Park was a satisfaction, Motherdie—*in its way.* I shall write you from Florence,[133] if all goes well with my plans—so you may hear from me fr[om] that side, by New Year's!

Remember me at *10 A.M.* on Dec. 5th, and if you are not too busy let me find a letter in "S. S. Normania" sailing Dec. 5 Hamburg American Line—foot of First Street Hoboken, New Jersey. When I get there I shall carry the note that comes with this precious box all round with me, and never let it go. Will write again before leaving.

Love to King & Belle[134]—
your own child,

Rose

---

131. Hepsibeth Anna Coffin Ames (1840–1917).
132. This suggests a recent visit in Massachusetts at South Park, likely after the marriage of Evangeline and Henry Whipple.
133. Florence, Italy.
134. Possibly Eveline Isabelle Bense, Jane Marrs's niece.

Rose Cleveland to Evangeline Whipple, St. James Hotel,
   Jacksonville, Florida
November 26, 1896
Thanksgiving Day

Almost dinner time, my dear Grand Mother—and I am just in from a trip through the steaming mud (cold here indeed! I wonder who calls it *cold;* it is the same nasty, grip-y[135] way it was last year this time, or worse). As I am exactly in the *middle* of the stream, you are so good to send the prescriptions.

I hope I'll have a chance to write again. Shall try to the last minute [to write] as to trunk, for saving and sending away and leaving in the house, and under a great pressure, for *me*. I could not leave home for even King's wedding, or a family visit. So I am here at work instead. After a little private Thanksgiving service this morning, I pitched in and got a good deal done. Then this P.M. drove, under a large box, Pussy & I, to Shorey's.[136] We hoped the villagers would think our box full of nice things for the poor—now—what do you think. A *great* box of Baileys![137] tied up with this stranger's ribbon, for all the world like my Granny's!! came last night—all colors & sorts, as Granny has it, with a bar of her *safe* peppermint in the *middle*—a lovely finish beneath! And *now* Pussy & I are going to *sort* it and make a little dish for *George* (Mrs. V.'s son) with wife & baby, to go with the turkey dinner I sent, *and* for Old Williams herself—who cannot say enough in loving remembrance of you—and whose silence is more than words! And for the *Shorey* girls, who think you are beautiful & say in *fortissimo*[138] that they [sic] are very few persons like Mrs. Simpson.[139]

---

135. That is, inclined to give people the grippe (influenza).
136. A Holland Patent dressmaking business operated by two seamstresses.
137. Probably candy.
138. Italian: very loudly.
139. Though Evangeline had married Henry Whipple in October, the Shoreys called her "Mrs. Simpson."

And now I must stop—for I am a tired little excited thing. Will write again before sailing—Room 37-S.S. "Normannia" Hamburg Piers, Hoboken, sail Dec. 5 10 A.M.

7:30 P.M.

And now the dinner is over, & all fed & treated to turkey & candy. Old Mr. Hamlin[140] & old Mrs. Candler,[141] my right & left tottering old neighbors, being added in the distribution of the candy, so that now poor Granchile's box looks sorry & G. C. looks sorry—but Granny would weep (too much left now for any safe & sound nights). And Pussy has gone and I am at a busy desk and it is eight or seven A.M., & I slept none to speak of last night, and, O, what a fine upset my rooms are in!

And here comes yours now of the *18th*—with prescription.[142] I shall let Evelyn have it to try but I believe I will hope for the best and go it alone. Then if I lie groaning all the *12* days, I will repent and go to my Grandmother and say I have survived, and take it from Evelyn's bottle! (a good way out?)

Shorey girls have made the Redfern[143] *green*, as you suggested, with a good jacket, and the old Sorento silk (quaint) with a nice, light, short skirt, & done a lot of bobbins to save worry and time. I am going to take what I can force into one trunk and my tin steamer trunk & valise—and leave the rest. *Your* long ulster Tirney has found a tolerable match for, & I am having long sleeves made in Utica & shall feel so fine in it. Too good for this steamer, but I have nothing else warm enough.

I am going to take Pussy to see me off and have a little time in New York, which will divert her. It is Evelyn's and my Xmas present to her. I will write you from Florence about Auntie

140. Possibly a relative of Adelaide "Fiori" Hamlin Thierry.

141. Possibly a relative of Amelia Candler Gardiner.

142. The prescription was likely a remedy for seasickness.

143. Probably Redfern & Sons, a British couturier with branches in France and the United States as well as England and Scotland. In its heyday (circa 1880–1920), it competed with the leading fashion houses of the time, including the House of Worth.

Harris,[144] and *if* we come back there later & she would like a trip such as you speak of I will let you know. But I am afraid it is *too late* for her now. But she shall know how you thought of her & that will do her great good.

I have the thick & middling flannels and shall keep warm. I *long* for the *freeze* that does not come. Now I must fly to other things & not work too hard or too late, or I would sleep, & I have too much to do tomorrow to allow this. I am better and taking as good care of my worthless self as if I was worth it.

I, too, will send a telegram from Utica Sat. morning to King & Laura—a note from King this A.M. *would* leave me in doubt as to whether it would or could even "happen" if I did not know the fact about it. I am sorry they have been so sudden and I *so* unable to contrive any gift—~~They~~ I will manage it later.

Bye—with remembrances to the bishop—
Granchile

Rose Cleveland to Evangeline Whipple, Maitland, Florida
Weeds—Nov. 27, 1896

Dear E—
The day is nearly past and I have not been out. Yesterday was a very tiresome day in Utica, but I got everything done—dentistry, the cloak fitted, & numberless errands. The cloth Tirney found is a surprisingly good match, and the cloak will be exactly what I want and need. It will keep me warm all the

144. Ellen Matilda Orbison Harris (1816–1902) was an American Civil War nurse and a member of Philadelphia's elite society whose long-term humanitarian work likely inspired Cleveland and Whipple. Between 1870 and her death, she lived in Italy—from 1881 onward as the widow of Dr. John Harris, the US consul to Venice (Eaton, *Birth Place of Souls*, 262, and Africa, *History*, 439). *Auntie* was, and remains, an affectionate honorific used for women regardless of blood ties. In 1897, Harris was living in Florence, where she likely supported social programs through the English churches, including St. Mark's and the Holy Trinity.

way across the wintry seas. Pussy is having a little cap made—toke-style[145]—for me from the old sleeves at "Sessons" to wear on ship—for which enterprise we can only *hope* for the best.

I am afraid I cannot get away from here before Friday, as I am arranging to have the unoccupied rooms (except library which I use for storing) rented, if the right tenants turn up during the summer months. It makes it a very close piece of work—and there seems to be no end to it all.

My neuralgia has all gone, and, except for too much fatigue, I am all right.

Yours of the 26th came last night. No box yet—will report its arrival. Among old letters I found this from Mr. F. Simpson,[146] which *possibly* you may like. I send also King's last. It is so characteristic. I sent "heartfelt congratulations to Mr. & Mrs. Kingsmill Marrs" from Utica at 10 A.M. yesterday. Hope it went off (the marriage) but shall not feel certain until I see it in cold type.

I am trying to straighten everything *up*, in case of fire—so to speak—or, to put it more pleasantly, "if anything should happen to me," since we must never mention in polite ears the one certainty by name. Well—I think I have got things in shape to provide for all such contingencies—or shall have after the visit I expect from Mrs. Irish to-morrow. Enough said?

As I "leave" the Lee County Florida land to you,[147] perhaps you would like to let Mr. Robinson send tax receipts to you, in my absence, so that nothing can arise to embarrass the matter in the future. If so, address him and tell him to address you on that subject until I return to this country: R. G. Robinson, Esq., Zellwood, Florida. I would like to *pay* the tax, however trifling, myself, if I can have it sent me—but you can keep receipts, please, in my absence. If that is right let me know,

145. A toke—more often spelled *toque*—is a brimless hat.

146. Frank Ernest Simpson, Evangeline's stepson from her first marriage, to Michael Hodge Simpson.

147. Cleveland was tidying her legal affairs and splitting up her estate with Whipple, much as she might have done before a divorce settlement.

and tell me that you have satisfied him, so that I shall not have it on my mind, or neglect it.

I did not mean to speak of the "Roseti smile" on *your* picture, but the Roseti smile in general, and perhaps because I recall so vividly the method of its manufacture in my own case.[148]

Pussy will be wild over the shoe buttoner and slipper slide—& Williams tearful (in secret) over *any* attention. I am too full of business to write more now—will write again before leaving. My rooms are in a wild state of chaos! but I hope order will come out in due time.

That every good and happiness may constantly be yours, pray.

Your beloving
G.C.

I don't realize I am going—have not time. Just feel that strange things are happening.

Rose Cleveland to Evangeline Whipple, Maitland, Orange County, Florida
Dec. 1st 1896
Weeds

Only a moment, dear Grandmother, in reply to yours of last night. Pussy will be in before I finish and I will leave you the address of the surgeon who made her well, i.e., saved her from being an invalid for life.

My doings here are of the most terrible description, with trunks, lawyer, mares (I have got a *good* place for her in my absence) and all the thousand rest. I marvel that there is any part of me left to tell the tale.

In packing away things I do not find that invaluable only

148. Cleveland referenced a portrait the Roseti photography studio, 297 Fifth Avenue, New York, took of her, possibly one housed in the New Jersey State Archives: Department of State, Cleveland Family Records; see page 14.

ambrotype of my brother.[149] Do you remember whether you took it *with* the Webber (I remember you took that) to get it copied? If so I shall feel safe about it. Only of course ~~we~~ I won't have it copied now.[150] Tell me if you know just where it is. The address is—"Dr. Gill Wyley,[151] 215 West 43rd St., New York." Pussy sends her love, and recommends the doctor for a fellow sufferer. She says Mrs. D. will feel *safe* as soon as he grasps her. The post comes in with a letter from Mrs. Cleveland[152] asking her to visit her at the *White House*! Mrs. Leaming's[153] management, I suppose.

I enclose this funny note from King—hope they will stay as much married as they are now. I shall hardly see them as I cannot get away from here before Friday noon—and have engagements at the hotel with *Tirney* &c for the evening, but will see them if they come.

I shall be glad, of course, when I am off! The unendurable state of things has arrived—and one cannot live *in* it. I shall write again, and will report arrival of box.

"Our life was but a journey & a march."

R.

---

149. Because Cleveland calls the ambrotype "invaluable," it could have been of her brother Lewis Frederick Cleveland, who, along with "five servants," was lost at sea on October 22, 1872, when the steamship *Missouri* caught fire off the coast of the Bahamas en route to Havana ("Another Steamship Disaster," *Baltimore Sun,* October 31, 1872). The *New York Herald* reported that he was intending to open a hotel in Havana (November 9, 1872).

150. The sharing of family mementos suggests intimate cohabitation. Cleveland's habitual use of the pronoun "we," which she crossed out and replaced with the singular "I," indicates her reluctance in accepting the end of her relationship with Whipple.

151. Possibly civil engineer and gynecologist Walker Gill Wylie (1849–1923), an innovative surgeon who practiced at Bellevue Hospital in New York.

152. Frances Folsom Cleveland.

153. Possibly Josephine Bennett Leaming (1836–1905), who married her brother-in-law, Jonathan Foreman Leaming (1822–1907), in 1888, a year and a half after the death of her sister, Eliza. Jonathan Leaming was a medical doctor, dentist, and senator from Cape May, New Jersey, who served in the New Jersey state senate 1862–65 and 1877–80 (Scannell and Sackett, *Scannell's New Jersey's First Citizens,* 587; Stevens, *History of Cape May County,* 352).

Evelyn Ames to Evangeline Whipple, Piney Woods Hotel,
Thomasville, Georgia
AM BORD DES SCHNELLDAMPFER NORMANNIA,
HAMBURG-AMERIKA LINIE
December 5, 1896

Dearest Evangeline,
I have not written, but you know my heart and remember all
I have said and written to you. Do you not? Your November
letter to me was delayed a very long time, being in the Boston
house while we were out of town. I could not understand why
you did not write me as well as my precious Millie, but your
note just came so I know. Rose is writing you, I believe—We
are writing goodbye to our dearest ones now. And the pilot
will take the little notes back.
Goodbye then, Evangeline—God bless you both.[154]

My love to you both
Evelyn.

Rose Cleveland to Evangeline Whipple, Maitland, Florida
postmarked December 7, 1896
AM BORD DES SCHNELLDAMPFER NORMANNIA,
HAMBURG-AMERIKA LINIE

Goodbye, dear Gran—Mrs. Ames, Susie, & another one—Clara
Fuller, Mrs. Leaming, & Pussy have just left—and Evelyn and
I have come here. She writes Millie, I you. She also hopes to
write you, and in case she has not time, sends her love to you
and the Bishop. The *glorious* flowers are here—the jacques[155]
superb and eloquent. I gave a little bunch of them to Pussy
only, and I know we both would do that. She has gone off

---

154. Evangeline Whipple and Henry Whipple.
155. Jacks-in-the-pulpit.

brandy—bearing herself finely. Mr. Leaming is determined to have her go to the White House Monday—for a day with the children.[156] I had your otter cloak on. It is *so* warm and fine for this purpose, and so good looking—all but the *fur*, which *little creatures*[157] had mangled. I tell you this that you may be on your guard for other things there. I shall have new otter put on on other side probably. It is *just* right now.

King and Laura came and staid a long time last night— Laura telling of her trials immediately, funny & heroic. King looks like a very contented old husband.[158]

I am sorry to say that *box* did *not* reach me. Will Thomas will *keep* it when it comes, subject to *my* or *your* order. Everything seems comfortable on board here, and I hope we shall have a pleasant time. Will write on arrival at Florence. Until you hear another, address me care *Magray & Hooker* as of old. Now I must stop. I have read your letter and shall keep it always. And now no more words.

All my heart is full for you.

[*Rose*]

With kindest remembrances to the Bishop,
I am always, unchanging,
Your Myself.

156. Grover and Frances Cleveland's children.
157. Likely moths or rodents.
158. Kingsmill Marrs was forty-nine and Laura Norcross fifty-one years old when they married in 1896.

Letters

PART II

1896–1899

Cleveland and Ames sailed out of New York aboard the steam-ship Normannia *on December 5, 1896, bound for Europe. Their first destination was Florence, Italy, which they reached via Spain, Algeria, Naples, and Genoa. Later, Cleveland and Ames spent time in Austria, Hungary, Greece, Turkey, and Egypt before returning to the United States in 1899.*

Rose Cleveland to Evangeline Whipple
AM BORD DES SCHNELLDAMPFER NORMANNIA,
  HAMBURG-AMERIKA LINIE
12 December, 1896

Beloved Second Mother,
Saturday night—a week and over out—and tomorrow we make Gibraltar, where we may go ashore for an hour or two, long enough to see the place, they say, and where these letters will be posted.

We have had a fine voyage so far. All has gone well. In the state room were the glorious flowers—the superb jacks,[1] a pink and exquisite enormous bunch of violets for Evelyn, done up in violet paper with violet ribbon & a strange violet *lace* over them, the like of which she, nor, of course, *I*, had never seen. My roses were the envy and despair of all, and kept splendidly for many days. King & Laura also had lovely flowers there, and a big box from Mrs. Ames.

The boat is very comfortable, its immense size preventing motion.[2] The weather has been good most of the time, but three days this week were very rough and a smaller boat would have pitched terribly. This one rolled like a huge cradle, and, altho' battered about a good deal, neither of us were sea-sick, and have not raised a meal. We have been on deck most of the time in all weather & got on finely. Very agreeable people on board—a son of Sec'y Morton[3] & others we have a good deal of talk with: Mr. Gould & his wife of St. Louis, who are the magnates of *Clearwater,* Florida, every winter. He told

---

1. Jacks-in-the-pulpit.
2. The Hamburg America Line offered weekly express service between New York and Europe. An 1896 brochure boasted the company held the record for the fastest time across the Atlantic from New York at six days, ten hours, and thirty-two minutes, "while maintaining ultimate safety with great comfort to their passengers" (http://www.norwayheritage.com/).
3. Julius Sterling Morton (1832–1902) was Grover Cleveland's secretary of agriculture from 1893 until 1897.

me he had a lot of oranges last winter, and was selling this winter at $2.50 per box on the tree.

We passed the Azores on Thursday, sailing between two of them, Corvo & Florio: beautiful, bold, rocky coast with dazzling white houses in clusters, the first land we have seen. We are approaching the coast of Spain now. To-morrow Gibraltar, Monday Algiers, Tuesday Naples. Wednesday, Genoa, and perhaps *Florence the same day.*

We are both very well and getting a great deal of good—I hope, I believe—from the rest; we sleep, eat, and talk—reading some. Evelyn has been reading Flaubert's "Salambô" [*sic*] in the French, which makes it a different thing, and drilling me a little in French. We are also reading Fairbairn's "Place of Christ in Modern Theology,"[4] which you gave me, and which justifies all the praise of it, and William James—(of Harvard's) *Psychology*[5]—in pieces. We have met a very clever man to talk with—the rest are only about average.

Laura and King came to see me Friday night in New York & we had a good talk—but I wrote you of that.

Now I must stop—for letters must go to the family & to Pussy with them. Evelyn sends you her dear love & much more about the *violets* (which I cannot repeat) & which she will write soon.

With the best love of
G.C.

4. The Scottish theologian Andrew Martin Fairbairn (1838–1912) was a Congregationalist scholar associated with Oxford University.
5. William James published his two-volume *Principles of Psychology* in 1890.

Rose Cleveland to Evangeline Whipple
SÜDBAHN HOTEL, SEMMERING [6]
Dec. 27th, 1896

My dearest Granny,
Such an embarrassment of riches—such a many things I want to fill this vacation hour with, and now it's nearly twelve and Evelyn will come immediately and then it will be dinner, & the rest—and the day will be gone before I know it!

Well, I shall push all aside the dear new Xmas books—your *loveliest* one this A.M. arrived; Mrs. Crosby's; King, Laura & the family's—even dear Motherdie will come *second*—and have a word with you first of all. I have just dipped into the last chapters of one of the Xmas books—(LeConte; *Evolution & Its Relation to Religious Thought* and find some ideas so exactly what I have been writing that I am in high good humor at this surprising corroboration, not surprising because it ought to be, but for reasons less complementary to our poor humanity— yet if it were poorer I might be less pleased, being afraid it would be said that I plagiarized!)

Well, let that parenthesis go.

I lay all books aside, only holding on my knee, as I write, the shepherd's calendar, and raising my eyes now and then to see the beauty of its cover—you knew just how it would please me—lambs, dog, shepherd, blue cloak, pipe, hat & all!

Evelyn is writing you, and will tell you how it happens that the dear great Present (worth so much money!) is pinned in my pink silk wrapper pocket to be made payable to one—and to be a constant kaleidoscope of *all* wonderful "things that Rose would like" turning & turning in the gayest Christmas colors in my dazzled brain, *until* one of their wonders gets ahead—and then *presto,* the transformation!

Meanwhile jacques[7] & jonquil & white holly flower are

6. A town in eastern Austria, forty-six miles from Vienna.
7. Jacks-in-the-pulpit.

perennial in my memory of this Christmas day & Granny! & Evelyn must tell you the rest. It has all been bright and dear and cosy—our little salon was a joy, our little gifts to each other overwhelming surprises—our neighbors across the hall—from Frau Mama Excellenz to the *tochter*[8] Baronnessina & Herr Baron—were in and out with holly & red cheeks & boisterous cheer from early morn till late mid-night, with Merry Xmas license—our charming hostess was some acquaintance—all helping the Yule log roar (Evelyn will relate its *tragedy!*). But best of all, in the dusk before light (~~dark~~at *halb-acht*[9] here on the mountains!) in our curtained room, came our Lumière-Kellnerin,[10] Poldie (Leopolde), with a Xmas tree *Engel*[11] from top-most branch, red, green, blue & white candles and set it forth & lit it before our wondering eyes,[12] saying the Christ-Kind hat es gebracht;[13] our poor, dear, sensitive, lovely, proud, seen-better-days Poldie!

As I write, the sun gilds everything in our room, which might look like a toy shop if the mighty *Rax*,[14] the huge pile that bulwarks our horizon yonder, did not tower in its majesty, white & glorious in its splendid dignity in the distance, while gay firs wane between!

But I *must* stop—the next to Motherdie, & then Laura & King. *Now* it must be dear Mrs. Crosby, whom, as you see, I do not attend to, for I will send the characteristic bits instead of repeating her misstep.

Love, love, love & around & best of bless[ings] for Granny,
from Chile

8. German: daughter.
9. German: seven-thirty in the evening.
10. French and German: light-waitress.
11. German: angel.
12. Possibly a reference to Clement Clarke Moore's 1823 poem "A Visit from St. Nicholas" and its lines, "When, what to my wondering eyes should appear / but a miniature sleigh, and eight tiny reindeer."
13. German: the Christ child has brought it.
14. A group of mountains in the Austrian Alps.

Rose Cleveland to Evangeline Whipple
Vienna—Sunday P.M. Jan. 3. 1897

Dear Evangeline,
I shall not wait longer to hear from you, but send a note by way of report if not a reply. My 4th since leaving—one from harbor, New York, one from Gibralter [*sic*], one from Florence, before this. We had a lovely ten days in Florence, [in] spite of cold, damp & rainy weather. The Uffizi was a little warmer, at least, the death-like, cellar-y chill a little broken by a row, few & far between, of little stoves, but San Marco, the Belle Arte & others were dangerous & dreadful. However we went & looked an hour & then finished off with photographs, of which Evelyn is making a collection. She got all the San Marco Fra Angelicos and Padua Giottos—and gave me, for Xmas, a *glorious* ~~Holy Family~~ Madonna of Botticelli's "Il Magnificat"—the one in the Uffizi—in carbon. She had another she got last summer, the one in the Louvre—and the two relieve our walls from barrenness.

We left Florence last Monday P.M. Spent the night en route, at Padua, where we visited the Arena chapel[15] for the Giottos and went on at 1 P.M. breaking the night at Gortz, the frontier station. We left there just as the sun was sending a faint herald ahead—far ahead—of himself in the eastern sky behind the cypresses and reached Vienna at 9:30 P.M. We were fortunate in having a comfortable 1st class apartment to ourselves for the entire day, and regular stops for dinner & supper: & the most superb scenery, of course. I shall never forget the sunrise—or its reflection on the half horizon of snow mountains opposite.

Just here came lunch—of chicken pureè, mutton chops with cream potatoes, bread & butter & *beer*—(we order everything a là carte & have most meals served in our salon). We are

15. The Scrovegni Chapel.

Rose Cleveland by Schemboche, Florence, Italy,
inscribed "For my dear Bishop Whipple, with the
love of Rose E. Cleveland." *Allyn Ford Collection,
Minnesota Historical Society.*

settled to our surprise and satisfaction in this best hotel—the Imperial.[16] Mrs. Crosby told me about it, down there in Kran. It is very well-located for opera, theater, &c. on the Ring near Yosef Plaza & the Burg theater. We came here on our arrival expecting to stop only for the night & hunt our housing the next day, having several addresses from Miss Mack & others. But we found we could have these very good rooms—one for sleeping, one for salon on the third floor—at a price no greater than the good first pension rooms and every way more desirable. We pay for the room service & light included (a concession to the length of our stay) 6 florins ($2.40;[17] $1.20 each). Heating is about 25 each/50 cts a day extra—& all meals; but the expense of having them served in our salon is so very little that we are doing that almost entirely. The cuisine is exceptionally good and we think ourselves very fortunate.

We have seen Miss Mack twice, once in her own house: she is very kind & good, looks better than when we saw her, has a great English (American) clientele and is very like herself. Asks with the greatest interest about you, and declares you have forgotten her: ~~says~~ speaks sparingly of Faniska:[18] kindly, but a little severely, I can see.

American friends are not lacking. Evelyn has a Boston family here—*I* a Buffalo! Not what we planned for but not to be avoided but controlled. So far I am not charmed with Vienna—it has no immediate charm. But I think we shall like it. Evelyn tackles Leschetizky[19] to morrow: I don't know how it will work out.

Now I must write Pussie and then dress & turn out ~~to the~~

16. The Hotel Imperial, located on Vienna's Ringstraße (the Ring Road that encircles Vienna's historic Old Town) at Kaerntner Ring 16. The building was constructed in 1863 as the Viennese residence of the Prince of Württemberg and made into a hotel in 1873.

17. At $2.40, the room charge was equivalent to about $70 in 2018.

18. A cousin to the Princess Cantacuzène, Elisabeth Sicard.

19. The Polish violinist Theodor Hermann Leschetizky.

for a walk which I propose shall be to the Augustiner Kirche,[20] where I will find myself hoping for some vesper service.

I hope to hear from you everyday. My address: ~~Old~~ Anglo-Austrian Bank, Vienna. Our salon is large & we have a nice piano in it. No view. Some English primroses we got yesterday & some Florence photographs. Evelyn sends love. Will write more as things turn up, and put on the rose-colored sheet last night for the first time in your honor. Exquisite to look at & feel!

[Rose]

Rose Cleveland to Evangeline Whipple
SÜDBAHN HOTEL, SEMMERING, AUSTRIA-HUNGARY
Jan. 16, 1897

My dear Evangeline,
Your last—postmarked Dec. 31—reached me just as we were starting for Vienna[21] Friday A.M. and was good company on the train with its enclosures. Shall I return them? The photographs you promise have not yet arrived, but will look in on me any mail now, and be very welcome.

I am glad you think we look *well* in the little card, and I think I may venture to say that we *are* as well as we look. It seems to me we look just harmless: and nothing else, but that is a great deal if it is the true expression of the character, which I dare not affirm, tho it *looks* so.

Your Xmas is, as always, a *great time* for all concerned, and as no one better than I know [sic]. By the way, *I* have made up my mind about what I "would most like" out of my little green Xmas of Granny's: It came to me in bed the other night at

20. The fourteenth-century Gothic Augustinian Catholic church in Vienna.
21. Vienna is forty-six miles from Semmering.

Vienna, and I can tell you about it— *some,* now, and more later. I "would like most" to send it to Auntie Harris for her wise, watchful, and prayerful expenditure for those poor Italians, for whom she is ever doing all she can, for body and soul, in league with such good & noble people who somehow always seem to feel that she is *able to help.* I saw one while I was there; a fine woman of most noble history, attainments, and character, and I saw how wistfully Auntie Harris was watching & waiting for the needed help. Of course I am not up to that sort of thing myself just now, but if my Grandmother makes it possible that is another thing. So I am writing her now and shall give her myself, God knows what "poor Italians," and, I hope, yourself, the greatest pleasure, in that choice of Xmas gift from you!

I shall keep the note pinned in the pocket of the pink silk wrapper (on at this writing) which is my Sunday evening costume: and I enclose the counterpart of the "white wool-y flower" which came with the red roses. I got it from a wistful, limping man we met in our morning walk this morning. Nothing so white, and nothing so wooly!

We spent Friday & Sat. in gay, great Vienna. We are there for a night or two every fortnight. One room, on the Ring, at our first old Imperial, where the old Austrian floor *kellner*[22] & all of them treat us as if we had come home every time, looks out on a perfect Paris of lights and shadows of humanity and gives the most powerful contrast possible to the great mountains, stars & forests that surround us here. We went to a fine concert by *Emil Sauer,*[23] the pianist—all very superb: hall, artist, people, everything. But after two days of rowing in town, it is wonderful to get back here, drive up through forests and stars *to* forests and stars, and open the door on our cozy salon, all warm & lit, *ganz geputzt,*[24] and the supper later laid!

22. German: waiter.
23. The German pianist Emil Georg Conrad von Sauer (1862–1942) studied with Franz Liszt and became a famous composer and music teacher in his own right.
24. German: completely cleaned.

I found out last night a long letter from Miss Mander.[25] She has been ill, but is now in Ireland recruiting, in her way, by recruiting those suffering people. She is a truly heroic character, as she shows herself to me.

I heard from Faniska. Here is her last, which I am just replying to. It may amuse [you] to hear her side of the wonderful Fanny Zeisler[26]—the old fashioned *pianiste* I idolized so in my last to you—did I? Telling you of her great concert in Venice? *Such is life!*

How lovely Florida must be now, i.e., what you describe is lovely. I am so pleased to think of Motherdie so well & happy. I want to write her & to King & Laura, to whom I am indebted over & over, but must wait. So many letters to write, and so many friends neglected. You will, I know, make my *devoirs*.[27] We still enjoy our lovely books. Evelyn revels in their illustrations, but those those [*sic*] "eighteen wild rabbits rabbits [*sic*] sitting in the moonlight in your front yard" gave her wild excitement and a never-as-yet-excelled "thrill" of delight.

Now *I* must stop, for supper time approaches. We are going to have cream toast made from English bread brought from *Wien* over our own coals, which I make with [illegible crossed-out words] a chicken and orange marmalade.

Love to everybody. Is Miss Bryant in Florida this season?

–G.

I suppose my little package of Xmas cards did not reach you. I ventured nothing more valuable to anyone.

---

25. Amy Mander, a member of a prominent English family from Wolverhampton and a graduate of Newnham College, Cambridge, had been involved in Irish nationalist politics since the 1880s.

26. Fannie Bloomfield Zeisler (1863–1927) studied music under Theodor Leschetizky and became a popular concert pianist in both the United States and Europe.

27. French: obligations.

Rose Cleveland to Evangeline Whipple
FROHNER'S HOTEL IMPERIAL, VIENNA
[January] 22, 1897

My dear Evangeline,

It is nearly ten o'clock and I have just come in from a drive; vast powers beset me, but I am anxious to end the day with a reply to your last, received day before yesterday, from Faribault. Now you are on the water, and being rocked to sleep, I hope. May wind and wave favor!

We went out right after dinner and took a cab to drive around the *Ring,* the great circular drive, past the palaces, parliaments, museums, university—such a noble group of splendid buildings!—and then the curve of the Donau.[28] At the long bridge we decided to go on out the Prater,[29] and so we had miles of it—past the Venedig-in-Wien,[30] a perfect Vanity Fair[31] of electric lights in every form, music in every tune, from familiar Bowery dances[32] to the majestic national hymn. Cafes by the acre, people by the square mile, and then the long stately avenues, growing quieter and quieter until it was almost a country hush, broken by the frogs, of oppulent [*sic*] horse-chestnut bloom and foliage. And at the end the great Lusthaus,[33] where we were eating and drinking and be-merrying. It is a magnificent pleasure ground, on a great, airy—not to say windy—scale, as is everything in Vienna. The city

28. The Danube River.

29. Wurstelprater Park is often called "the Prater."

30. "Venice in Vienna," a theme park (one of the first in the world) that had been built less than two years earlier, in the spring of 1895.

31. After its appearance in John Bunyan's *Pilgrim's Progress* (1678), and, to a lesser extent, William Makepeace Thackeray's novel (1848), the phrase *Vanity Fair* entered general use as an expression meaning "the whole world."

32. Cleveland might refer to music played to accompany Bowery waltzes, also called *Apaches*—partner dances that emerged from the Parisian demimonde of the 1890s.

33. A historic house, open to the public, at the edge of the Prater.

certainly has its own *cachet,* which develops and comes to stay, when once it has come at all.

We are leaving in about two weeks, and are pretty busy now, dividing our time unequally between work[34] and play. Last night we went to the opera to hear Glück's *Orpheus and Euridice* [sic] followed by the *Cavalliera Rusticana.* The great Greek myth was wonderfully rendered: god and man, Hades and heaven, and the fair [illegible] furies were there for the eye, and all the meaning of that tragic myth was sung through one—ears to one's soul. One's heart ached for the valorous, death-defrauding Orpheus, struggling in vain to keep the faith and obey the will of the Olympians. But Eurydice had her way, and the allegory read itself in the catastrophe. The singing was superb, the orchestra Titanic. I have never more enjoyed an opera. The after-piece was splendid—you remember it? The acting was finer than I have seen it. The other night we heard Bethooven's [sic] *Fidelio*—something not to be described for solemn majesty and triumph.

I had a nice letter from Laura the other day; you will of course see them in London. They sent their pictures, both as *perfect* as any thing can be. They look so nice and married and much prettier than they were before.

I have not seen "Stephie"[35] since my return; shall see her to-morrow and take her with us on the drive to Schönbrun [sic].[36] We hear a great deal now of the empress[37] again, apropos of the terrible death of her sister, the Duchesse d'Alençon,

34. Cleveland's reference to "work" suggests that she continued to translate Augustine's *Soliloquies* while traveling.

35. Cleveland offers no concrete clues to Stephie's identity. Her train of thought, however, which leads to a discussion of the Hapsburg royal family, suggests that the woman could be Princess Stéphanie of Belgium (1865–1945), Empress Elisabeth's daughter-in-law and the widow of Crown Prince Rudolf.

36. The Hapsburg royal family used the palace at Schönbrunn, built in the 1500s, as a summer residence.

37. Elisabeth of Austria, made Empress of Austria and Queen of Hungary by her marriage to Franz Joseph I in 1854.

in the frightful Paris fire;[38] she it was to whom Ludwig[39] was engaged, you know. We had a very minute account of that episode from an Austrian the other day—all very extraordinary, not easy to put on paper. The empress is, naturally, terribly affected, and stores it in her usual illness—of the head, with strange isolation and contumacy. She is not liked here, and spends as little time here as possible. The emperor consoles himself with a matronly actress,[40] who has been faithful to him, it is alleged, irrespective of twenty-thousand florins yearly,[41] for his part of the contract toward that domestic happiness, to [which] all Viennese seem to add their blessing!

I am afraid I am wandering, and dare not read this over, but now it is written I will send, hoping you, too, will not read. I know enough, [in] spite of those yawns, though, to realize that.

When you receive this you will be about plunging into those ecclesiastical vortices which await you, as you follow the bishop in his appointment. May every day be fair and all so for your good and happiness!

Address as before, as I have not yet decided on my next post-office. Evelyn sends her love.

Always, always with love,
Rose.

---

38. Sophie Charlotte Augustine, Duchess of Alençon, died on May 4, 1897, when an elaborately constructed charity bazaar in Paris (Bazar de la Charité) caught fire, trapping many of the shoppers inside ("Fire Horror in Paris," *New York Times*, May 5, 1897; "The Paris Dead List," *New York Times*, May 6, 1897).
39. King Ludwig II of Bavaria (1845–86), sometimes called "Mad King Ludwig." Evangeline Whipple acquired numerous objects from Ludwig's estate during a European trip prior to 1890. Some of the items are in the collections of Shattuck–St. Mary's School, Faribault, Minnesota.
40. Katharina Schratt (1853–1940).
41. Equal to about $232,500 in 2018.

Rose Cleveland to Evangeline Whipple
Venice, March 13th, 1897

My dear Evangeline,
Yours with the enclosed reached me two days since, and to-day I have a note from King from Taormina,[42] enclosing a note from you. Not the one you promised me written after your return from Biscayne Bay[43] but before going, at the time you thought you had lost our letters! And that we had lost yours. But yours to me was after you returned and had heard from me, and before this time you must have had several more.

I wrote you from the seminary a week or so since, and even at that writing could not be certain about whether we would go to Constantinople and Athens or not. A day or two after we decided, in spite of encouraging talk from our US ambassador at Vienna, and a telegram from Mr. ~~Tripp~~ Terrell that same day, to give up the East and come to the West. A sort of sixth sense seemed to warn us that all was not as smooth as it seemed—and so, with a discretion which was our better part of valour,[44] we shifted quickly and began to feel that Venice would console us as nothing else could.

We left our Alpine roost in a gay snow storm and slid down the mountain roads to the station over snow enough for runners, and past fir forest bending under heavy snow blankets, where before, two days before, we had been lying on beds of pink heather blossoms whitened only by Christmas roses. We had, of course, our misgivings about Venice in March. It seemed a big leap from Corfu. But we came steadily on, reaching here at 11 at night, leaving the seminary at 10 A.M., and went to the Grand Hotel for over Sunday.

A great place comprising the four palace[s] below the

42. Near Mount Etna in Sicily.
43. Florida.
44. See Shakespeare's *Henry IV, Part I*, V.4: "the better part of valour is discretion."

Brittania & Pension Suisse: full, just now, of ministers & scientists in attendance on the health conference here over the bubonic plague. We could get only one double room, too small, at a huge price (for us)—so we went out to hunt and finally found our present, most fortunate resting place: a dependence of Hotel Suisse and a place recommended last summer to Evelyn by Duse,[45] who lived here six years. It's in the Babarigo [sic] palace,[46] and we come up three flights of marble steps, then we enter a huge salon or hall, dark and darkly frescoed with arms and portraits, in the centre of which is a grand piano; many windows and many mirrors. Crossing that to the right we open our double doors and are in our own territory—a very large front room or salon on the grand canal, with all its sights & sounds & sunshine—and behind it two smaller rooms. They are all clean and comfortable. The back rooms' windows open on roofs of all dimensions and heights, and we are glad to get night air that travels across their motley enclosures, rather than direct from the canals. It all seems sweet and sound, as we have it: with two stoves for morning and evening and *excellent* meals, in our salon, served by a little Venetian with Titian-red cheeks and black eyes & hair. All this ("and heaven too!")[47] for *nine francs*[48] per day! Already we have got our huge salon twisted round to something quite cozy, with its lounge & easy chairs and our books and pictures, which get an almost daily addition. Yesterday it was two colored photographs (Naya's[49] latest achievement) of the Carpacio [sic] mandolin player and Saint Ursula's bed-room.[50]

45. The Italian actress Eleonora Duse (1858–1924) was known by her last name alone.

46. The Palazzo Barbarigo Minotto, located on the Grand Canal.

47. From the quotation attributed to the English clergyman Philip Henry (1631–96): "All this, and heaven too! Then we serve a good Master."

48. Nine francs was equal to about $50 in 2018.

49. The Venetian photographer Carlo Naya (1816–82).

50. In addition to a famous image of a boy playing a mandolin, Vittore Carpaccio painted a series of nine canvases depicting the life of St. Ursula, including the *Sogno di sant'Orsola* (*The Dream of St. Ursula*).

To-day's plunder stands propped under the lamp at our round table where we write, and divides our attention with yourself and "Anna Lee." It is a little marble [one], very old, much mended and not at all clean—but looking out of its marvelous old broken drapery with a face beyond words for steady grace and perfect, sensitive chiseling—a woman's, I believe—a portrait, altho Evelyn wishes to believe it an ideal head—but holding its secret all these centuries, until one aches with guessing it; and leaves its yellow pallor to itself. We found it in a little nasty shop on our way home from the academy this P.M. Evelyn *saw* it, but I *got* it. The man asked eight francs but I gave five,[51] which he took happily.

Venice is, I believe, the most beautiful city in the world, and I am surprised to see so much [sic] simple old Italian surfaces everywhere. We are walking a good deal in the little streets and gazing at all things. Of course the Piazza is the same wondrous jewel as ever—the Lion flaps his wings wide over the book, resting his paw on the top of his tome.[52] The Duomo[53] scintillates like a jewel—the lions of the harbor still keep up their ancient watch. You know it all.

And I hope you will be here in cold weather—not hot—some long time and out of season! King wrote from Taormina en route for Naples and Rome. He may go to Florence before we return to Vienna, May 1st. If possible I shall try to carry out your *wish* for Auntie Harris for two or three months in the summer—I will write more of that later. But write Miss Bryant.

Much love from Evelyn, and best wishes for you both, always with love,
Rose

51. Probably five francs, or about $27 in 2018.
52. The Piazza San Marco is the home of the *Lion of Venice*, a bronze statue of a winged lion resting its front feet on the pages of an open bible. Portions of the statue date to the thirteenth century, when it was created and installed on the Column of San Marco.
53. The dome of San Marco (St. Mark's) Basilica, Venice.

Rose Cleveland to Evangeline Whipple
Vienna, May 4th, 1897
Hotel Imperial

My dear Evangeline,
We arrived here last ev'g from Ischl,[54] where we spent a week. This morning we went for our letters waiting at the bank for us, and among them I found yours of April 10th, with the one to send Mrs. Lawrence. I have just enclosed it to her with a word or two in favor, which may help your wishes with regard to the sale. They may feel timid about offering the price they can afford. You must give Mr. Austen the proper instructions to encourage them *if* they make any overtures that way. At any rate, I have done all I can think of, to properly bring on the crisis.[55]

Now that I have started this I suddenly realize that you are to sail in fourteen days, and I do not know where to address you.[56] A moment's thought suggests that if I send this in care of Motherdie it *may* reach you in time—but as I do not know where she will be in New York I shall have to address to Dorchester.[57] I will try it, for what it is worth, and trust that you may find it somewhere; if not it will be no great loss. In your next you will surely give me your London address. Mine will remain *here*, until June: and I will give you the next as soon as it is determined.

Yes, certainly I received the letters sent me to Florence— the ones you speak of as in this: "to the Florence Bank." I answered them, and acknowledged their receipt several times. Among my letters is one fr[om] King, which, lest he may not

54. Bad Ischl, a spa town in Austria.
55. Cleveland was relying on Whipple to manage her land in Florida. This note could pertain to Florida, or possibly the sale of the Weeds in New York.
56. Evangeline and Bishop Whipple were traveling to London to attend the fourth Lambeth Conference, which started in late June 1897.
57. Dorchester, Massachusetts, where family members of Elizabeth Bense, Jane Marrs's sister, lived.

repeat to you the items about Auntie Harris, I enclose. I have had not a word from her in reply to my two letters, but of course I make no wonder at that, and what King tells in this is reply enough. It would be preposterous to expect her to write. But I see how it has been; she had had this plan of her niece for her, which probably made my suggestion, in a round-a-bout way of yours, as you gave it to me in one of your last letters to me before I left the Weeds, less vivid, so she did not feel it worthwhile to bother with me on the subject, quite apart from what I wrote her later of my inability to be in Italy this summer. And so, as it turns out, she is disappointed in *both!*

I would give up all and go down to Florence in June for her sake, *if* I could feel that *I* could dare take the responsibility of taking her anywhere, *and* that she would be really pleased about it. It is hard to know what is the thing to do, with justice all around. Perhaps you can get some word from her direct. Among my letters was one, too, from Miss Bryant—most like herself. I also had one from her a few days before. She seemed glad to have heard from me.

I take it this from you—April 10th—is in reply to my last from Venice, though you do not say so; but the letter to Mrs. Lawrence must be in reply to the suggestions that contained, so I conclude it has reached you. Please mention receipts of mine, when you write, so I may have the comfort of knowing they reach you.

I am very tired after my journey and the excitements and work of this first day, with the horrible unpacking & settling them on in, and I have staid away from some friends, where I was expected to night, to write these letters, but I fear you will wish I had gone to the friends (some nice Buffalo[58] people). We are feeling very much at home in our old rooms here at the excellent hotel. They have been all done over in our absence and seem fresh and nice. Vienna seems very agreeable now,

58. From Buffalo, New York.

Evangeline Whipple and Bishop Henry Whipple by Russell and Sons, London, 1897. The "photographers to H.M. The Queen" took this photo when Evangeline and Bishop Whipple attended the Lambeth Conference in London in 1897. *Collections of St. Mark's Cathedral.*

and is really a splendid town—but I am too stupid to write, and so I must stop.

With every good wish and love, yours, as ever,
Rose.

Rose Cleveland to Evangeline Whipple
Sunday, 11-30 A.M. [June 21,] 1897
Salzburg [Austria-Hungary], *Hotel Nelboeck*

My dear Granny,
Yours of last Tuesday (Cromer)[59] reached me last night. You have, by this time, learned that yours to Vienna came all right, and that I am in pleased anticipation of my Scotch cape & hat, and that I shall have them, all warm and gay for me, when I return to Vienna last of October.

Now I must write for the steamer, for I dare not wait to mail until to-morrow. I do not worry about the letters—mine or the registered one, sent by the banker, *Berger,* but I shall be glad to have your telegram assuring me of receipt, naturally. However that has nothing to do with this letter, which must take to you the very truest and most earnest feelings of my heart for you—!

No matter about not *seeing* me—time enough for that.[60] The great thing is to be sure of what there is to see, or, perhaps, what cannot be *seen,* but only felt. It is not to be summed up in this—that you may depend on me, for all that a true & tried friendship can ask? And *I* on *you?*

With our separate disciplines and developments, we must grow toward realities, more and more, and therefore I dare to say so much, and to hope that the standards of this true

---

59. A town on the south coast of England, in the county of Norfolk.
60. Evangeline and Henry Whipple had planned to meet with Cleveland during their trip.

friendship will be the same, because each will be *true*: and there is but one *true*. So be as easy and tranquil about me, as I am about you. As never before, we can afford to be.

I am enjoying my stay here very much. My first trial of hotel, "Mirabell," was a terrible failure, but this is a great success. I have a fine room with windows look[ing] S. E. & S. W., nice old-fashioned lounge & chairs in big flowered cretonne[61] of pink & black, and I made old "Sophie" change my dreadful *scarlet* rug to another which goes admiringly with them— everything most comfortable. Both windows look into noble trees & over fine lawns, with perfectly kept flower beds & gay shrubs. Breakfast & supper are served in my room by a fine big boy, with excellent English & English manners. "Sofie" reminds *me* of Williams, in her earlier days—a nice elderly Austrian maid. As I wished quiet I am in a dependency just across from the more lively hotel, where I dine, in elegance, at 1 P.M. Sometimes I take supper out in the heights, at that fine "Forteresse" Restaurant, which commands the wondrous view, which Humboldt[62] called one of the three finest in the world, I hear.

Also I find here what I am needing, a really excellent bookstore, with an intelligent man who has agents in Paris and London, and who lets me look at his books *en examen*,[63] and this week will give me just the chance I want in that way. I am reading to-day *L'Homme* by *Pere Didon*, the great R. Catholic author of the *Life of Christ*, and am delighted to find an apparent breadth & depth, which gives one hope; though, alas, the bigotry & blindness, i.e. ignorance & prejudice, which make *his* Church the "*seule*" and makes the rest of us but poor creatures, exists. But that does not prevent my delight in his goodness & intellect.

I shall be here until the 7th, on which date Evelyn will join

61. A type of cloth.
62. Wilhelm von Humboldt (1767–1835), the German diplomat and philosopher, or his brother Alexander (1769–?).
63. French: in review.

me, bringing Millie here to ship, per Orient Express,[64] to Paris, after having given her a grand good time. I have thought it better to stay by myself, as I could do more so, and leave Millie to have her beloved & adored Evelyn quite to herself—as she should, after and before such long absences; for it will be perhaps a year before we return to America. Evelyn has always a great affectionate thought of you—and sends "currents" of them to you. She is, as ever, "little great Evelyn"—very much in earnest over her music[65] and *every thing else,* full of goodness and candour. She has severed her connection with the Theosophical Society,[66] as she has found its leaders not to her mind—and wields now a very free lance in the world of religious thought and faith. But, [in] spite of her lack of *name,* I stand rebuked before the spirit of her love and faith in God.

Oh dear, it is late—I must hurry it off, or it may miss your steamer. Every best wish for your happy & easy voyage—every good hope and trust for the comfort & good of you both, from your affectionate
Rose

I enclose this bit about Florida to interest you?—

Rose Cleveland to Evangeline Whipple
Bad Gastein [Austria-Hungary], August 7, 1897

My dear Evangeline,
Yours of July 15 reached me duly and was, as ever, most welcome, although my reply is tardy. But I cannot give as a reason for that tardiness the one you give for yours, that I am

64. The long-distance luxury passenger train that ran from Paris to Constantinople (now Istanbul).

65. Evelyn Ames was an accomplished pianist.

66. Theosophists emphasized brotherhood, individual exploration, and comparative study of world religions rather than strict religious dogma. In 1895, factions of the Theosophical Society separated, fracturing the organization.

in any social rush—or in a rush of any objective sort whatever. I can however say that I am occupied mentally to the extent almost of pre-occupation and that I have to exercise a real sense of duty—nothing less—(and you know I hold that there *is* nothing *more*) to "render unto Caesar the things that are Caesar's"[67]—i.e., to make the signs of remembrance (for there is no lack of inner remembrance, apart from the signs) to absent friends, and to give myself the sufficient relaxation and exercise that are necessary to keep the balance in this subjective-objective compound of life. This is my only reason for tardy answers to letters, or any other dereliction. Whether it acquits me or not must, I suppose, depend somewhat if not wholly upon the nature of my occupation, and its relative value &c., all of which is the unknown quantity. But I hope I am learning something of value to others, as well as myself.

Also, a big also, I have nothing new to tell you. Nothing could be a greater contrast than your situation, as you describe it, and my own. I have made no new acquaintances, and my sole society is in my books, my sole recreation in Nature, as a spectacle human nature as well! And I can tell you of no events; and you know this little *Bad,* with its mountains and valleys—'everlasting' in this quiet stability, its cascade pouring its foam and passion into the stormy Ache[68] that rushes roaring through the peaks and valley on and on to river and lake and sea. The Tauern Range, snow clad that walls the valley, the sharp triangle that stands in the gap between it and the Stubner Kogel, clear against it snowy Sonnblick, as is its counterpart on the shiny sands of Egypt. You have seen sunset and moonset here,[69] as I do—and you remember perhaps

67. Matthew 22:21: "Render to Caesar the things that are Caesar's, and to God the things that are God's."
68. The Großache, a river in Germany and Austria.
69. Evangeline Whipple had traveled to Austria multiple times, possibly during her honeymoon with Michael Simpson in 1882–83, and with her parents and brother in 1887. Additionally, the *Buffalo (NY) Morning Express,* May 22, 1893, reported "Rose Cleveland Returns" after an absence of two

such scenes; the moon as it hangs out its warm torch over the Sonnblick when all else is dark as death—and as still. The promenaders gone from the promenade. The lights of the hotels only clustered, like a swarm of fireflies in the depth of the valley (I am above all that and look up the valley, and a little *down* on the Cascade). All this I have day and night, and little else, outside: every physical comfort.

Evelyn has been with me some time until a day or two, and is now again with Millie, who still travels I shall but will settle down with Evelyn for a little before she leaves at Ebensee (Ischl) where I shall go by September 1st or 3rd. She sends her love to you always. I am so pleased that you are having so gay and good a time. You will also enjoy your Scotland trip this lovely August. Please let me know at once the exact day of your sailing and the latest day upon which you can receive a letter from this region—say, Vienna, altho I shall hope to write a reply from here within the three weeks left me here. I want and hope to send you an important letter to catch you before you leave, but may fail of it, so *please* give your first address on returning, which will be of any length.

I hear from Miss Mander now & then—she sent her love to "Sweet Mrs. Simpson" and hoped to see you. I hear from "Aunt Fanny," who writes with a new & sweet tone of humility and goodness. Not a word from Auntie Harris. Has she gone?

And now I must stop, with every good thought and wish for all time from
Rose.

Cleveland continued to write letters—now lost, but referenced in the following—to Whipple throughout the fall and winter of 1897–98. The trail of extant letters picks up again in May of 1898. ∿

years in Europe and the Orient, accompanied by "Mrs. Marr [*sic*]" (Evangeline's mother, Jane Marrs) and "Mrs. Simpson" (Evangeline). Cleveland's reference suggests she and Evangeline visited this spot together, likely in 1891–93.

Rose Cleveland to Evangeline Whipple
HOTEL HAJEK,[70] MODLING-VORDERBRÜHL, STATUIB DER
ELECTRISCHEN EISENBAHN, TELEGRAMM: HAJEK MÖDLING.
TELEPHON NO. 1
Vorderbrühl [Austria-Hungary] A.M.: 15 May, 1898

My dear Evangeline,

I am very much afraid I have not written you since I was in Athens, which is nearly or quite a month. Since then we have made acquaintance with Constantinople and Buda Pescht,[71] and found the place we wished, very near to Vienna, and settled down in it. My last from you was written from Florida, but a note from Laura, written in Tennessee, on the way North, told me that you were en route for the summer quarters, though not where they were to be. I suppose, of course, you will be in Minnesota for a while at least, and then perhaps at South Park. Perhaps you are there now. But I will address this to Fairiboult [sic], for it will surely find you somewhere.

We had a charming and profitable trip. I wrote Laura— whom I had been owing for several letters since before Xmas—a gossipy (for me) letter about it, and have repeated the "tale of travel" already to so many, that I will not risk a possible repetition of her letter to you, as you may be there at its receipt. But there was a great freshness and novelty about it all, and the sights, if not all pleasant, or suggestive of pleasant things, were wonderful and stirring, and sometimes marvelously beautiful. But I shall surely become tedious if I get wound up on either Turkey or Greece.

You see where we are, but I imagine you do not know the place, as unless one stays long in Vienna one is not apt to hear

70. The Hotel Hajek was near the Mödling-Vorderbrühl electric tram station. The town of Mödling—within the Austrian district of the same name— is about nine miles southwest of Vienna. The Mödling and Hinterbrühl Tramway carried passengers from Mödling to Hinterbrühl beginning in 1883 and was one of the first electric tramways of its kind.

71. The destinations of Athens, Constantinople (Istanbul), and Budapest suggest that Cleveland and Ames traveled on the Orient Express.

much about it. It is, however, a most joyous little place, such as one rarely sees except among German people. It belongs to a prince who makes it a pet & pride, and there is no end to its bucolic charm. To day we went out at eleven, after break-fasting and reading the war news,[72] no *news* really, with our book and struck into the pine forest, choosing a path we had not before explored. On and on we went—until pine forest changed to beach, and the stately gravel path to the little *Fussweg*[73] amid thickets of all Spring leaves and blossoms, a place for Botticelli; good Spring maidens to tread their dances in.[74] Here we spread our Roman blankets and lay down on the yellow heather, whose scent was like that of wild roses and something else nice & different. Then we went on and came out past noble views, in Hinterbrühl—*we* are Vorden-brühl. There we turned in at a restaurant and got our soup, and *fleisch*, our *gemüse*, and our *mehlspeise*[75]—and two glasses of beer, and then turned into the little bright electric train and glided back to our own place, through every sort of glisten and twitter that spring can get up. Now we have had our nap and settle down to our letters, until cocoa time, at five. Then we take our book and go into the garden and read, and at seven saunter to the *Mairei,* the Lichtenstein milk place, where we have brown bread and warm milk and honey in a little table under huge horse chestnuts. A big dog lies in front, and the others caper around. The pretty milkmaids stride past with their huge tins and go to the watering trough to wash them. It is "all cows and china" and we feel like happy Mrs. Skewtons.[76] The paths are hung with white & red lilacs in

72. The Spanish-American War had begun less than a month earlier, on April 21, 1898.

73. German: footpath.

74. A reference to Botticelli's *Primavera,* also called *Allegory of Spring.*

75. German: meat, vegetables, and dessert.

76. In Dickens's novel *Dombey and Son* (1848), Cleopatra Skewton comments, "What I have ever sighed for, has been to retreat to a Swiss farm, and live entirely surrounded by cows—and china."

bloom, and the most wondrous yellow blossom I ever imagined. Whole trees are like golden wisterias every where, and in the depths of the woods it is just the same. It is quite Aladdin like and past belief. We are in the most comfortable hotel imaginable, and altogether are well satisfied. A half hour takes us to Vienna, and we go in for anything at anytime. The other evening we went to hear "Walküre"—a new Siegmund and Sieglinde—beautiful and charming.[77] But I have outgrown Wagner, I think.

I can imagine the interest you and the Bishop are taking in the war; I remember how his sympathies were for Cuba.[78] We have a daily German paper which gives us the latest news, and the N.Y. *Herald* and London *Times* complement it. We are hoping for a speedy end to the war. Of course we will not cross the water while this state of things exists.

Do write when you can. We saw the Washburnes [sic][79] in Constantinople; William asked after you with much interest— Evelyn sends love, and with love from myself, as ever,

Rose.

Address as before, to Vienna.

77. Cleveland and Ames attended a performance of *Walküre*—the second opera in Wagner's Ring Cycle—at the Vienna State Opera (Wiener Staatsoper). At the time, its director was Gustav Mahler.

78. Bishop Whipple first visited Cuba in March 1871. By November 1871, he had sponsored the Cuban mission of Reverend Edward Kenney, who described his work in Cuba during 1871–79 in letters now housed at the MNHS. Whipple visited Havana on behalf of the Domestic and Foreign Missionary Society in March 1872 and in February 1887 (Henry B. Whipple papers, MNHS).

79. William Drew Washburn (1831–1912) was a businessman, politician, and railroad magnate whose namesake flour mill was absorbed by the Pillsbury Flour Company.

Rose Cleveland to Evangeline Whipple, Faribault, Minnesota
Sept 14 1898
photo postcard, Cortina d'Ampezzo,[80] *Italy*

See how Cortina has changed since we were here![81] A noisy,
crowded town! And no souffle. *Über prachtvoll!*[82]
Why do I not hear from you?

R.E.C.

Rose Cleveland to Evangeline Whipple, House of Bishops,[83]
Washington, DC, care of Bishop Whipple
Meran [Italy], October 2, 1898

My Dear Evangeline,
Here we are at Meran[84] again, and finding it *beautiful*. We are
enchanted with it this time, seeing it in its freshness of before
season, instead of staleness of after season, as we did before.[85]
Everything is spic-span, and nowhere except at Gastein have I
seen an approach to the perfection of public appointments—
walks, seats, &c.—as here. This should be as it is, for each guest
must pay a weekly tax for twelve weeks, the least one florin:
we have each 11 ½ florins[86] per week: and, as multitudes of
people stay here many weeks, it must roll up a fine treasury

80. A ski and health resort in the Italian Dolomites mountain range.
81. Indicates Cleveland and Whipple had visited Italy together—Cortina
in particular—prior to 1896. They traveled extensively in Europe and "the
Orient" from 1891 to 1893 ("Miss Cleveland Returns," *Buffalo [NY] Morning
Express,* May 22, 1893).
82. German: quite magnificent.
83. The Whipples were attending the General Convention of the Episcopal Church, held every three years. This one was in Washington, DC, from
October 5 through October 25, 1898.
84. A town (*Merano* in Italian; *Meran* in German) in the north of Italy.
85. "Season" here refers to the winter tourist season, though Cleveland
may also have in mind the winter social season (November through February)
observed by upper-class Americans and Europeans.
86. Equivalent to about $130 in 2018.

for Meran bursars to dispense. We shall stay only two weeks from yesterday, being due at Venice on that day.

Also our location is vastly more agreeable here than it was before at the huge "central" and most expensive "Meraner Hof." We are higher up in the fine "Villa von Weinhart," a largely private house, where we have a sleeping room and fine salon, with long, broad covered balcony on the top floor, which therefore commands a fine view of mountains, vineyards, old castles, & c. For this was the least taxes I ever found at any public house. We pay each 4 and ¼ Florins per day, or around $1.60 per day![87]

I hope you will come someday to Meran: the fruit, at this season, is *superlative;* the grapes *par excellence,* and we are eating them à la carte twice a day! And already imagining good results. For the first time we are dining at *table d'hotel* and meeting some good country women; and others, and liking the change very well. I have written Miss von Mack to ask for the address of Baroness von Pausinger's sister,[88] who hunted after me in vain (of course without my knowledge) when I was here before. I hope we shall meet her.

We are beginning to think a great deal of Egypt, and the excitement is coming up. I shall be so interested to see how things have changed since you and I were there.[89] We expect to go to Ravenna[90] after Venice and then to Florence, and from there to Egypt as direct as possible. Evelyn's mother and

---

87. About $50 per day, each, in 2018.

88. The sister of Baroness Helene Paula Von Pausinger Erggelet (1871–1956) was Elisabeth Von Pausinger Stork, a professor at Swarthmore College in Pennsylvania and a children's book writer.

89. On March 14, 1892, the *Philadelphia Record* reported Rose Cleveland was writing a book on Egypt and "has gone to that far-off country in search of material." Cleveland, Whipple, and Jane Marrs traveled together to New York on the SS *Etruria,* and Cleveland went "as far as Palestine" during 1891–93, according to the *Buffalo (NY) Morning Express,* May 22, 1893. Photographs in the Massachusetts Historical Society show the Marrs family in Egypt prior to Dana Marrs's death in 1892.

90. Ravenna is a city south of Venice famous for extensive architectural mosaics.

sister may join us for that trip, but also may not. In Florence we expect to see Mrs. Crosby & her daughters and some other friends. What do you hear of, or from, Auntie Harris? I get *no news from her* whatever. Now it is four o'clock and I must write two more letters before grape time, and then go for our walk—*such walks!* Address me care *Blumenthal,* Venice.

With love from Evelyn,
always Yours
Rose

Rose Cleveland to Evangeline Whipple
Meran [Italy], 6th Nov[ember], 1898

My dear Evangeline,
Your last nice newsy letter from Washington came the other day and was much enjoyed. I am so glad you have dipped into that life in our own land as well as abroad. A little of it is a good thing; but a little goes a good way, do you ever think so?

Mrs. Johnston was not there, as she has just sailed from Paris and will be slow enough settling, I expect, as she does not love "the novelties" (as my Russian friend used to say) she left there, now-a-days. Also my friends the Addison Thomases[91] live there now, but probably were lingering in their Newport house when you wrote. I am not clear whether you return to Minnesota or go from Washington to Florida, but as this will reach there late in this month, I will venture Florida. As Laura writes me they are going about this time.

We are somewhat hurried off by the news by cable-gram this week that Susie Ames sails yesterday for Genoa. Apparently Mrs. Ames does not come, but there may be a surprise awaiting us in her arrival also at any rate it hastens our trip to Egypt, which we shall start as early as Dec. 1st and return to Florence probably in February.

91. Colonel Addison Thomas (1845–1908), who lived in New York and Newport, Rhode Island, but wintered in Washington, DC.

I am not needing *Helwan*[92] yet, but shall not forget if I do need it. So far as my health goes I think I should prefer to stay here, for the air and life generally agrees with us both—particularly, and I recommend it in case you ever want to cool off from Florida. We anticipate much pleasure in this lovely trip, though I hardly think things are as nice there now as they were when you took me up and down the turning Nile. Some nice countrywomen of ours who are here tell us diverse tales of recent travel there.

Faniska's sister is here and we see her often, have had tea with her at her little apartment in the "peasant house," as she calls it, a plain little villa a little outside the place, occupied below by the peasants who own it. She is very like her sister but not so large—quite a *grande dame*—speaks the same English—and likes to talk, and talks well. Has some superb old bits of things in her tiny rooms, and fills all space and absorbs all attention in the cafe where we get her cocoa—"never goes out" but twice out of the four times we have been to see her; is "eating at her cousin's the Princess Cantacuzene"[93] and we meet her in her *roll-wagen*[94] (almost as much of a roll for her faulty but delightful Roller as Faniska would be!) on her way back; and vivacious tales of her "dretful" [*sic*] servants, just discussed, and assurances that she is "very agitated!" She seems great and noble in her way.

Evelyn is most grateful for your trouble about the bag—begs that you will leave the bill for it as soon as you receive it, when she will write herself.[95]

It is Sunday evening, and we are going to have our supper

92. Helwan, a resort town on the Nile outside of Cairo, was a favorite destination of European travelers because of its hot springs, reputed to have healing powers.

93. A Russian royal title from Ukraine, likely a reference to Elisabeth Sicard, who was Princess Cantacuzène.

94. German: carriage.

95. This could have referred to a commissioned bandolier bag made by Anishinaabe beadwork artist Sophia Smith in Minnesota for Bishop Henry Whipple. See page 175, note 114, for more information.

up here, as a sort of celebration. Next Sunday we expect to spend in Milan and you will know just what we shall see.[96] I anticipate it; as our sight-seeing has been so moderate that a little past now seems a really great privilege; and in spite of the comforts of Germany one can keep a flag for the Charm of States. I expect to see Mrs. Crosby and some others in Florence—*of course* Auntie Harris, to whom I wrote just after hearing about her from you. Love to dear Motherdie, and greetings to all the rest from us both, and always the same love for yourself,

[*Rose*]

Rose Cleveland to Evangeline Whipple
Firenze [Florence], [November?] 21, 1898
Bellini [Hotel]

My dear Evangeline,
Here we are and here is Florence and the Arno and the Ponte Vecchio, and the Tournabuoni [*sic*],[97] and Vecaresi (mending my bag clasp), and Giacosa[98] (taking our centimes too often), *and Auntie Harris,* lying in bed all the time now, but with her hair still curled and shining white, and her eyes still so blue and her cheeks so red, her brain so keen and her voice so clear; all as much as ever, and *more so, only* she can never walk again and never, probably, use her right hand or arm again, and is likely any day to pass away, because likely to have another stroke or paralysis, which she would hardly survive; indeed she can survive no shock of any sort.[99]

96. *The Last Supper* by Leonardo da Vinci is in Milan at the Convent of Santa Maria delle Grazie.
97. The Palazzo Tornabuoni, the chapel of the same name, or the Via de' Tornabuoni, all in central Florence.
98. Probably the Caffè Giacosa, a coffee shop and bar near the Via de' Tornabuoni that attracted wealthy Florentines from its opening in 1815.
99. Ellen Harris was eighty-two years old. She lived for four more years and died in Florence in 1902.

She has weighed on my mind, and I have made her my *business*—for I felt the time had come. She has a lower floor in the same place, for which she pays 200 francs 8 sous,[100] but nothing looks as it used to because of course she could only be put into bed on arriving and kept there, and there is no one to arrange anything. She has one good woman, and another comes in for the night, as she is, of course, wholly and entirely unable to do anything for herself. She does not suffer acute pain often, but of course great discomfort from the terrible confinement in position.

It seems terrible, worse than ever than [when] she was alone, and from some things I heard I suspected she might not be able to give herself all the comforts she needs, so I went *alone* to see her, and got it all out of her. She, by degrees, let me know that she had lost 4/5 of her income by the total failure of Gov. Beaver[101] *and* her brother;[102] and that now she was obliged to think too much of expenses—did not feel able to have a ~~hard~~ trained nurse & c. I told her her friends, you first of all, could never allow that—and that I should tell you, to which she made no objection. I could not find out *what* sum would lift her out of her troubles, but I know a present in *money* would suit her best. Evelyn & I are going to give up our Xmas presents to each other and give her the money! Say, fifty dollars,[103] which we shall take her on Thanksgiving day. I know you will send her another for Xmas, as we shall be in

100. About $1,000 in 2018, presumably rent for the month.

101. James A. Beaver, governor of Pennsylvania (1887–91). His finances were volatile throughout the 1890s, particularly after the Panic of 1893 and again in 1897. See general note on series seven (business correspondence and papers, 1867–1912) of finding aid to the James A. Beaver papers, Penn State University Libraries, https://www.libraries.psu.edu/findingaids/1433 .htm#aspace_SC_HCLA_1433_800fed31c2fb41c56b730e55c4fa022e.

102. Ellen Harris had four brothers: Edmund Burke, James Henry, Thomas Elliott, and William Penn. In 1897, only William Penn and Edmund Burke Orbison were living. Edmund was hit hard by the Panic of 1893 and withdrew from public life, possibly the reason for Ellen Harris's drained bank accounts (*Mount Union Times* [PA], July 28, 1899).

103. Equivalent to about $1,400 in 2018.

Egypt by then and we hope to be back here in February, when I will report again.

She has no real dependable friends here now—but *one good* one whom I have seen & whose card I enclose—you may like to send your present through her, or write to her for something. Auntie Harris thinks so much of you and your letters and is the same dear little wonder.

This is all about her this time. We like Bellini very well, but I do not know how long it will last. Forgive this—it will be its own excuse, for I am not fixed for writing here, as work shows.

Love to you
Rose.

Rose Cleveland to Evangeline Whipple
Pagnons Luxor Hotel, Luxor, Upper Egypt
Tuesday, Dec. 20, 1898

My dear Evangeline,
Here I am in the writing room of this hotel, waiting to hear the verdict of Dr. Wallis Budge[104] on some things: an amethyst scarab, a *Ka*, & two little blue colius [*sic*] leaves, or flowers, and a bit of alabaster; they are "four pickings." *Everything* is poor now—but I think Evelyn will like them if she can know they are genuine, and I suppose this great man's word will settle it for her. I had the good luck to meet him this afternoon at the Am[erican] Mission, and found him delightful.

I do not know where to begin to tell you about our experience thus far. I sent you all an Egyptian Xmas card the other day, but have not been able to write; there is so much to say, it staggers me. Firstly, we came from Naples to Alexandria in

104. Sir Ernest Alfred Thompson Wallis Budge served as the keeper (curator) of Egyptian antiquities at the British Museum between 1894 and 1924.

68 hours: three nights & two days, and all but the first night very good. That was very bad, and I was promptly and heroically ill, but well over it, with the night. We came on to Cairo the same day (Nov. 29th) and got nice rooms at Shepheards,[105] where we staid a week. Cairo is much less interesting, it seems to me, than it was; the trail of the tourist is over them all,[106] dragomen and shop men more insistent and noisy, with less to sell; no more decent antiquities, any amount of cheap trash for which immense sums are asked: no hope of buying anything really good or pretty. Shepheards is much improved in appointment and the table is good enough, but the air is frightful, influenza is said to be epidemic there, and typhoid fever has ~~been~~ occurred, according to all accounts, which I can well believe. We found it so uncongenial an atmosphere that we spent the next week at the Mena House,[107] which suited us much better. The *Desert*, the Pyramids, the Sphynx [*sic*], are all there, in their majesty and dignity, too great to praise in words. You know it all. Our *Ibrahim* has retired:[108] is in Cairo, where he condescends to sell antiquities sometimes, and his tall & dignified but childlike son represents him, consenting to take care of unprotected ladies, as did his father before him.

The Nile is, of course, very high yet, and everything is different, as I found out early in the trip, from what it was in February, so many years ago. But if not so warm, it is still *Egypt,* and there is but one Egypt.

Now I must go up to my room for a little rest before

---

105. The original Shepheard's Hotel, a famously luxurious hotel in Cairo, attracted European tourists, politicians, and military officers between its opening in 1841 and its destruction by fire in 1952.

106. An adaptation of "the trail of the serpent is over them all"; see page 198, note 39.

107. A luxury hotel in Cairo, opened in 1886; the first swimming pool in Egypt was installed there in 1890.

108. This reference suggests that Cleveland and Whipple hired a man (Ibrahim) as a guide during their 1893 trip to Egypt.

Dec. 26, Luxor.

Evidently just then the great man appeared. He sat down with the prompt & business air that becomes the Curator of the British Museum, took my little blue mummy[109] & promptly wrote under the hieroglyphs, which I beg to be excused from copying: "Osiris, builder of the Amun temple, Tscheset-Ra" (the temple of Karnak) adding his autograph by way of official affidavit. So it seems my mummy was a veritable *find*. One of the soul-bodies of *Tcheshet* [*sic*]—already addressed as Osiris & Ra. Budge said it was a good thing, expressed much interest in it—asked rather jealously where I got it, and, so I felt pleased, and Evelyn did yesterday morning. I wound a green ribbon around him, pinned the little scarab on his breast, and put him in his sarcophagus, which, all by chance, I made out [of] a Cook's Nile Steamer book[110] and a blue photograph film box, winged scarab, lions, lotuses & all, with an Osiris left over to stand up at the end for *judgment* of the same.

So our Xmas went with some merriment, for I found in the enclosed stocking (in which the maker calls special attention to the silk "clocking") a tiny package containing the marvelous Coptic coins, the like of which I never saw or heard of— part of Old Mohammed's—the same mysterious old rag-bag he used to be, of urbane manners & committed craft—*hidden* store, which Evelyn induced him to show her.

Susie Ames left us mysterious packages which disclosed tiny gold donkey & camels, with other pretty things, and, by some mischance, King & Laura's bundle of Christmas magazines came Xmas Eve, & were left unopened until the morn. I bid our Abdulla bring my roses at 7:30 & at that hour the most stupendous edifice of yellow herbs & limp greens, with two

109. Ancient Egyptians buried their dead with *ushabtis*—miniature figures intended to do labor for the deceased in the afterlife. Most were shaped to resemble mummies; some were made from faience and blue in color.

110. May refer to one of the travel guides published by Thomas Cook & Son. The company maintained a fleet of steamboats that carried tourists along the Nile.

glorious lilies & some exquisite roses stood in, which yielded, by careful discretion and selection, three charming arrangements of flowers. Evelyn was not able to get up so we spent the day until dinner in our room, except that I took a two-hours' gallop on "No. 8" to the Coptic Convent at sunset. You remember the charming road or path? The sand, only spring green everywhere now, in place of harvest yellow, then, with the perfume of white bean flower rising in the clear air, and donkey equal in speed & ease to any horse I have ridden.

We go on Friday to the second cataract:[111] are enjoying it all immensely. To-day we take tea at the Am[erican] Mission, which is doing an immense work here. We sent up two sovereigns Xmas Eve & he put in praises for the poor—of whom Mrs. Munch tells us sad tales. Hope all my little bits of cards reached you. I believe I have lost lots of letters.

[*Rose*]

Evelyn Ames to Evangeline Whipple, Lake Maitland, Florida
MENA HOUSE HOTEL: PYRAMIDS, CAIRO
Address [to] Whitby & Co., Florence
Jan 27th, 1899

Dear Evangeline,
The sun has just gone down behind the last great drift of desert that breaks like a wave against one of our sitting room windows. Rose is lying well wrapped up in silk blankets before the open fire, making a brave fight against a severe increase of the grippe which has never really let go its dreadful hold since it first fastened upon her weeks ago. You will remember how we fled out here from Cairo and got relief enough to start up the Nile on the appointed day, treacherous old

---

111. The Nile has six relatively shallow stretches with rapids, known as cataracts. The second, called the Great Cataract, lay close to the Egyptian border with Sudan and was destroyed by the creation of Lake Nasser in the 1960s.

"*serpent du Nil*"[112] with its northbound hiss—pitchless and deadly. We have had a great experience of mental realizations, many very deep ones, that must come as one looks into that old past through its strange memorials, so beautiful and colossal, with all they reveal of human maturity and immaturity. We have had much aesthetic enjoyment as well, and have revelled in graceful alabaster jars, and little wonderful inscrutable bronze Osirises, long strings of rose, pure carnelian beads; we have played our humble part in "spoiling the Egyptians," but as Rose says, the "Egyptians have spoiled us," too.

I am mending but Rose is not. I don't believe in all Egypt there is good air for her. We are flying from the country[.] Helwan is *crowded* with invalids, only grand rooms to be had, and people with sensitive *throats* complain, although they often improve in other directions. Much of Rose's trouble lies in her throat now—her one wish is for snow-clad pine hills & mountains, always her panacea. She longs & pines for Vallombrosa, but if that is not practicable, as far as hotels are concerned in the matter of warmth and food, we shall fly to Meran, and if that is not bracing enough, to S. Moritz,[113] or even little S. Ulrich. Despite these apparent uncertainties, the turn of events will bring quick decisions, and we have good friends all along the way. So don't be too anxious, but it would wring your heart to know just how hard & constantly persecuting circumstances have been to fix this racking cough upon her that wears her out night and day.

Rose keeps her elasticity of temperament and declares it is nothing that will not yield to the right air, but she says this is not the Egypt she knew in her first visit here. And she "loathes" it.

She has promised to meet some friends at Shepheard's, tomorrow if possible, so she is resting. I wouldn't let her

---

112. French: serpent of the Nile (possibly the Egyptian cobra). Also an epithet for Cleopatra (see Shakespeare's *Antony & Cleopatra*, I.5: "He's speaking now, / Or murmuring 'Where's my serpent of old Nile?'").

113. St. Moritz, Switzerland.

write but it is so long since she has heard from you that she is desperate. She has had no letter since leaving Meran. ~~and its~~ She wrote you from Meran, from Florence, and from here, a month ago, and sent Christmas cards from the Nile. She is anxious to hear what of the bead bag?[114] Is the "one & only" Indian artist dead, or just capricious and unmanageable? I have been waiting weekly to hear the amount of my indebtedness, and that is why I have never written to tell you of my delight in your 1,002nd tale, of fair, cruel Fatima and [the] jeweled tree and the hapless prince and all its true flavor of the *Arabian Nights*.

I hope you & the bishop are both well. Florida is much preferable in every climatic respect to Egypt.

Goodnight, with love,
Evelyn.

Rose Cleveland to Evangeline Whipple
HOTEL BRISTOL, NAPLES, CORSO VITTORIO EMANUELE.
VIEW OF POSILLIPO FROM THE HOTEL; A. LANDRY, PROP.
~~Jan~~ Feb 12 [18]99

My dear Evangeline—
Your note ~~of~~ addressed to Venice came to me with Laura's a few days since, and altho dispatches have been sent in all

114. This comment could refer to renowned Anishinaabe beadwork artist Sophia Smith, wife of Reverend Frederick Smith (Kahdahwahbeday), an Anishinaabe lay minister trained by Henry Whipple who worked in the Episcopal churches on the White Earth and Red Lake Reservations in Minnesota. Sophia Smith created a gashkibidaagan, or bandolier bag—#1520 in the MNHS's museum collections—for Henry Whipple. Two portrait photographs of Smith holding the bag, circa 1900 (Bishop Henry B. Whipple Indian photograph collection, AV2002.169.98 and AV2002.169.107), are marked with a note: "This was the last fire bag [another word for bandolier bag] made for Bishop Whipple," indicating Evangeline Whipple could have brokered a commission for this piece, paid for by Evelyn Ames. See Anderson, *Bag Worth a Pony*, 203–4.

directions—New Hotel & Shepherd [*sic*] included—for the letters you speak of as sent to me, not one has yet turned up, and this note, telling of them, is their only representative from you for about three months or near that time. Meanwhile I have written you steadily from every place, over & over, but how can I ever know you have rec'd them?

Well, they are no great loss, that is a consoling truth, and now I hope we can both be more certain of getting what belongs to you.

You will hear from Laura that we have escaped from our land of bondage and are in great comfort on the hill over the Bay of Naples at this hotel, which you remember, of course. I have improved a great deal in a week, altho suffering from a little set back yesterday & today, owing, I suppose, largely to the curious fog that has set in and lifts but slowly, a little at noon today, thickening again just now at sunset, and softening Capri & Vesuvius all but out of sight. Catching and holding, as in a luminous veil of mystic rose, the sunset light over town, sea, & land. I am hoping to hear that Vallombrosa[115] is practicable, for nothing short of high pine air will balsam the unhappy throat and several anatomy that burdens me.

Mrs. Crosby is in Florence, and we were to have met her there before this. Now she will look into the Vallombrosa matter & when we hear, if favorable, we shall go there, stopping a day or so in Rome, and of course in Florence, but postponing our longer stay there until after the Vallombrosa experiment.

When I see you I shall have a lot to tell you of Egypt & what I cannot write; but it can wait. Also some few lovely trophies to show you, although nothing so rare as the lapis scarab

---

115. A Benedictine abbey in the mountains of Tuscany, about fifteen miles from Florence. Nearby are seven botanical gardens dominated by the pine and beech forests of the Arboreti di Vallombrosa. Many English and American writers visited the abbey, including Mary Shelley and Elizabeth Barrett Browning, who both lived in Bagni di Lucca a generation prior to Cleveland and Whipple.

you gave me—that has been so much admired and envied.[116] Its like is not to be found. But great treasures have been unearthed since you & I were there.

You will know how rich and pleasant it all seems here. I go out mornings & stay in afternoon & evenings, and live a lazy life, to my sorrow, but not an altogether profitless one. We are reading new books on Egypt & Pompeii, and in the evening *Paradise Lost*[117] from a pretty little copy sent me Xmas by Millie Candler. By the way, have you heard of her engagement? She is to be married in the fall to a young Mr. Gardiner of Boston, and is wildly in love with him.[118] Evelyn expects to be at home in time for her wedding as we hope to sail not later than August next for our land.

Amy Mander is at Baden-Baden in a bad way after a heroic campaign among her poor in Ireland. She is writing me to try & stay with her somewhere, but I am afraid it will not be possible this time, but we shall surely see her, and try to get her to go with us for a fortnight in Ireland or England somewhere in June; perhaps Scotland, for I want to have Evelyn meet her. She seems a very grand character to me, as I see more of her.

I forgot to say in my letter to Laura that I shall make all effort to see her friend in Florence, of whom Auntie Harris told me with great appreciation of her good services.

The papers interest me, and "situations" are serious in all directions. Our own less vivid, of course, as I can get no accurate lights or perspectives on it from the poor material what deals with it. The English papers, of course, are more worth

116. Whipple's Italian will, preserved in the MNHS and dated April 19, 1929, left to Carolyn (Carrie) Hastings Lawrence "the Egyptian necklace which belonged to her said aunt (who wished the said necklace to be preserved in the Cleveland family as an heirloom)."

117. John Milton's "Paradise Lost" (1667) contains the line, "autumnal leaves that strow the brooks, in Vallombrosa," leading many to suppose he visited the Vallombrosa Abbey. This may have been the driving reason for Cleveland to visit Vallombrosa.

118. Millie Candler married William Howard Gardiner on June 3, 1899, in Brookline, Massachusetts.

reading, for nothing divides honors (!) with the *N.Y. Herald* as yet, claiming to be American news, and one day confuses if not contradicts the previous one. I am hoping the President will come out clean & strong from this army scandal[119]—and to day I read ~~what~~ (for the first time hinted at) that the Inquiry, so far, rebukes Miles[120] for not reporting officially at the right time to the right headquarters—i.e. the president & secretary of war—on the bad beef, before rushing into newspaper print all over with it. It strikes me that may suggest the truer 'other side' to all this *pro*-Miles bravado. I never doted on Miles; but my knowledge of him is but slight.

Now I must stop. Begging for news at once to care of *Whitby, MacKay & Co* (Whitby & Co is enough), Florence.

With love to dear Motherdie, and cordial greeting to the Bishop and "Billie."[121]

Evelyn sends love.

Yours Ever,
Rose.

Rose Cleveland to Evangeline Whipple
Hotel Bristol, Naples, Feb. 18, 1899

My dear Evangeline,
At last the wanderers[122] to Shepheard's Hotel & the New Hotel are here, and with them our lovely books. Evelyn wants to write you a note about hers herself, but I am not sure she will

---

119. In 1898, a court inquiry found that the US Army had supplied spoiled beef rations to soldiers in Cuba during the Spanish-American War. Many died from food poisoning and dysentery. The resulting scandal led to the resignation of Secretary of War Russell Alger on August 1, 1899.

120. Nelson A. Miles, commanding general of the US Army.

121. If the Whipples were in Faribault at the time, "Billie" could refer to William Milligan, the caretaker of their home.

122. The missing letters.

be able to, as she wished this P.M., as she has letters which absorb her energies and will use it up, I can see. They concern Millie Candler's aunt & her two sons, whom [she] is *supporting* and *educating;* now one of them has fallen very ill, must lie by in St. Margaret's Hospital for weeks & have a very critical operation performed. Evelyn has but one thought, that of "standing by," and far from feeling any sacrifice, ~~and~~ which this extra may invoke for herself, seems to feel only that *she* is the one receiving in the opportunity to help, or, more accurately, to do *all.*

Millie, also, is marrying a poor man, whose prospects are good, and who has not seemed *ready* just now, and you will know how much that opens up for Evelyn again. But she has enough, as any one has, who cuts the coat according to the cloth, and is content (all the above severely private).

I am delighted with Miss Scudder's book[123] and shall write to tell her so; and very glad to have it. A thousand thanks for the gift and the selection.

We are both mending, and shall move on this week. We are thinking now of making the round trip to Castellammare, Sorrento, Amalfi, Cara, all by carriage drives of a day each. This week, for the purpose of being out in the air, from Cara we shall go to Rome, staying there only two or three days as sightseeing (galleries & churches) is out of the question for us now.

Now the dinner gong goes, and soon our good dinner will be brought. We dine in our rooms, as eve'g out of them seems not to agree with us.

We went to church this morning, and it was a great treat to see ~~things~~ways I am used to, and hear words I am used to. The minister is a Scotchman—is one of those shrewd, canny Scots

---

123. Wellesley professor Vida Dutton Scudder had published two books in 1898: *Christian Simplicity* and *Social Ideas in English Letters.* Her social circle included the poets Katharine Lee Bates and Katharine Ellis Coman, who maintained an intimate partnership for twenty-five years, and, after 1919, Florence Converse, her own long-term partner.

of the 'newer sort' who "gongs over the fundamentals" in a clean, clear way, good to hear, his touches clever and pleasant & precise as those of the Pompeian frescoes.

This P.M. we have been driving in the forest and Capo-dimonte. I wrote you last Sunday, Laura the week before & Motherdie this week. My address until April Whitby & Co. Florence.

Always [illegible],
Rose.

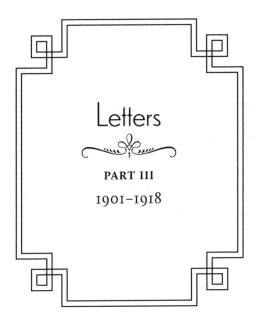

Letters

PART III

1901–1918

Cleveland and Ames returned to the United States and their separate homes by the summer of 1899 but continued to spend much of their time together. In March of that year they paid a joint visit to William McKinley, Grover Cleveland's successor as president, in the White House. In August 1900, Cleveland and Ames bought property together on a two-mile-wide spot of land off the coast of Camden, Maine: Seven Hundred Acre Island, also called Acre Island, in Penobscot Bay. It is adjacent to Islesboro, where Cleveland and Ames had previously spent summers together in the village of Dark Harbor. They then undertook the long-term project of establishing a working farm on the island while still living for much of the year in Boston, Florida, and upstate New York.

Henry Whipple died at his home in Faribault, Minnesota, on September 16, 1901. He was seventy-nine years old. Cleveland wrote the following letter of condolence to Evangeline Whipple, who was widowed for a second time. ~

Rose Cleveland to Evangeline Whipple
[September 1901]

All the languages in the world, you *darling*, could not possibly express my sympathy—the *perfect* love which I feel for you.

Always remember this, and when you read the words just written think also of all that the heart leaves unvoiced, unexpressed, except as you feel my thought and sympathy and unerring interest during *all* of these coming days.

That they are to be days *brimful* of just the experience which is next, and which will be glorious in the results, I am assured in my own soul, and my prophecy, dearest Evangeline, is that they will be the *blessedest* and among the *most joyful* days of your life.[1] These years of days passed with this friend[2] whose nobility and loveliness of character I feel as sure of as I do of your own nobility and loveliness.

Ever yours,
Rose.

1. This is an odd statement from Cleveland, considering that Whipple's husband had just died.
2. Was Cleveland revealing a clue that Evangeline's relationship with Henry Whipple was primarily platonic, or was Cleveland hoping this was the case?

Evangeline Whipple in her widow's cap, circa 1901. *Courtesy of the Cathedral of Our Merciful Saviour.*

Rose Cleveland to Evangeline Whipple
Faribault, Minnesota, December 26, 1902
Walmouth, Wayne, E[ast] N[ew]. Y[ork].
Dec. 26

Dear Granny,
When I arrived here Tuesday evening Sue[3] showed me my Granny box, which I insisted on lugging in my own arms, in a jealous, exclusive way, to my own room. Safe there I allowed it to stay unopened, unpacked until Christmas Eve, when, before getting into bed, I unpacked it and laid each beautiful package on my table, so the lavender and violet and pink and green showed in the early light Xmas morning, the bouncing box of candy roses outside, in the middle. Duly on the morning I opened each. Everything pleases me, and I feel petted and spoiled and natural Granny's Grandam; book pleases me. I am pleased.

The most wonderful thing of all is Motherdie's gown & slippers, for all the world hers, and how she *did* it after last summer I cannot make out, and so let it go with the other miracles of love and goodness; but *this* gown will have no chance to wear *out,* though I shall wear it and wear it. When you come to Naples[4] you will see how *full* my closet door bag will be. I can see it bulging in every pocket *now.*

Mrs. Yeomans begs me to give you her especial thanks for the thought of her this Christmas, as ever. She will enjoy reading that remarkable book, and eating that fine candy. You will find at Maitland, I hope, a little remembrance from her, in a bit of her daughter's clever work. The "prayer &c" is before me in all its good words. I'll venture they (The Bells) rang bravely yesterday![5] If I close my eyes & ears I can hear them too. You

3. Cleveland's sister, Susan Yeomans.
4. Naples, Florida, Cleveland's winter home.
5. Evangeline Whipple paid for a bell tower at the Cathedral of Our Merciful Saviour in Faribault, Minnesota, with one tolling bell and ten chiming

ought to have put in the prayer with "For those who hear" and "for those who do *not* hear also" and there we would all be in it. But we are all in it anyway.

Let me know when you are going to Maitland. Address at the Weeds where I shall be after all a little while, as I have found a second *Williams*,[6] I hope. How I wish you could look in.

You used to scold me for not praising my brother[7] more. Here is a slip which Sue handed me & I have just been reading. If you can strip off the rather tiresome hero-worship in the writer, it is pretty correct for his best side—the real man, & will, I hope, satisfy you. Please return.

This cannot take enough to Motherdie, but what I can I send, of grateful love for her dear work & thought for her Rose. Who made the slippers?

[*Rose*]

Rose Cleveland to Jane Marrs, Maitland, Florida
The Weeds, Jan. 4, 1903

My dearest Motherdie,
How you ever did that pink nightgown I cannot imagine— perhaps you didn't. But you are in it anyway, and nobody else could *think* it, whoever sewed it. And the *slippers*—did Belle do them? It seems so like *always,* and I like always things. I have to wear such hateful, ugly gowns now—or did before this came; but now this will dress me up over the worst of those old, white, short, *poor*-looking "outing flannel" which is just nothing but old-fashioned cotton flannel. I think *you*

bells, finished in 1902 as a memorial to Bishop Whipple. Inscribed on the tower: "This tower is the thanksgiving of many people for Henry Benjamin Whipple, first Bishop of Minnesota and is the symbol before men of the supreme value of a righteous man."
   6. Cleveland's longtime maid.
   7. Grover Cleveland.

ought to wear pink French flannel, Motherdie nightgowns. Evangeline and I could make them for you.

I had E's note from Chicago last night, and do hope you realized her plan and arrived in Maitland yesterday. It will be great fun watching your house go up on four legs, and I expect other things will be done to it. Perhaps I can hop in there, but I do not think I will leave here—or the North—before Feb. 1st. It may be necessary for me to go to Maine this month, but I hardly think so. It is an unexpected treat to be here in my old Weeds. You would laugh again and say again—"Rose, you are the luckiest person"!

I thought I could not find anyone to open the house and do the work—the excellent people, as I think I wrote Evangeline, whom I had put in here *forever* having flown after three months—to a larger wage in October. So I posted up here two days before Xmas to see about my horse, who they had been writing must be helped into Spirit-land on account of her ills of body. I came just for over night and stopped at the hotel, my dear old Adelaide[8] coming along with me. The next morning I had Meg[9] off frisking for the winter having some dentistry done and laughing her croakers to scorn; found the very woman for the job, put her in two back rooms, and took the A.M. train for my sister's where I spent a lovely week, and come back here two days before New Year's to find a nice warm house, clean, lovely rooms and everything comfortable. So I am resting in the old place with old faces and scenes before me.

I am writing Evangeline, too; make her answer *at once* because I must hear before I can make any plans. I certainly expect to look in at you in a month's time, God willing, and expect you and E to go to see me at Naples.

With love,
Rose.

8. Adelaide Hamlin Thierry.
9. The horse.

Rose Cleveland to Evangeline Whipple, Maitland, Florida
envelope postmarked Holland Patent, New York
Jan 5, 1903

Dear Granny

I am crazy to do as you say, but being the *Wind* I cannot tell where I will blow next—perhaps to Maine, perhaps to Florida. But it is only a question of time. I—and Evelyn—will surely bring up at Maitland on our way down very early in February if not before.

Meanwhile I am wondering why I do not hear from Lester.[10] I sent him $20.00[11] in a letter from Maine before I left (he cheekily asked for $40) and Evelyn & I each sent him a Xmas gift of a V cheque;[12] but I hear nothing from him.

It is important that I know if anything has occurred to make it impossible for him to fulfill his engagement with me which was that he should go to Naples and get the house ready for me as soon as I could provide him with company. (I think he is afraid to go alone, as he refuses to do so.) Now Mrs. Haldeman will be going down with her family before or by the 15th and will let him know when her train passes Maitland so that he can get on it and proceed under their oversight. She will look after him and advise him what to do about the house if he is uncertain.

Now Gran, will *you* let me know in a word if I can depend on him[?] I am too tired of servants and houses to go there and have to tackle both, and [when] he goes and does as he agrees I shall feel like giving it up, I am afraid. He said he knew a nice woman (colored of course) who might go along to wash and get breakfast & supper (dinner we take at hotel) while he did the house & the waiting. Please inquire into this woman to see if she is his beau. (I shall not object but insist on the marriage

---

10. Likely a caretaker who worked for Cleveland in Naples.
11. Equivalent to about $515 in 2018.
12. Possibly "V" as in "verified" (i.e., a certified check or banker's check).

Evangeline Whipple in her Faribault, Minnesota, garden, circa
1903. *Courtesy of the Cathedral of Our Merciful Saviour.*

ceremony and a honeymoon fast). If not can you raise one for me. I have a person on the hunt for one in Jacksonville but she will probably fail.

By a mischance I have the keys of the house with me, but send them, with this, to you, begging you to give them to Lester. Of course it was a mistake & the house should have been opened often. "I'm wae to think upon yon den."[13]

The snowflakes are idling in the air, which makes me think that my old Grandam is prying with my things, and *I must* go and get in among them and BLOW.

Wind.

Rose Cleveland to Evangeline Whipple, Hotel Somerset,[14] Boston postmarked from Camden, Maine
Acre Island–Oct. 6th [1904]

Dear Wingie,

Yours here last night. You have been naughty to not write before—we have been hoping for your visit. Now the winds do howl and the rains descend, and *our* house is closed, cook & waitress gone, and we in the Beach House with *substitutes* as best we can while the works get finished. [In] spite of awful gout and other protests I cannot agree to leave while so many things remain unfinished—but I am pushing for all I'm worth, and hope to get off soon.

Now Evelyn and I are going to try to get to Boston next week for over Sunday, arriving at 355 Commonwealth Ave.[15]

13. Robert Burns's poem "Address to the Devil" ends with these lines: "But fare you weel, Auld Nickie-ben! / O, wad ye tak a thought an' men! / Ye aiblins might—I dinna ken— / Still hae a stake; / I'm wae to think upon yon den, / Ev'n for your sake!"

14. The 250-room luxury hotel had opened in 1899 at the corner of Commonwealth Avenue and Charlesgate East in Boston (400–16 Commonwealth), about a block from Evelyn Ames's family home.

15. Evelyn Ames's family lived in a brownstone building at 355 Commonwealth Avenue in the Back Bay neighborhood of Boston.

Friday morning or Thursday eve'g. Your "ten days" will be up then and we will have *some* fun; if there are *any* little girls at your house.

Now I must get ready to *survey* all the afternoon for a *road* on the island with the dearest of Maine surveyor[s]. And *now* I must write to the man who wants to sell us 50 sheep, for which we are building a *pen*. "History repeats itself."

If there are some good days and you can come back with me Oct. 17th for a picnic we will try for it.

Anyway, if all goes we will see you next week & talk.

Ever your gran chile

Rose Cleveland to Evangeline Whipple, Hotel Somerset, Boston
postmarked October 14, 1904
Tuesday A.M.

Dear Wing,

It looks now as if we—I—*could not* leave on Thursday. So I write to ask *when* you are leaving—if you could run here for pot luck over Sunday, leaving Friday 7 P.M train to connect at Portland[16] with Frank Jones (steamer). We will be there & have your state room. Telegraph on receipt of this—*yes* if possible.

Evelyn wants you to call at Herricks[17] (Copley Square) for her Friday afternoon symphony concert tickets for yourself or someone you want to send (give your name in calling for it).

There is little possibility that I can get away before next week Saturday.

In rage and love,
Rose.

Tickets to be returned to Herricks as it's a season [. . . writing off page]

16. Portland, Maine.
17. A theater in Boston.

Rose Cleveland to Evangeline Whipple, Maitland, Orange County, Florida
T. G. YEOMANS & SONS, FRUIT GROWERS AND EVAPORATORS,[18] *WALWORTH, N.Y.*

Nov. 25th 1904

Dear Grandma,

I came here Wednesday and stuffed myself full of good things yesterday fr[om] which I am recovering today. Spent two weeks at Weeds, Evelyn leaving me on Saturday of first week. Williams in attendance, but my new woman very severe with me, but one to respect and keep. Already she announces, as a wonderful thing, that "she likes me—I don't know how much;" which I leave to simmer for future use.

Sue is well, but her husband miserable,[19] very weak and ill—they may, if he's able to, go to Florida later. If they do and wanted it, could they get the little house we had for a month or two? I go to New York Sunday to meet Elofun[20] and have another conference with Mr. Emmett. On to Boston Tuesday, to Maine ~~Wednesday~~ Thursday, hoping to get back Saturday night and be at the Weeds again by Dec. 8th. Do a little more fixing there and after that I am uncertain. I may stay there, may go to Boston, may come here, may go to my grandmother's.[21] I have work to do, if I am able, before going to Naples.

It was lovely to have the *little* visit I had with you—so much better than nothing that I cannot complain that it was not

18. Susan Yeomans's husband, Lucien, managed T. G. Yeomans and Sons from about 1870 until the business was sold in 1905.

19. Lucien Theron Yeomans (1840–1906) was a Republican state assemblyman and apple grower; his family operated a plant nursery business.

20. Perhaps a phonic inversion of "Evelyn," referring to Evelyn Ames.

21. "Grandmother's" implies Evangeline Whipple's house, either South Park in Massachusetts or in Maitland, Florida.

more. But I feel pretty certain of the future. Give love to dear Motherdie, and send me a note to the Weeds.

With love from Sue,
Your own Granchile.

Tell Lester I have his letter and give him my warm sympathy at his sorrow. I shall write him if I do not see him soon.

Rose Cleveland to Evangeline Whipple, Maitland, Florida
Weeds, Dec. 22, 1904

My Grandmother,
That box sets behind my old sofa here in the library and just aggravates me. In three days I can open it—Xmas Eve!

Pussy is here for 3 weeks—arrived last night, and is now seated in your room,[22] white fur, feathers & all—but no honey or doughnuts—grapefruit (my own crop) and some *postum*[23] instead. I have a new man in the place of the incomparable Simeon, and though he knows less than anyone could about his business, still I believe he will be a comfort, and I shall take him to Florida with me. I have had awful, thrilling, and dangerous experiences with my new woman, and finally *retreated* from the encounter. This man-mongrel, jack of all trades and good at some, will keep me going and give me protection and now all goes well. But oh, the scuffle with old rooms, garrets and rubbish to get to it. But Clevie got her back up, and through well-nigh licked to her death, still struck and struck and now am *Upper Dog,* in triumph![24]

---

22. This suggests Whipple had lived or had often stayed at the Weeds.

23. Postum was a Post Cereal Company coffee substitute made from roasted wheat bran, wheat, and molasses.

24. Cleveland had exacting expectations of her staff. This account demonstrates she also had a sense of humor about it.

And now if you were here! You must come the first chance. The snow falls with that noiseless peace: white everywhere except on my green spruces and red bittersweet which hangs, snow tufted, out my library window. I love it, and soon Pussy and I will draw on our leg things and other things and go out in it. I [am going] to get a carpenter to come and divide my back room (behind *your* room) with a little sleeping room to open into the kitchen (Simeon's) for the man—the rest of it to be a little upstairs dining room. I have arranged my library so I use it for sleeping and am as cozy as *can* be, and will be cozier. But I am getting my "orange cough"[25] and will be eager to flee to my old grandmother, after the holidays. As I can not be there on Xmas, I am sending you and Motherdie a Xmas light with my best filial and grand-filial Xmas love, with Pussy added in, so Merry Xmas and every good joy to you

from
Granchile C.

Rose Cleveland to Evangeline Whipple, Maitland, Florida
Weeds, Dec. 26, 1904

Grandmother & Motherdie!
I opened it Christmas Eve—Xmas Eve-angeline[26] it was. The silver strange stringers please me much, and I shall run things *in* now just because it is "fun," you old monster! Dainty handkerchiefs please me *much*—and Mrs. Clap tickles me to death with her hooks & vanities and Kentucky wits. And the Archbishop's addresses from dear Motherdie, all in this country, are just what I need & want, for I did not see or hear

25. "Orange cough" probably referred to a physical need to visit the warmer climate of Florida.
26. A word play on Evangeline Whipple's name and a commentary on her generous gift giving.

him, and did not, in my Penobscot Waters,[27] get reports of all his speeches. I read the one delivered at Old Trinity aloud last night to Adelaide Hamlin, who is staying with me. She enjoyed and endorsed it, although its message sadly rebukes our too-selfish lives.

I resisted all seductions and settled down here with a new, perfectly pleasant but displeasing, because incapable, man servant: a plumber, a carpenter and a paperer, never minding compliments of the season. Evie would laugh a short wild laugh if she saw the tinkering that's going on; and I will detail it to her in good time. Adelaide—alias "Fiori"[28]—is here for her three weeks vacation and we are jogging along as of old. Awful beastly East wind weather is on, and poor Clevie is a-cold[29] and piles the green logs on the library fire and tells green Norman to go and shake the rusty furnace, and thinks of Granny's house,[30] all jasmine and rose and tea room, and wishes she were there, where, D.V.,[31] she will be before many moons have waxed and waned. So keep the mules in harness for I come on the second or third Nor'Easter[32] to stay with Gran & be her

Gran Chile

Adelaide sends Happy New Year, with love.

27. Cleveland's home was on Seven Hundred Acre Island, Maine, in Penobscot Bay.

28. Adelaide "Fiori" Hamlin Thierry.

29. A reference to *King Lear*, III.4, and Edgar's line, "Poor Tom's a-cold."

30. In Maitland, Florida.

31. Abbreviation of *Deo volente* (Latin: God willing).

32. An intense storm, typical to New England, with battering northeasterly winds.

Rose Cleveland to Evangeline Whipple, Maitland, Florida
Jan. 6, 1905
Weeds (all covered with snow)

Dear Grandmother,
What made you think I was going either to start or to arrive
on the 3rd? It may be (but I doubt) the 3rd of February, but
here I am, and here is Pussy, and tomorrow Clara Fuller and
Genevieve DeAngelis are coming to dinner in my tiny dining room looking with its one window to the western hill—
Charlotte Corday and St. Elizabeth and St. Catherine (one in
marble and one in Eisenach embroidery) and St. George and
St. Abe Lincoln all hung around it—and all of us old girls gone
out from here and there gathered with grey hairs from all the
quarters of the earth, and Norman, the Maine lumberman,
stumbling around like a bull in a china shop! And next week
if I can I will ask all the country folk in to see Pussy and have
tea and see my "things," of which, by their standard, [I] have
an egregious and magical multitude.

On Wed. Pussy goes, and then I must settle down to for
[*sic*] other work. But I shall drop down on you in Feb. and will
give you ample warning.

With all love, your measly
Granchile

Fiori will write to unburden herself of doings and sends love.

Rose Cleveland to Evangeline Whipple, Maitland, Florida
Jan. 19, 1905
The Weeds.

Dear Grandmother.
The fireplace here in my library had [a] wide place between it
and the wood for sparks to fly in and burn the house down.

So the man is here with Portland cement filling them up so I will be safe—and he is humming low to himself and me as he works, and the job is keeping me from pulling on all my things and walking to Stittville[33] to see if the Shorey girls will fix my dress & collar to go to my Grandmother's in—& I don't like it. But I think I better sit *by* until he is done, and so I will commence to write you now instead of waiting till evening as I intended.

Now Granny, I think it will be Friday, Feb. 10th when Elophun and I start, but maybe it will be the 13th. You did not ask Elofun, did you—but you see she has to be along and could stay in *my* room[34] with me, and perhaps you will let her, she wants to *so bad.* We could only stay two or three days, because I have two great goose men going to keep home for me, who must be presided over on their arrival at Sanford[35] by boat, about the 14th I suppose, & gone along with.

I did so want to go down to you & stay a long time, but I would have had to leave the house here all unfinished, and the man—a treasure *as treasures* go—all untrained & probably lost, and there was nothing for it *but* to stay. But two days will be better than nothing, and I will let you know whether it will be the 11th or the 14th. I think it will be the 11th.

And I hope it will be so that you & Motherdie can come to Naples—I feel as if it was going to be better than ever there this year, perhaps because I so feel the need of the vacation. I am standing it very well though and enjoying my snow, ice, cold and even *thaws.*

Now I must run, only begging you will send a letter word in reply at once to

your cunning Granchile

---

33. Stittville, New York, about three miles east of Holland Patent.

34. Indicates Cleveland had a dedicated room at Evangeline Whipple's home in Florida.

35. Sanford, Florida, about fifteen miles from Maitland. Passenger boats traveled along the St. Johns River.

Rose Cleveland to Evangeline Whipple
Naples, Florida
Feb. 22, 1905

Dear Wing & Motherdie,
It is late to report but I will take this bit of time to begin. We got seats in the chair car at Orlando, changed at Lakeland to a clean comfortable day coach, reached Ft. Myers about 12 midnight, an hour late. Took the "Royal Palm" carriage to hotel and got the last room. So /moral/ be sure to engage seats in Drawing Room car *in time*. And let me know as soon as you can be *sure* and I will engage two connecting rooms for you by telephone[36] from here at the Royal Palm Ft. Myers. Probably cannot get them with both. The hack[37] (a new back board) starts at 7 A.M. Tuesdays, Thursdays and Saturdays for Naples. On the alternate days a nice launch runs. Hack arrives about 5. Launch at 1 P.M., leaving at 7 A.M. If the day is fine I think the launch would be less fatiguing. If you bring only one steamer trunk *it* could probably come with you whichever way you come.

I am writing this from Marco,[38] where we came on Saturday, for fun. We are going to Naples this afternoon. I never have seen such a Naples; the freeze has left ugly marks. My "man" was disgusting, had his horrid family in my (kitchen part) house, & "the trail of the serpent is over them all."[39] The two men are cleaning, but we have been at the hotel so far: [I] shall probably go in the house this eve'g: the "grounds" look so brown and the dry leaves & branches of the cocoanuts [sic] crack so in the wind that I do not *care* for it. But perhaps it will

36. By 1900 there were nearly six hundred thousand telephones in the United States, a number that had grown to 2.2 million by 1905. Though not yet common, the technology was available to Cleveland and Whipple (http://www.elon.edu/e-web/predictions/150/1870.xhtml).
37. Hackney carriage.
38. Marco Island, Florida.
39. "The trail of the serpent is over them all" is a refrain of the poem "Lalla Rookh" (1817) by Irish poet Thomas Moore (1779–1852).

be better bye & bye. Anyway we can have *fun* on the 'water.'
Do not let anything hinder you. I believe Motherdie can be
comfortable & it can be *made* to do her good. We are going
out to lunch with so *rara avis*,[40] whom I shall show you when
you come.

We had such a good time with you. Be sure to write as soon
as you *can*. We shall look for you two weeks from to-day?

With all love to both
Rose.

Rose Cleveland to Evangeline Whipple
Saturday March 5, 1905

Yours with its bad sad news[41] came duly, and I have been
waiting to know what to say as to my movements. Now it
seems certain we will be here in April, and that you & Motherdie must come.

I found the house in an awful condition, everything wrong
inside & out—a long story of the victimizing of the *employer*.
My cook became insolent, and I dismissed him, after he made
his poor apologies. This last week I have had my boy and two
most undesirable helpers and some of the work has been
done which should have been done before I arrived. Elofun
& I have had some fun over it, and now in a day or two we
are starting on a cruise for fun and hoping to run down a
cook, for I do not want to go three times a day to this house.
If you know of a decent woman who would come, [send] her
on—promise her any wages you think will bring her—what
your conscience will permit—but with an eye to *next year*, as I
shall induce Lester to come next year, and if the woman could

---

40. Latin: so rare a bird; presumably, Cleveland and Ames's unique lunch
companion.
41. The "bad sad news" likely involved a canceled trip.

come with him again, after this year it would be well. *I shall get one &* have a triumphant orgie [*sic*] here yet this year—so don't you forget it.

It is just getting like Naples, this the first day. *Write soon &* let me know how Motherdie is. The weather has been splendid but too cold for Naples weather, & I suppose it is with you. Now plan for the April moon,[42] about the 10th or earlier: we will have the better time for these adversities.

with our united love & sympathy to dear Motherdie,
Your Rose

Rose Cleveland to Evangeline Whipple, Faribault, Minnesota
Naples, March 15, 1905
Wednesday P.M.

Yes, dear Granny, we went and we saw oh, such sights—and we are back today just one week from the start plus the extra day getting here. And your letter is here and I obey your behest and let not a mail go without the word you ask.

But first let me ask *why* you make no mention of your next moon visit here. I beg *be definite* and set the day. We are counting on it, and hope nothing will prevent. Surely if Motherdie can come you need let nothing. You will find the house just as you found it last year—but perhaps the kitchen will be different, inasmuch as no cook is in it—I have had no luck in any hunt for one as yet.

We take our continental breakfast here, and dinner and supper at the hotel, which is often delightful, not always: is, in fact, as you know it. But you and I could supply fish and oysters and have there what we could have here. Motherdie could drive up each time—there is nothing easier—and,

---

42. It's unclear why Cleveland was marking time by the phases of the moon; the habit may be related to her farming venture.

except for mosquito-pest, would enjoy it. We could case her in a net for each trip.

The April moon's first quarter begins on the 12th, full moon the 19th. If you could, leave home April 12th, arrive the 13th or 14th, as you please, to have a day & two nights in Myers, and stay as long as you can. We would probably make the trip back with you as far as Maitland on your way North. We will have a launch at our service while you are here and keep on the water all you like—over it and in it; for our baths have not commenced yet.

One Saturday we expect to run (in a launch) up the coast for a few days, touching at Myers,[43] Punta Rassa, Sanibel, and points up the coast to Tampa and back, reaching here again by Saturday, 25th. After that we will commence our baths but wait for you. There is such a lot to tell of the wonder & beauty we have seen, I cannot even begin. We had a big launch, the front half of it all our's [sic]—slept on the floor in the open air on the water—they bring you back by easy stages in the launch. If you like that idea telegraph at once.

Yours,
R.

Rose Cleveland to Evangeline Whipple, Faribault, Minnesota
Naples
March 25, 1905

We see no wisdom in your Lenten sacrifice, Wingie. That box will go full all the same and carry the same freight of goodwill, whether you come or not. I know there are other reasons, and shall take no stock in all your fine excuses. We are just home from another seven-day cruise, this time up the coast, and have had a fine time, of which I will tell you when I see you, not before. I cotched an old Mammy who is

43. Fort Myers, Florida.

now making jell-cake in the kitchen, and who says, "If you all will jas show me how you likes it, I guess I can tucker it out." Awfully cunning & quite clean. The weather is at last like Naples—the bathing superb, and we intend to stay until April 14th. Your two rooms standing ready & empty—come along quick, if only for a few days dips—I swim better than I did and will take you way *way* out and jump you up & down. We will have a launch and shoot all over the water—I know where you can catch a tarpon.[44] Mother will lose her earaches. Now telegraph when you will come & I will have a launch at Fort Myers for you and we will laugh & be gay day & night.

Elofun says she *will* have the pin cushions that we got for this house but I tell her they are in the box by this time and well on their way to the reservation.[45] I feel a reservation on the subject.

Answer this *at once* & say when you will come.

Rose

Rose Cleveland to Evangeline Whipple, Maitland, Florida
postmarked April 23, 1905
Easter Sunday
355 Comm[onwealth] Ave.

Dear Granny,
We reached Orange Park duly and passed a pleasant, preach-y eve'g [til] midnight there, getting on our way at 7 A.M. next morning, reaching N.Y. three hours late, so took the Fall River boat and reached here the next morning at breakfast, late. We go to Maine Tuesday, if plans are not upset, and I hope to get back to New York so as to see you there by May middle.

---

44. A species of fish that grows to between four and eight feet in length.
45. Evangeline Whipple was probably collecting items for Anishinaabe and Dakota communities in Minnesota.

We had the loveliest time at your house, and look back and forward to it. I called to see Miss Adams on Friday in the place where she holds court in her white cap strings and oatmeal crackers and tea, her books piled by her side and people dropping in. Very affectionate and full of affectionate messages to you; talking all the time on "themes."

I have been trying to go to church, but could not get in to any. Dr. Gordon's no standing room even in halls. Trinity guarded by policemen. Arlington ch[urch] (Paul Frothingham's, whom Miss Adams calls the unequalled except by Dr. Gordon) ditto, and so the others, I supposed, so I went into a "hall" and heard a New Thought or such like expound his mysticism in phrases one might hear in lay pulpits—to his milliners and dry-goods clerks—learning a good deal, meanwhile, and pleased to have a chair and no music or flowers. Then I stopped at Vida Scudder's, and sat a while with her and her little black satin mother and aunt, having the least of talk.

Now Evelyn, who is calling today, and I await the dinner, and refrain from going down until we know the guests have departed. A great display of flowers and Easter gifts. Mrs. Ames sends you her love, and says you are "noble looking." Evelyn sends all love to you both.

Now drop a line when you will be in New York. All love to both of you dears, from,

Rose

Rose Cleveland to Evangeline Whipple, Maitland, Florida
Dark Harbor, Maine
Late summer, 1905

Dear, Darling Wingie,
If you think I do not *appreciate*, you are mistaken. Your dear little letters are precious, and your verses cute besides—but—I am a poor old thing with much work and little play and I ache

a good deal, and everything, work or play, is a "job to be done," as Grover used to say of his various works.

I have just come home from our little Sunday afternoon meeting in the "little red schoolhouse"; and I preached, and Evelyn read and played. There were a lot of farmer and "help" folk there, and it was the last meeting for this year. We have had a busy summer. My sister Anna Harding, and Mary Hoyt,[46] and Richard Hastings and wife (missionaries) have been here, and Carrie Lawrence[47] of my family, and several other friends have been here—now the season is waning, and our cook and waitress go on Sept 2. Then the laundress (herself an excellent cook, and the chambermaid) will turn in, and we will take in some sail and settle down to six weeks more of it. About the middle of October I hope to get *off*, for I need a change. It is doubtful if Evelyn can go so early. Last year in October you talked as if you would go for a while. Can you not manage it this Fall? Let us go *off* away from all care and get rested, Wingie. I know you need it. Elofun will be going along later, and if you can stay we will plan something which will make up for the last Everglade trip. It is wrong for us to take [on] the all-work-and-no-play *rôle* too long; Jack will get a dull boy if we don't do something about it. Now talk it over with dear Mother-die and be *bold and firm* and write *definitely* in your reply.

I have got things in train for the Weeds and Florida so both places can be left—this winter better than any other. Can't you do the same and let us have the *luxury* of Egypt's warmth? We are going from a sense of *duty* and that justifies a good time.

Oh, I know you are worrying yourself to death. Love to dear Motherdie from us both,

And your Gran'chile.

46. Mary (Minnie) F. Hoyt (1858–1958) was the first woman invited to work as a civil servant in the United States.

47. Carolyn Hastings Lawrence, daughter of Cleveland's oldest sister, Anna, and her husband, Reverend Eurotus P. Hastings. She married R. A. Lawrence.

bault, Minnesota

acation for a month, o on over to London) for a fortnight—or : winter after Jan. in m Paris to Sicily, and Malta. Why can you year and go with us? e month in England. Maybe I will repent go to Florida myself, hurting yourself with urs. It is your duty to rne in upon me that)t I will go, all alone,

Evelyn at Paris twisting along, I worrying seven men over impossible jobs, which, however, *get done,* by sole dint of my hypnotizing them to do it: and I come out of this effort as if from a knot hole or a needle's eye, have an hour or two of jaw aches, and then go for 'em again. But *I* am going to have a vacation—and you must. Evelyn goes down to Boston on Saturday, the 15th. I stay and wind up up [sic] a week or two longer plan to spend a few days in New York & Boston first week in November, then go to Weeds for a month. Then *off!*

Here comes Elofun from the "sing" with the "help" all hands (four women, seven men), where she played the "organ." The night is *superb,* as soft as Florida almost. She (E) sends love & says *come,* we will have *fun.*

Your G. C.

Rose Cleveland by Alice Hughes, before 1911. Alice Hughes (1857–1939)
was a leading and prolific London photographer, operating from
1892 to 1911. She was legendary for photographing only women and
children, including members of Europe's royal families. *Courtesy of
Professor Marcello Cherubini, Bagni di Lucca.*

Rose Cleveland to Evangeline Whipple, Faribault, Minnesota
Weeds—Nov. 15, 1905

Dear Ole Grand Mother.

Yours of the 13th came this A.M. as I was on the way to the Shorey girls to get them to turn some sleeves of 1903 upside down so they would do for California 1905. (They begged if you came here that I would drive past so they could *see* you). Now *Gran,* you old thing, you've *got* to stop here as you pass on the 8th, & let Motherdie and Mary Whip[ple][48] *go on & on.* Spend the two days here; there will be flakes and flowers & honey & doughnuts & *sleep.* I will write Motherdie if you don't.

You see Wingie I have at last consented to go to Florida by way of Cal[ifornia]. Evelyn (who spent last Sunday here) is crazy to go, and I feel myself drawn by Sue, who is spending the winter in a house with an empty upper floor, at Los Angelos [*sic*] with her invalid husband.[49] There are other reasons and *so I go,* starting about New Year's & coming back by Florida; but I may not see you there—so *make* a way & *stop here en route.*

I am getting so rested I do not care about Clifton Springs[50] *this* year, but next perhaps. No day is long enough for me, and I feel that as long as I can be kept *as* comfortable as I am now in the house—there is no place like it for refreshment. But after all it just happens so this year.

---

48. Possibly Mary Webster Whipple (1842–1916), first cousin to Bishop Henry Whipple, or Mary Mills Whipple (1825–1911), Henry Whipple's sister-in-law. The latter moved to Faribault, Minnesota, with Reverend J. Lloyd Breck in 1858 and was the first teacher at the Seabury Mission. In 1861, she married George Whipple, who worked as a pastor alongside his brother, Bishop Whipple. George Whipple died in 1888, and Mary entered a long widowhood.

49. Susan and Lucien Yeomans began visiting California in 1901 because of the latter's poor health. They moved to Long Beach, California, in 1905; Lucien died there on February 5, 1906.

50. A spa town in New York with sulfur springs where Cleveland and Whipple took treatments.

I see—it's a Church Fair,[51] and you are making slipper bags (a new kind, of course) & toothpick holders, & will sell your eye lashes for a hundred dollars a lash. It will be the *coat* of the missing box over again but if it does me out of my visit you will be sorry. I go to Hartford for Thanksgiving, on to Boston & Maine & back here by Dec. 6th. So set the day & train & I will meet you & push you up here hard.

G.

Rose Cleveland to Evangeline Whipple
The Weeds, H[olland] P[atent]
Nov. 27 [1905]

Dear Wingie,

Where are you and why do I not get a word? "This is only a line—will write a *real* letter soon—flying haste."

R.

Did you go to Clifton Springs?

Rose Cleveland to Jane Marrs
Holland Patent, New York
December 19th, 1905

Dear Motherdie.
I don't know where you are—the Fair Lady has not deigned to tell me—so I take it for granted you are in Maitland though I am aware that it can very well be otherwise.

Evangeline wrote you were going and I wrote she should stop here, and she said (after saying in other letters a great

51. Evangeline Whipple organized fairs at the Church of Our Merciful Saviour in Faribault, Minnesota.

many other things) that they (at Faribault) were *getting up a fair* (I know she hated to tell & looked guilty writing it, for you know *that missing box!*), and so after that I understood, and knew I would not see or hear from her any more. But Christmas comes but once a year (and we, you and I, are *glad* that it does not) so we must all have peace and good will and *say* so. *I* feel awful guilty myself because I have just veered right around and am not going to California and Florida but am going to Europe! I think it's my duty to go, as Miss Ames is in much trouble and worry over some things about her house that can be better settled there than here. We sail on Jan. 2, S.S. Saxonia, Cunard line, Boston. Perhaps I shall not be able to write dear Evangeline again—for this is of course to *her* as to you, and she must have a letter at the steamer for me. I am not very keen about it and feel *now,* as I have a cold and a low spell, as if I would rather sneak down to Florida. I need to be back in late April. You can imagine I am crowded just now—Xmas, even in my modest way, bringing its extra excitements and work. I expect "Fiori" to morrow for three or four days, over Christmas, and then three days of work and I am off.

I am sending you a patriotic book, which I hope you will find interesting, and a yellow book to Evy, which a friend's friend wrote & [sent] all the other things in it.

I read today in the *New York Times* that I am living in Paris and, at present, writing a play for Sarah Bernhardt, who has two acts, three yet to come![52] How's that for a "Queen of Acre Island."[53] I tell you, Motherdie, it's a queer world.

---

52. "Sarah Bernhardt, it is understood, is about to purchase a five-act play in French written by Miss Rose Cleveland, a sister of ex-President Cleveland. Miss Cleveland has lived for many years in Paris, where she makes her home. The play deals with an episode in the French Revolution, with a leading part designed especially for the great French actress, and is nearly completed. Mme. Bernhardt has already two acts of the piece in her possession, and the final contract is soon to be concluded" ("Gossip of the Theatres," *New York Times*, December 17, 1905). No extant evidence supports the article's claims.

53. A story in the *Washington Post*, reprinted in half a dozen additional papers, had declared Rose Cleveland to be "absolutely queen of the island." It

Now I'll have a word later with E—but it's *dreadful* how many time-tables & letters with directions I have from my sister & King & Laura for California!

Now only just the sweet old wishes for the sweet old time's [*sic*] (and love to Miss Whipple and with you.) Will you take my Naples home a while this winter?

[Rose]

Rose Cleveland to Evangeline Whipple
June 17, 1906
260 Beacon St. [Boston][54]

Bunker Hill Day—in the morning, and I sit, Wingie dear, in Evelyn's beautiful house in the rear room, fifth floor, hearing the sounds of engines on derricks seen by Italians [who] do not want their holiday, and seeing the placid river which they are making narrower on this side by the dredging of a "boulevard" over a "Subway Trolley R." to beautify Boston. Evelyn has gone to "Ruby's" for a fitting; and I happily settle for the coveted hours at my desk. We are here until Monday next, the 22nd, having spent three weeks at the island in preliminaries, which would amuse and interest you.

Now the maids are up there getting the house ready for us and we are passing here. I have just written a note to your [Miss] Adonis, whom I promised to go to see on June 1st, but instead stopped in Maine until the 8th, so explain to the

added that "by enforcing her rules rigidly, Miss Cleveland and her associates are enabled to be as much alone as if they were dwelling on an uncharted island in the middle of the Pacific Ocean" ("Money in Maine Islands: Miss Rose Cleveland One of the Women Who Have Speculated with Success," *Washington Post*, October 8, 1905).

54. Evelyn Ames's home was 260 Beacon Street, Boston, which she purchased on June 14, 1904, after moving from her parents' home at 355 Commonwealth Avenue in Boston. Peabody and Stearns, architects, designed and built Ames's Back Bay house in 1870.

august Sarah, whom I like very much. Her nurse tells me over the telephone that she is in Nahant with Mrs Fields for the summer and in better health than for years.

Now I must come to the point, for I will be cut off any instant. Evelyn will break in with accompanying letters and I will disintegrate. The point is to get your date for the visit you have promised us this summer. We count on it and shall be really offended and disgusted if you do not come. I am convinced that you can if you *will*. So come surely. Anytime you say and as long as possible. Try to spare us a month. You have *no idea* how willing you will be to settle down after you have been there a few days. You can choose between three empty houses beside the one we live in, where your room is the only one besides ours; you have your own bath, and your kingdom complete behind your closed doors; and all our joint acres to spread out in.[55] The only thing you can ask for is a crowd. You will have to be satisfied with us for the most part.

The latter half of July is taken; any other time between the 23rd of June & September is clear for your date—so give it! Evelyn's heart is extraordinarily set on a long visit from you. Set aside the whole month of August if possible, & make it possible. Of course you can. There is every reason for it this year. Come to stay with us for August and go to England with me for September. Address answer to Dark Harbor, Maine.

Yours
C.

Jane Marrs died on June 26, 1906, at the age of seventy-seven, in Faribault, Minnesota. Whipple buried her in Maple Lawn Cemetery, Faribault, in the Whipple plot—a choice that suggested she intended to stay rooted in Minnesota. ⌁

55. Cleveland and Ames owned about two hundred acres and three "cottages" on Seven Hundred Acre Island. It is noteworthy that Cleveland offered Whipple a private house during the stay.

Rose Cleveland to Evangeline Whipple, Faribault, Minnesota
postmarked June 28, 1906

The awful news has just reached me. Wingie—*awful* for you, for King, for all of us, to whom she was "Motherdie."

Nay, but what a sudden stop comes here! Not "was," *is* Motherdie. Our faith cannot have it otherwise. *She is the same* Motherdie, only passed into perfect peace and rest, while *we* struggle in vain for it. Let us see it as it is—is gloriously and forever.

Ah but how my heart bleeds for you, poor Wingie, poor King. Never was Mother more idolized—never can she be more missed. I have trembled for years at the thought of what this will be to you both. Yet I trust God for you.[56]

Oh, Wingie, come back with King and hide away with us here a while. Motherdie would like it so! I have no words, but great grief, great sorrow and suffering in yours. This is to you both, my dear old friends, and God bless you and help you.

Rose

Rose Cleveland to Evangeline Whipple, Faribault, Minnesota
postmarked from Lincolnville, Maine
Acre Island
July 14, 1906

My dear, my dear,

At last I conclude I can send you a word direct, as *King* writes you are much better and gaining. Oh, I know how heavy it is, Wingie, how dreadful, how it hurts. The thing I dreaded for you always has come now—come from God—and I can only pray that when Motherdie flew away, she came back to be an Angel of Light and Peace in the very core of your heart,

56. Cleveland's tone is noticeably more anguished here than in the condolence letter she wrote to Whipple after the bishop's death.

as God's messengers can. Any way He can send one, can be one Himself, and I trust you will have the Light and the comfort, in full measure.

Your poor, tired, battered nerves have bowed before the blow, but I feel certain have not broken. You will rise like a cedar of Lebanon after the snow has bent it.[57] The snow will melt and you will feel the *Sun* of the Universe all through your being again, for action and accomplishment.

But do you not need a change—a big one? Why not come, you and anyone or ones you like, and sit by the sea awhile. A big, clean house can be yours, if you would have your staff of friends & servants, and if you would creep off to our hill-top, we shall hide and brood over you, and *show you* the sights that Motherdie would have loved, and tell you the tales she would have laughed over, and we shall see her light & hear her laugh all the time. So come if you will—we will love it. And Motherdie would say *go,* perhaps you will feel.[58]

But perhaps you have plans for other things. Let us know them—but I cannot feel it wise for you to stay in your rut, all sweet and lovely as it may be.

Now my fingers are just too bad to keep on guiding this pen—perhaps it is already a misguided one, and so, with love to Mrs. Scandrett,[59] greetings to they who may remember me who are with you, & dear love from Evelyn, who weeps unceasingly at your grief.

Yours,
[*Rose*]

57. The Psalms contain multiple references to the cedars of Lebanon (ancient symbols of endurance), including Psalm 92:12 ("The righteous flourish like the palm tree and grow like the cedar of Lebanon") and Psalm 29:5 ("The Lord breaks in pieces the cedars of Lebanon"). A reference to them also appears in the Song of Solomon.

58. Cleveland's reliance on the memory of Jane Marrs to arrange a visit with Whipple may be based in sympathy, but it can also read as a method of coercion.

59. Jane (Jennie) Whipple Scandrett.

Rose Cleveland to Evangeline Whipple
Dark Harbor [Maine]
Oct. 14, 1906

Dear E,
So glad you went off a week. Did it do you good? Of course it did.

I have so much to gossip about. It is no use, with my bad hands, to try to say anything. I am going to Clifton Springs to try to get rid of it in a three weeks tubbing[60] or whatever—can't you join me there about the 25th or so? *Do.* Write me [that] you will to 355 Commonwealth Avenue, where I will stop two or three days. We hope to leave here on Saturday or Monday.

Great doings here this summer and fall. Superb weather—just now turning a little cold.

Evelyn sends all love. While in Boston we will try to auto[61] out to see King and Laura over tea time.

Love, and do come to tub and rub with
C.

Rose Cleveland to Evangeline Whipple, Faribault, Minnesota
January 9, 1907
The Weeds.

Dear Wingie.
I came here an hour ago from N. York, where I have been two days, away in all two weeks and two days—much longer

---

60. That is, soaking in the sulfur springs mineral baths at Clifton Springs Spa. Its bathing and massage treatments (rubs) treated various maladies, including arthritis. Cleveland was sixty-one years old and likely suffered from arthritis in her hands.

61. Cleveland had adapted from driving horse-drawn carriages and buggies to automobiles.

than I planned to be gone, but Evelyn needed me to push her house along and the time went and so I am late here and settle down *at once* without preliminaries to my letters and then to my work. Of course it is an experiment how long I can stay here, but just now it seems very pleasant, little snow and the air superb. Pussy is here but going to Chicago in a few days, where she will spend the rest of the winter at least.

I find lovely things here for me—the *Life of Leland*[62] in your own *beat-the-world package* among them. It does indeed bring back Florence, and those first visions of it, with the long beard, skull cap & incessant discourse of the facile Hans Breitmann.[63]

Mr. L. never was satisfying to me personally, or in memory, but he is his biggest best in these pages, written *con amore*[64] evidently. And reading for [illegible], is reaching you and all that setting of you and me in those days.

Glad the *Open Road*[65] stirs you up.

The "remedy" in two parts has not yet put in an appearance but I will try it when it comes if not too scared of it.

You don't say a word about Florida—are you not going? & when? I want to go awfully, but shall wait and see. I find this book of Naples here & enclose to further stir you up to the *Open Road*. But Wingie, I have got to sell my lovely camp down there—I cannot carry so much house & land property with no money to carry them. So I am going to shut my eyes

---

62. Elizabeth Robins Pennell had published a biography of Charles Godfrey Leland (1824–1903) a year earlier. Leland was a journalist and writer whose work explored folklore and language.

63. Leland published *Hans Breitmann's Ballads*, a collection of comic poems describing the misadventures of a fictional Prussian soldier (Breitmann), in 1871.

64. Italian: with love.

65. Probably *The Open Road: A Book for Wayfarers*, compiled by E. V. Lucas. The book, first published in 1899, collected excerpts of literature intended to inspire travelers. Coincidentally, E. V. Lucas was Nelly Erichsen's sister, Alice, who married solicitor Edgar Lucas. Erichsen lived with Whipple and Cleveland in Italy (Madden and Harkness, "Nelly Erichsen," 50).

and swallow hard and sell it, as soon as I can. Haven't you some bold, brave Fisher lads out there who would jump at it, if they knew about it[?] I will sell it for $3000.00,[66] land & all, furniture as it stands. It is insured for $2250.00 and if anyone wants it, it's the thing they want. I fairly choke over it, but I am not quite well enough to do *so much* planning for three places, and realize that I must give it up, if I ever amount to anything but an earth-worm, and I do want to. I am working desperately, & *determined* to do it or die, at my Augustine papers. For I am ashamed that they never get any farther.

I hear from my man at my grove that those wicked freezes have been again doing mischief in Florida. I do hope your grove escaped. Mine did, altho fruit in the neighborhood was hurt, and the crop so reduced that they are expecting fabulous prices for what is left. He asked me if I would take $5.00[67] per box on the trees?

All the same I shall sell the grove if I can see $5000.00[68] for it, just because I cannot carry it. I'm too old, Wingie, and I wouldn't be so old if I did not have to tend things so hard. It dries up all the founts of fancy & fine frenzy in my head.

Now write & tell me what *you* are up to or down to, for I've no doubt you are best off in bed. Why can't you come this way, & look again at my wintry Weeds; but it's *cold,* Wingie.

Well, I'll see you, "as I pass," *if* I go and you go to our beauteous, best Florida. Keep me posted & sell my pet place for me quick, so I won't decide to keep it to my hurt, and its hurt. It's all painted new, but it will *run* down if I don't tend, and I'm too busy to tend, Wingie.

Now write quick. Did the Cal[ifornia] last quake give King a start? God bless you ever.

Yours, C.

66. Cleveland was willing to sell her beachfront Naples cottage for the equivalent of about $70,500 in 2018.
67. The equivalent of $117 in 2018.
68. The grove's worth was equal to $117,400 in 2018.

Rose Cleveland to Evangeline Whipple, Faribault, Minnesota
postmarked from Holland Patent, New York
Weeds
Jan. 24, 1907

Dear Wing—
I have just *scratched* all over a page with my *bad* hands, a note to Mrs. Crosby (10 Francis Avenue, Cambridge, Mass) who has lost her queer, great son *Ernest Crosby*: her only son, and a distinguished man.[69] She was badly broken when I last saw her— & this will be a sad blow. Oh, well, it's all in life here & there!

And I must go on & scratch just enough to let you know the bottle & box & letter all came—so good & kind & *well meant*. I rub—or Pussy does—the hands & now and then I take a thing out of the box, but Wingie it's no use. It comes & goes and I've just got to stand it. On the whole I'm very well off.

Lots to say, lots to hear, but I can't write to night. Let me hear, good old Wing, and keep *your* hands well, anyway.

R.

Rose Cleveland to Evangeline Whipple, Faribault, Minnesota
postmarked March 30, 1907
HOTEL WESTMINSTER, COPLEY SQUARE, BOSTON/W. A. BARRON
Easter Eve.

Beloved Wing,
Yours of March 29 just received, enclosed by "Sue" from Brooklyn,[70] which I left on Monday, having been there the

---

69. Fanny Crosby's son, Ernest Howard Crosby, was a writer, a pacifist, an advocate of radical social reform, and an intimate friend of Leo Tolstoy. He died of pneumonia on January 3, 1907, at the age of fifty-one. "Death of E. H. Crosby," *New York Times*, January 4, 1907.

70. By 1907, Susan Cleveland Yeomans had moved to Brooklyn from Long Beach, California.

best part of two months, all total, working interoperably to get my Augustine translation, with *Notes & Introduction,* done. Sue copied for me and goaded me on, and I have really *worked* and got the thing almost in shape.

I came here last night to this hotel, where I stayed two months once, you know, and feel at home. I wrote Belle to get me a room which she did and met me, and made it seem less bleak. You know I am trying to sell my Florida house and one man seemed "almost persuaded" but wanted to see photographs of it, so I bethought me of the ones you took of it,[71] and wrote Belle if she would send any she had for him to look at, which she promptly did. But now he wants to wait until next fall to decide! So that away it goes—as you know.

Belle looks fine and talks as she used to—I see much of Motherdie in her. She and Annie[72] are coming to call tomorrow ev'g—shall be glad to see Annie.

Poor little Evelyn—she had to go South after all and went to Columbia, where Susie lives. Took her factotum & staid in hotel—went late to Charleston: arrives home to night. I shall stay here.

She will go with me to Maine I expect, as I must go next week to oversee some early spring work. I hope to be back to the Weeds for the best part of May. Pussie has gone abroad, returns in May or June.

Now Wingie, what do you mean by an "arrow"? Is it the letter?

My address for Boston will always be, now—260 Beacon St., Evelyn's house. Did you know Mrs. Crosby had lost her son? I shall try to go and see her tomorrow—She is living now in Cambridge.

---

71. Evangeline Whipple was a prolific amateur photographer. Examples of her photos exist in the collections of the Cathedral of Our Merciful Saviour in Faribault. Whipple took many of the images reproduced in her book *A Famous Corner of Tuscany* (1928).
72. Probably Jane Annie Bense and Eveline Isabelle Bense, Jane Marrs's nieces.

I am pretty well but a little cough lingers and breaks out when least wanted, so I dare not go to church tomorrow, as Belle asks me to, and provides a seat. *Too bad* to miss these lovely services.

But I must send up some rare old books lent me as a special favor from the library and need all my time. When are you coming East and can you not set a date for a visit to us in Maine this summer? *Do,* Wingie—you ought to spend a month with us. Life is not long enough to miss each other always. Let's plan to meet!

A happiest Easter, Wingie, & God bless you!

[Rose]

Rose Cleveland to Evangeline Whipple, Faribault, Minnesota
June 20, 1907
Dark Harbor, Maine

Oh Wingie, why are you not here—with your work—to be rested? To rest us!

It is too bad, and I am not willing to take your last refusal as an *ultimatum,* and shall hope you may find some way to reverse it.

We came here a week ago, have had very trying weather most of the time, but in it all manage to keep comfortable, in our beloved nest; and no weather can take away the glory & beauty of this nature or be as bad as it is anywhere else. Today a fog softens everything and the scraggy old trees of the orchard look spectral sitting with their thick cover of blossoms all webbed up in it. I am as busy as I want to be, with constant small matters to get and keep straight; but I have my books and some days manage to get a good deal of reading done. My translations of the *Soliloquies* with my introduction and *notes* is finished, and I posted it off as I went for the train last Tuesday morning to hunt a publisher. If it fails I will publish it myself someday.[73]

I was just taking a train out as King & Billy[74] came in a while ago in Boston. It was awful, but I hope to see them some later both here and there. It is such a comfort to feel that King is settling in the old place,[75] & Laura loves it so, too. I spent most of May at the Weeds, *Sue* with me a part of the time prodding me on to a finish with my Augustine & giving me all sorts of comfort.

When I have a chance I will look up that picture of Grover & Richard & send you– probably.

[*Rose*]

Rose Cleveland to Evangeline Whipple, Faribault, Minnesota
Acre Island, Sept. 18, 1907

Well, Wingie, I have been deep in your letter in a deep Morris chair in a half hour's recess from my works, while I came here from the fields to get the letters—to and about my poor ailing brother (not so ill as the willing, malicious papers put it, nor so well as the devoted, adoring ones do)[76]—and in the depths I sink way out of my present, as did you—to wake with a start as I look at the clock and see the hour—4 P.M. In one hour I must ring the "knock off" bell, to meanwhile go to give the

73. Little, Brown & Company published Cleveland's translation of Augustine's *Soliloquies* three years later, in 1910.

74. Englishman and photographer William Wilson Barker.

75. Kingsmill and Laura Marrs lived in South Park—Whipple's Wayland, Massachusetts, home.

76. Contradictory stories appeared in newspapers across the country throughout mid-September, including "Cleveland Is Very Ill; Former President Reported Failing Rapidly" (*Washington Post*, September 15); "Cleveland Declines to Die; Jokes About Report of His Fatal Illness" (*Washington Evening Star*, September 16); "Grover Cleveland Reported Dying" (*Paducah [KY] Sun*, September 15); and "Cleveland Losing Weight But Says He's Not Ill" (*Buffalo [NY] Enquirer*, September 16).

carpenter, who comes every day from Dark Harbor, the letters, egging in an errand or two on the poor pack horse to save time from sending our boat over.

This man, with four others, and the oxen are moving an old monster of a barn from one end of the long hill crest to another where I want it, and by wh[ich] operation (wh[ich] no one else would think possible or worthwhile) I shall have a $600.00 barn good enough for less than $100.00[77] down the hill and through the woods to my clearing, next [to] where Titanic work goes on, and I must meet all emergencies.

The filly has lost a shoe. *How* to get a horse-shoer here in the shortest time!

The oxen are on the hill and only they can plough some not-clay corners and root-y mounds in the clearing (wh[ich] must be seeded in 5 days, I say (!!). And so it goes, enough to make a horse laugh. (I am sure the filly does!) Then more woods road and I trot to the chopping place, where the "contract" men are at work and clear 2 acres or more (the contract, wh[ich] *I* write, says) perfectly clear of everything I don't want, smooth and nice, ready for seed (!!), and the pleasant "contractor" *signs* to his own price and his own time, in perfect innocence, I *think,* of what he agrees to. But he does not, and I wait for developments. Silly man!

Evelyn is in Boston, our home closed, I in the little spruce-forest one wh[ich] I have rescued from a low estate and made very cozy. And here, in a fireplace dining room (where real mahogany and a *crane* remain), with a sitting room, a sleeping room, bathroom and dressing room (everything on the first floor except the kitchen places), I abide and run my race: up at seven, beginning the day's trot and keeping it right up until 5 P.M., or after. Then the kitten (Alonzo the Brave)[78]

77. The equivalent of about $14,000 in 2018 dollars, versus $2,350 for the hauling.

78. The name of the hero of a British choral ballad as well as Matthew Gregory Lewis's corresponding poem "Alonzo the Brave and the Fair Imogene" (1796).

and I sit by the fire and go to bed. The mail comes; a good old tedious Swede factotum and her son serve me.

Why are you not here? There is endless whim and fun, and deep design in it. Sometimes of an ev'g I get off and away in my books, but the water and wine do not mix. Yet there is great life in it.

I go to Boston for over Sunday Saturday [*sic*]—back here Tuesday with Evelyn and whom I make work. How long to stay I wait to see.

Again, *why* are you not here? Let me know.

Anyway, you have sent me much and I am enriched. Love *Banf* [79] and worthy of your, *our,* [illegible word].

"*Write!*" This is unheard of from me.

[*Rose*]

Rose Cleveland to Evangeline Whipple, Faribault, Minnesota
Weeds—Jan. 15, 1908

Wingie—
Yours of the 9th here to-day. Had gone first to Holland Patent, *Florida*: which accounts for delay and makes me the more anxious to get off the reply by next mail, which leaves in a few minutes.

Since I wrote things have happened which place me in a position of suspense as to General Walters, and will not allow me to be where mail cannot reach me, for it must be at once attended to when here. As in your case I cannot keep you waiting by making all this knot of affairs clear to you in this, but will depend on another chance later.

"Suffice it to say" that I *cannot* probably go to Florida. If I can I will: but you must not depend on me, for it is more than unlikely.

79. Probably Banff, the Canadian spa town in Alberta that catered to wealthy tourists beginning in 1888.

No time for regrets, but they are *boiling.*

Now why not send those darkies[80] from Utica, or Rochester direct, ahead of you, & you come on here to the Weeds for a breathing spell. *Make* it possible, as you can.

C.

Rose Cleveland to Evangeline Whipple
Feb. 2, [1908]

Dear Wing,

Suddenly I seem to *have* to go to Florida. Perhaps it will fall through but I do not think so for good reasons, which I will divulge later. Now *perhaps* I will have "Sue" with me and *perhaps* be alone.

Write me at once where we shall meet and when: Jax[81] or Maitland.

"Flying haste,"
R.

Will reply at once, on hearing, with further demands. Will probably leave here Saturday—so write at once.

Rose Cleveland to Evangeline Whipple
PINE TREE INN, ALBERT A. LeROY, PROPRIETOR, LAKEHURST, N.J.
March 7, 1908

Dear Wingie,
I write this to show you that we are not at *Clifton Springs,* having at the last minute changed and come here on the

80. Whipple employed at least two African American people as domestic servants.
81. Jacksonville, Florida.

recommendation of my niece, who knows the place. It is about two hours from New York, beyond the famous Lakewood on the Central R[ail] R[oad] of New Jersey. The region is not seashore but a lake region, and flat—sandy soil-covered, with pine woods, a good deal like Florida. The air is fine and the walks in the pine woods very nice. The house excellent—altogether a nice place to know and come to, very quick and simple as compared with Lakewood; almost like Maitland or Naples as compared with Palm Beach.

I wish you could come and stay a while if you need rest. We are staying only through next week and expect to go back to Boston week after next some time. I have also found a nice little English-y inn sort of a private house in New York (62 Madison Avenue, The Bayport), which you would like.

After leaving here I plan to be in Boston a while, then go to Maine and oversee some work there in April and back to H[olland] P[atent] for May. Do try to plan to give yourself an outing sometime soon, and be our first guest in Maine in June late or July early.

Do—and let us count on you. It is time.

Now the sun sinks red over the pine trees. The hotel stage [coach] has come with its load of Sat. night guests, and the darkness descends. We must dress and descend also—get a good dinner at a little table, the N.Y. *Evening Post*; perhaps exchange a few wintry words with some condescending "Waterbury" lady; and come back to our own rooms to read and go to bed. Not a very exciting or fruitful life, but best for Evelyn just now. She is improving—working over piles of bills and business papers, as you used to. She sends love and love—and so do I, dear Wing. The world is a lonely place.

[Rose]

Rose Cleveland to Evangeline Whipple, Faribault, Minnesota
Dark Harbor, Maine
July 16, 1908

Dear Wingie,
Your words came and meant much.[82] I have not been free
enough to answer any but I am wondering when I shall have
the promised date for your coming. We are asking no one,
and only our familys [*sic*] and the oldest friends come now. It
is your time.
　　We hope you will come. Let me know any time to Sept. 1st,
the sooner the better.

Yours ever & ever
R.

Rose Cleveland to Evangeline Whipple, Faribault, Minnesota
631 East 23rd St.
Brooklyn, New York
Sep. 19, 1908

Wingie,
I received yours postmarked the 13th when I arrived here from
Boston last night. Things happened and I had to go there for
two days. Evelyn sick—must get away. I had almost decided
on Clifton Springs and found letter from there in reply to
inquiries among my letters waiting here.
　　Your letter makes me miserable. I want to go and do not
see quite how I can. Have just written E. to see if we could
change and go to Florida. Am a little afraid it will make too
much work getting ready for poor little *her*.
　　But in a week's time, perhaps it will clear up. If you could

---

82. Grover Cleveland had died on June 24; Cleveland may be referring to
condolences she received from Whipple.

come *here* to New York next week we could meet anyway and manage it all right. The only way I can see now is for you to do what is easy for *you,* and for me to do what is possible for *me* (with poor little needy Evelyn) and submit results. Complications kill one.

Your old-time self is so in your note—but this must fly. Answer here.

R.

Rose Cleveland to Evangeline Whipple, Faribault, Minnesota
260 Beacon St., Boston
October 30, 1908

Wingie,
I am right here, and well enough, but can whine when expedient. Am pleased that you are anxious if by that you will write.

I have been waiting to get to the Weeds to write you a long letter but will send this leaf. Let me hear at the Weeds when I go day after election[83] if you receive this. Are you going to Florida? Let me know your plans. I expect to stay in Weeds, with exception of Thanksgiving, until the New Year. After that?

Nothing [very] new. Am rushed today. Thankful you stick to

Your C.

If so.

---

83. The 1908 presidential election was held on Tuesday, November 3. Republican William Howard Taft defeated William Jennings Bryan.

Rose Cleveland to Evangeline Whipple, Maitland, Florida
Holland Patent, New York
postmarked November 16, 1908
Monday, 7:30 P.M.

If all goes as you planned you are off for Florida at this writing. You seem very plucky to me, with your cargo of help & helped, and it does seem a pretty big proposition. But it's powerful & fine and you will get there triumphantly, my Wing. As for me, I fare along, and it is marvelous how much can happen in a short November day. Yet I am settled enough; but every day is different, and there is always a *must be* or a "better not put it off" never known to fail.

Today after the pretty poor night, after a Sunday too much in my library, *and* mice (for whom Rachel & I have just prepared a fine new tin trap, *handy* for them, & I quake in advance at the *sounds* that will announce capture, just at the entrance to the wood closet out this door of my library). I moped around and got something done on my Introduction and after dinner had my old lovely Mr. Jones cut down the vine of bittersweet, scarlet with berries, and he & I cut off the little branches and made a big branch for the garret, where they will dry & be beautiful Christmas [*sic*]. Then I *lounged* a little & then went over the fields in this southwest wind to see if I could find the old places where I used, twenty-five & more years ago, to gather the long trailing ground cedar & ground pine which mix so beautifully with the red berries. I paced across meadows under rail road culvert & over a fence and constructed a pontoon bridge across the creek and *got there* to the ravishing great mounds of deep moss trimmed and laced with the trailers like green embroidery, with here & there straight tufts of "princess pine" & squirrel berries, more beautiful than I remembered it. I stuck five wide-apart fingers under the trail & traced a long one branching everywhere & got some lovely long ones.

My pack & long tramp home made me see you toiling down the Beach Road with your awful pillow case of balsam!

Well, I got it, & when I came in letters—one of three sheets from Mrs. Scudder writing for herself & Vida too[84]—the[n] Clara Fuller's voice, who I thought at Ossining, came up the staircase, then Genevieve's, who b[r]ought a letter from her Italian relatives, the Capt. DeAngelis, who did such good rescue work at Messina, then Rachel with a fine tomato soup. I sat down with *bon appetit* for my cold chick & bread & butter & apples & nuts & milk, and now I shall read James[85] a little before I get too tired & then turn in, and think of you, my kind one—and try not to think of sad things—and press into the Real things & be thankful for Love & life—and this is to greet you with every pull & hug á

Gran-chile & Clevy.

Rose Cleveland to Evangeline Whipple, Maitland, Florida
Weeds—Jan. 6, 1909

Wingie—
At last I have seen my name in your bold bad hand[86] and have this beautiful calendar, which I see you have gotten up yourself. It is a masterpiece of work, pre-Raphaelite and beautiful. I don't see how you did it; but I appreciate it.

But why no word?

Evelyn thinks she wants to go down in Feb. to Florida. Now what do you want? I do not *want* anything but to stay right here and work on, but I may not be able to stand it. I am not as strong as I used to be, and can't throw off ailments as I used, but I do not want to leave my books and sure fire & food

84. Cleveland refers to the writer and academic Vida Dutton Scudder (1861–1959) and to her mother, Harriet Louise Dutton Scudder (died 1920).

85. Cleveland could have been reading the work of the American writer Henry James Sr.; his son William; or his son Henry (the novelist), who visited Bagni di Lucca, Cleveland's and Whipple's home in Italy from 1912 to 1930.

86. That is, in Whipple's distinctive handwriting.

and easy life—any old way—for regular nice folk living. *But I may have to.*

Anyway, let's meet somehow somewhere before another year rolls round. I take it neither of us feels like wasting time or strength. But I wait to hear from you, and with all love, ever

Your old C.

What fun for us three to go on a lark?

Rose Cleveland to Evangeline Whipple, Faribault, Minnesota
Saturday, June 19, 1909

Oh, Wingie—no word from you yet, and I am afraid to wait longer because my other maid has "accepted" the position I have offered her, to my surprise, with no ifs or ands, which would make it possible for me to withdraw if you preferred to have "Hoyt" around you. So I write to say so. But in case you have promised Hoyt[87]—or any of them—I can make work for them, for instance, if you have nice laundry to be done, or something like that.

But if you have no need of anyone (I can arrange for all our needs), just come free, and have a free time, the time of our lives, I hope, for physical and nervous rest. I am trying to shape affairs so I can get to the Isle of Guernsey (between England and France) in the fall. "There's a reason" but it would take too much time this busy, over-busy, morning to tell and can wait till we meet. I want to spend the winter there if possible. Would you? I just drop the seed hoping it may germinate.

Do not fail me, on Aug. 1 and earlier, if possible, for I shall find it hard to wait for

My Granny

—C.

---

87. Hoyt was likely one of Whipple's maids.

Rose Cleveland to Evangeline Whipple, Faribault, Minnesota
Holland Patent, New York
June 24th, 1909

Oh Wingie, *rise* in that might of yours which *compels* things, and say you *will* come August 1st. You said positively *you would* (I will quote your written words) and I have gone on that. Now you must keep your word. No matter *what* you find to do there. I need you and life is not long enough to always wait. You wrote asking my plans for the summer, before *you* dreamed I was to be so struck down. There is very much I want to tell you—my necessities for readjustment of plans incident to this "escape" of Evelyn's[88] compel me, probably, to go to the Weeds early in ~~Octo~~ September. And I do so want you here. I believe you will manage it. I shall get no one else & keep the whole month for you, & you will get so well & rested. In your reply to this *set a day* and then keep to it. I feel a terror lest if we do not meet and *take account of stock now* we shall not meet at all to any purpose.

No new friends for me! And no more striving to make things go or come. Only to do the day's work, Wingie! *And live.* But I cannot give up having you *see this place.* Do not make me! *You will thank me for insisting later.*[89]

[Rose]

---

88. Evelyn Ames, at the age of forty-six, married thirty-year-old Frederick Garrison Hall on June 23, 1909, in Watertown, Massachusetts.
89. After saying she would not contrive to make things happen, Cleveland insisted that Whipple come for a visit.

Rose Cleveland to Evangeline Whipple, Faribault, Minnesota
Dark Harbor, Maine
July 20th, 1909

My Wingie,
Yours of the 16th here yesterday. You must come. If it cannot be earlier than Aug 20th, as late as that will do, and I shall still have this house running until Sept. 8th, perhaps later. But I shall have to be here, in this, probably, or another, house, up to October, probably not later. I shall have a good old body to do some of the work and an excellent factotum to do nice things and between the two we could be perfectly comfortable ~~here~~ as long as we liked—or as long as I must stay. Wish me the fall ~~and winter in between~~ in Holland Patent, and New York to the New Year, and then either Florida or Guernsey. Do try to keep a loose foot for a real "change of scene" which I am sure you need as much as I do, and which I must have if you can get it.

So now this is all "the whole truth" as far as I can write or see it, and this much is fixed: that you can be here as long as you can and we can have, so far as I can see, as perfect a chance to "chew grass" as ever fell to deserving souls. Up to October 1st I shall have men and maids, horses and oxen, cows and sheep, pony and dog, cats and chickens, all to serve us, and a motor-boat and sail-boat with a splendid boatman to take us to easy places for rare sights, up to as late after August 20th as we like.

But do not be later than August 20th, whatever happens, and try and get it in all that work out there by August 15th, for the good months on the water to strange and rare places. After Sept. 20th it is uncertain, and I do so want a whole month of it.

Now I will send this, and you send me a word to assure me that you will connect with my train. After we meet we can talk of all the rest. But do plan for freedom if possible—to crutch around with your

Granchile

Rose Cleveland to Evangeline Whipple, Faribault, Minnesota
Sunday, Aug. 1, 1909

On my arrival last night from Tamworth,[90] Wingie, I found yours of July 28th. Yes, I shall spend September, *all* of it, here, and perhaps *all* of October, so come, surely. Everybody else will have gone by that time, except sister Sue who will stay just long enough over to look at you.

I will write you the most exact directions if you tell me when you can reach Boston—what time in the day. If you get there early enough to get the 9 A.M. train at the Boston & Maine Station, you can get tickets & check direct to *Dark Harbor*. The train goes to Rockland[91] & car backs down to boat for the 1-hour run to Dark Harbor. I [will] meet you at Rockland. You can bring *all* the trunks you want. The great world lingers a little after Sept. 1, but presently clears out for good, and anyway at our island there will be no one.[92]

Now Wingie, you say you dread boarding your servants. If you would like them to come here and would take the empty house, with all appointments for house keeping, you can have it and they would probably enjoy the change. If you have the feeling that it would be better, we can do it just as easily as to not do it. You can have everything your own way, and it would seem like old times. But would *you* have such a good time? Think it over & decide accordingly to your feelings—I shall like to be *your* guest, as well as to be another's, and no plan you can make can possibly interfere with my joy or yours.

We will talk over the "loose foot" business when you come. We both know a good deal about the foot that is not loose *now*. You will find a busy Clevie but you will like my busy-ness and stick by me in it all for it is all in glorious outdoors. Bring

90. Grover Cleveland's family had a summer house in Tamworth, located in the White Mountains of New Hampshire.

91. Rockland, Maine.

92. That is, Seven Hundred Acre Island. Dark Harbor on Islesboro attracted the East Coast elite, especially wealthy people from Philadelphia.

the darkies if you like & we will stay until they can be sent to Florida & skip somewhere else for fun ourselves, till you have to go; my two servants can be easily shifted.

[Rose]

Rose Cleveland to Evangeline Whipple, Faribault, Minnesota
August 11, 1909

I mean just the real *you,* Red-Wing Evie, chained or not chained. So come along, limping or flying, and begin to peer and beat the oxen and make trouble.

I am not sure I will *ever* let you go back, but perhaps, if it's a question of *pedestal* we will settle that when we discuss the loose foot. You will love it here.

I am glad you will not bring the darkies. Pale faces will do for us.[93]

If you take the 9 A.M. train Sept. 3 from Boston you will arrive at Rockland at 4 P.M. and at Dark Harbor Wharf at 5:45 P.M. where I will meet you, and tote you over. If all goes well we will reach here about 6:30. You can bring a house with you if you like. The oxen will pull it. Three weeks from today you start, but I cannot tell if it will be three weeks from tomorrow (Friday) or Saturday you will arrive at

Clevie's

---

93. It would be easy to explain away Cleveland's statements under the guise of her being a "woman of her time." Paired with the derogatory statements about African American people she made over decades, however, the comment "pale faces will do for us" denotes a deep-seated belief in white superiority.

Rose Cleveland to Evangeline Whipple, Faribault, Minnesota
AT THE SIGN OF THE TAVERN/BAGG'S 1794, UTICA, N.Y.
October 15, 1909
7:30 P.M.

Half an hour late!

Settled in "57" promptly, the heat [h]issing and good clean currents of air coming in the window, much improving the *flavor* of the room.

I was *expected*—the tall lean clerk, his son the bell-boy, and the amiable porter all kind to me—A small bottle of lithia[94] bro't—extra blankets & writing paper; the note to Herald, to Pussy, written, the bed opened & cooking, and now this little report to you, for *so far*. *The Chippendales*[95] waiting, & my big apple, and the *pellets* ready.

You have warmed and blessed me—I go to bed & to sleep I am sure—trusting our God of Love in our Master & Saviour His Son—and loving you as never before in all time and for all time.

Your Clevie.

Rose Cleveland to Evangeline Whipple, Maitland, Florida
H[olland] P[atent]
Dec. 22, 1909

Oh Wingie, I am so stunned with these papers of today, all taking up the awful Cook story.[96] I've been in Utica and

94. Lithia water—mineral water containing lithium salts—reached the height of its popularity as a cure-all health drink during the Edwardian period.
95. Robert Grant wrote *The Chippendales*, a novel about Boston society published by Charles Scribner's Sons in 1909.
96. On December 21, 1909, a Danish commission completed an examination of evidence supporting Frederick Cook's claim that he had reached the

reading off & on all day—and now by my library fire I review it all.

Well, I simply *do not know.* There may be some hideous mistake about it all—or poor Cook may simply have gone stark crazy—or the unbelievable *worst.*

Well, dear—we will wait, hoping for something better until there is no longer any ground for hope, and even then I shall have a theory of all the dreadful all, which could be, and exonerate Cook from the worst. Such incredible possibilities there are of muddles in this poor world of human nature.

Bear up, Wingie—all is not lost at the worst. I thought of you as "the next friend" mourner, and forgot almost all of the grief in yours.

Well, it's Christ-Mass, X-feast anyway, and that covers all scars and wounds and deformities. We can't afford to be sad to-day, for there is ultimate joy and salvation for the one most far from it now.

I am *not* opening my three packages, with the bold bad handwriting, dwarfing all the plainer ones around it. To-day, I went to Utica and got a few little trinkets for *my* baskets to be packed on Friday & sent or set round the same eve'g. Adelaide came there on her way up to Watertown to spend her holidays—and we had two or three hours together. She will drop in on me on her way back, but family unpleasantness makes it difficult for her to be here just now. She is well and nice and I took her your lovely package, which she will not open until Xmas day. I have things for Rachel & William, my dear old saints down stairs, and for old Williams (*fils*)[97] and for Sarah Hitchcock & her mother & Sally DeAngelis, and Saturday morning I shall open mine, and then walk gaily down the hill to eat dinner with "the girls"; to-morrow I commence

North Pole in 1908—a year before Robert Peary, who had been credited with its "discovery." The commission found that Cook's data did not prove the alleged facts of his expedition. Afterward, newspapers speculated that Cook had deliberately falsified his records.

97. French: (the) son.

a dentistry siege which will last the rest of the year i.e. for a week at least; and what will be left of me I do not know.

I am *cut up* to think my nice book, which I know you will *like*, will *probably* not reach you until you had forgotten all about Xmas—for the wicked book seller said—when too late to change—that he had *sent* to London for it! I am so *ashamed.* *Tell* those women with you it is *not* neglect & try to realize my wrath; & so God bless you, *my Wing,* for all time. I almost *cry* over our St. James Park photographs! Pussy thinks I look *so* well—"like my old self." Good night, dear! And heaven bless you. Pack all your baskets full! It is too awful to talk about—those oranges! Mine, too.[98]

Dec. 26, 1909

The day after, Wingie! And a day of unmixed malice in weather, would one say—a Northeast wind blowing with a steady, low roar all day and much of the night. Perhaps it had too much mince pie yesterday![99]

Well, I did not, but on the contrary a most excellent dinner between two friends, who have much interest in merry things and something to say about it all. The day was pleasant (stormy outside) from beginning to end in giving and getting, and looking at my many gains, the bewitching books easily first, with their inimitable cards and mottoes in the bold, bad hand of her I love so well.

The motor trip out is already in my blood, and I [was] well tuned up by the [time] we set sail, I am afraid. But more of this later. Everything went well. I am abundantly remembered by gift and letter, and have great cause for gratitude, which I feel very inadequately. But still, perhaps, it is seen by the great see-er!

98. A cold snap in Florida in December 1909 lowered temperatures to twenty-seven degrees Fahrenheit. Most of the orange crop was already harvested, and only "tender plants" were affected ("Not Hurt by Freeze in Southern Florida," *Atlanta Constitution,* December 31, 1909).
99. Cleveland shows her sense of humor here in a joke about passing gas.

I hope yours was full of joy, but I know it was clouded by
the sudden eclipse of your hero. Alas, what a tragedy. If Cook
has just been fooling all this time! I do not yet believe it, but
hold a theory which "helps the hurt which honor feels"![100]
Darling Wingie, don't be too sad about him. He is not so
bad as the *glad* enemies depict. I am sure of that.

I have not been out to-day as I feared creating a disturbance
by my cough, which is, however, better. And now for the long
pull of January—and then, sunshine and oranges and Wingie!
So brave up, Clevy, for tooth filling and book worming and
rounding up. Clara and Pussy and Genevieve will help, and we
know what is waiting after *all* is over, don't we?

Your
C.

---

*In 1910, Whipple's brother, Kingsmill, developed a serious illness.
Cleveland arranged for herself and Whipple to visit him in Florence, Italy. Travel documents in the Minnesota Historical Society
show they sailed for Europe together on July 20 aboard the S.S.
Saxonia, sharing a cabin for the six-day trip.*

*After Kingsmill died in Florence in 1912, Whipple and Cleve-
land remained in Italy. Whipple continued to direct the management of her finances through attorneys, employees, and family
members in America. In Italy she acquired three homes in the
town of Bagni di Lucca, in the mountains of central Tuscany,
where she and Cleveland devoted themselves to community work.
Both women developed a close friendship with the English writer
and artist Nelly Erichsen, who eventually moved in with them.
The three women supported Red Cross relief work after the start
of World War I.*

*In the winter of 1917–18, Whipple wrote the following letter
to Reverend Charles Slattery, rector of Grace Church, New York,*

100. In his poem "Locksley Hall" (published in 1842), Alfred Tennyson
observes that "the jingling of the guinea helps the hurt which honor feels."

and a former dean of the Cathedral of Our Merciful Saviour in Faribault, Minnesota. In it, she asked for donations to support Italian veterans and their families as well as refugees displaced by the war—some of whom were living temporarily in Whipple's and Cleveland's homes. After receiving the letter, Slattery forwarded it to an Episcopal weekly journal called the Churchman, *where it appeared as a letter to the editor in the edition published on January 12, 1918.*[101] ∿

Evangeline Whipple to Charles Slattery
Casa Bernardini
Bagni di Lucca-Villa-Italia
December 1, 1917

My dear Doctor Slattery,
Into your busy days I shrink from thrusting concerns from over the sea, but for the first time in my life I am impelled to ask help. My story shall be as brief as possible.

You know the circumstances which brought me to Italy— the illness of my brother which kept me here for several years. When the war broke out, duty kept me here. From the grim day of that mid summer of 1914 when I consecrated myself to the cause, my one thought has been for the soldiers and their families. I began with England and Belgium, and then with Italy upon her entrance into the struggle. I did not go into the hospital work at Rome or Florence, where the numberless flocked to offer their services in the more stimulating atmosphere of town-life, but decided to remain in this little town of Bagni-di-Lucca, which includes many of the surrounding mountain villages, and where the people are brave, industrious, and patriotic, knowing that I could do far more useful work in direct contact with the people, employing them in

101. Charles Lewis Slattery, "Help for Italy" (letter to the editor), *Churchman* 117 (January 12, 1918): 66.

Students at the Italian School in Bagni di Lucca, January 1919. Evangeline Whipple is in the center, back row, wearing hat. This photo was taken just two months after the death of Rose Cleveland. *Courtesy of Professor Marcello Cherubini, Bagni di Lucca.*

work for the soldiers, while helping and encouraging them in other ways.

I have been employing a large band of the poor women whose husbands and sons are at the front in war-work. Of course the expense of heating, lighting, and stocking the workrooms has become a serious matter as prices of everything are more than double. Especially is this so with wool, which must be used constantly.

You will have read of Italy's setback, of which I need not speak.[102] The refugees from the invaded places, like Gorizia, have inundated us like a tidal wave,[103] and the care of them is now added to the other burdens. They were obliged to flee in haste, and most of them are destitute of almost everything. Children in arms are constantly seen with nothing but a thin strip of old shawl to keep them from the biting cold. The difficulties of the food and fuel question, as of everything else, make the situation tragic. Shoes are now like rubies, but they are necessities in this climate.

Now I am helping to employ the refugees in my rooms, and work goes on at high pressure for the military hospitals in Lucca, at this moment. For example, within four days we have finished five hundred mattresses for the wounded soldiers who are being rushed in from the fields. In a case like that, however, the Government supplies the material, but I have to pay for the making and all else. Besides the hospital work, the women work steadily in knitting for the soldiers, and now I am trying to supply clothing for the refugees. Never was help so vitally needed. You understand that I am speaking of my especial undertaking. Of course, the Sindaco (the mayor) and Pro Patria are doing everything in their power, but they are overburdened, for in a country already reduced to extremities by the long war there is never enough. This will give you a

102. Whipple referenced the Battle of Caporetto (October 24–November 19, 1917), often called the greatest defeat in Italian military history.
103. The Battle of Caporetto displaced six hundred thousand people.

faint idea of what I am trying [to] do. I hope that I do not seem to be blowing my own trumpet! Far from it, I feel insignificant indeed in this great sea of sorrow and want.

Now comes the *raison d'être* of my letter. I know my countrymen well enough to know that could they realize onetenth of these necessities, not one hand would be withheld. I am asking you, who knows something of my ways and sympathies, if you think that there may be some great souls who would help one. If you shrink from asking this, in addition to the home demands, you must not do it. If, on the other hand, you have tried and generous hearts upon whom you count in times of stress, if you would echo my appeal from this gallant Italy, now fighting at white heat for honor and victory, it might bring me help for which my gratitude would be eternal.

Rose Cleveland and I are living together here, the other member of our house being Miss Ericksen [sic], the writer of many charming books on Italy. Miss Cleveland, whose voice is a power among the people, is all that you would expect her to be this time. Miss Ericksen is doing splendid work in sustaining loyalty in the village and factories of this province.

At home, while you had been admiring the almost superhuman accomplishment of the Italian fighters in the fearful Alpine regions, I have been giving many of them their woolen outfits, and receiving letters from hundreds of them from the trenches, for the men of the mountain villages [of] this Province of Lucca have had a noble record for bravery and high courage from the beginning, many of them having received medals. But after these years of hardship and constant fighting, and the anxiety of their suffering families, the bravest hearts must droop if not sustained by encouragement and so much of that can be done here. If I have to give up or curtail any part of it, it will break my heart.

Gratefully and sincerely yours,
Evangeline Whipple

The Spanish influenza epidemic arrived in Bagni di Lucca in 1918 and devastated the small community. Whipple, Cleveland, and Erichsen all nursed infected patients. When Erichsen came down with the disease herself while working in a makeshift hospital in town, Cleveland nursed Erichsen. Cleveland apparently contracted flu while adjusting a pillow for Erichsen, which caused her to cough directly in Cleveland's face. Erichsen died on November 15, four days after the signing of the armistice between the Allies and Germany; Cleveland died on November 22. Whipple wrote to her stepdaughter, Jane (Jennie) Whipple Scandrett, with details a month later. ∼

Evangeline Whipple to Jane Whipple Scandrett
Casa Bernadini/Bagni di Lucca[104] Villa, Italia
December 29, 1918

My dearest Jennie,
I was so glad to get your dear letter, and how gladly would I answer it with a long cheerful letter, fresh as it deserves, but I simply cannot write letters.

You will have heard long before this of the crushing & terrible tragedy which came to our household—both within ten days[105]—our house the centre of every activity and all of us so well, and in the thick of all good work, till the fatal Friday when our friend, the other member of our household of three, was seized by the awful scourge[106] and died within five days. The day after the funeral my precious & adored lifelong friend Rose Cleveland was taken by the same illness, and

104. Bagni di Lucca is an Italian town (*comune*) in Tuscany consisting of three small villages: Fornoli, Ponte a Serraglio, and La Villa (Bagni di Lucca). Whipple purchased three homes there: Villa San Francesco, Villa Burlamacchi, and Casa Bernadini.
105. It was ten days from the time Nelly Erichsen came down with influenza to Rose Cleveland's death on November 22, 1918.
106. Influenza.

five days later we were again winding our way to the *Campo Santo*.[107]

The light has gone out for me, but the work is too important for me to run away from. At first I thought I *could not* stay, but I see clearly that my record as a soldier must not be broken and I must stick to the trenches at whatever cost.[108]

The loss of this noble and great soul is a blow that I shall not recover from. I will try and write you about her splendid crusade against the epidemic, which was here more like the Medieval scourges in its awful sweep, but today I cannot.

I shall remain here. The people have made me a citizen of Bagni di Lucca, the only other one to have received the honor having been *Marion Crawford,* who was born here.[109]

Miss Cleveland's funeral was impressive & wonderful. The Ambassador at Rome sent the Amer[ican] Consul to represent him. By order of the mayor, all places of business were closed, and at every house was a flag at half mast tied with black. The mayor & other dignitaries & Amer[ican] Consul walked by the hearse holding the gold cords. Then the carriage with Mrs. Lawrence, Miss Cleveland's niece[110] and myself, then the Red Cross American & Italian nurses, and then the servants. Then all the people of the town—the comunal [*sic*] schools, the two large schools, both girls & boys of refugees,[111] one mine & one my friend's next bearing flowers, wreaths & the school flags at half mast. Then the great processing from the three villages of the town of the hundreds of refugees bearing their large wreaths. It was so still that you could not hear a sound all the way. She was wrapped in the American flag. The grave was lined with laurel. The casket was covered with

---

107. Italian: cemetery.
108. That is, she intended to continue doing humanitarian work.
109. Novelist Francis Marion Crawford (1854–1909).
110. Carrie Hastings Lawrence, Cleveland's niece, who lived in Florence.
111. Cleveland and Whipple administered the girls' school, and Erichsen the boys' school, for refugees in Bagni di Lucca.

crimson roses,[112] only the silver crucifix showing when it was lowered into its laurel bed. The consul & two others lowered the American flag over it and then masses of wonderful roses were thrown in and it was over.

Letters have come by hundreds testifying to the place she held in the hearts of the many who knew her in many lands. She was a great character—a passionate lover of her own country, a true friend of Italy, and her influence in these foul years of war has been wonderful.

Forgive me for not writing more, dearest one. Seas of love to you, & love to you all.

Evangeline.

After Cleveland's and Erichsen's deaths, Whipple continued to live in Bagni di Lucca. Jarrolds, a London publishing house, published her book A Famous Corner of Tuscany *in 1928. She continued to travel intermittently throughout Europe, for her health, for business, and for pleasure, and died in London from pneumonia and kidney failure on September 1, 1930. As she had requested in her will, she was buried next to Cleveland,[113] with an identical tombstone, in Bagni di Lucca.* ~

112. Cleveland identified with the flower for which she was named. She used it as a visual cue for her name on the cover of *George Eliot's Poetry, and Other Studies,* and Whipple often sent her rose bouquets. It is fitting that Whipple chose to drape Cleveland's casket in red roses.

113. Nelly Erichsen's grave is in the same plot, next to Cleveland's, with a flat, rectangular tombstone. The three graves underwent extensive restoration in 2012, partially funded by the Robert Neslund Memorial Fund, administered at that time by the Very Reverend James Zotalis at the Cathedral of Our Merciful Saviour in Faribault, Minnesota. The Comune di Bagni di Lucca, the Fondazione Montaigne, and the Rotary Club of Bagni di Lucca have continued to preserve and conserve the graves of foreigners in the English Cemetery.

The graves of (left to right) Nelly Erichsen, Rose Cleveland, and Evangeline Whipple in the English Cemetery, Bagni di Lucca, Italy, 2012. *Courtesy of Tilly Laskey.*

~ To the beloved and honored memory of Nelly Ericksen [*sic*] who died at Bagni di Lucca of the epidemic Spanish Fever Nov. 15, 1918 while working for the relief of the refugees in the Great War. Born at Newcastle on the Tyne, England. "Usque Ad Mortem Fidelis" (Faithful unto Death).

~ In sacred and loving memory of Rose Elizabeth Cleveland Born in New York, U.S.A. Author and philanthropist A loyal lover of her country And a true friend of Italy She died 22 Nov. 1918, at Bagni di Lucca stricken by the epidemic Spanish fever which, with her band of nurses, she was nobly combating among the refugees of the Great War. T. John.15.13

~ In loving remembrance of Evangeline E.T. Whipple born in Canton, Massachusetts, U.S.A. Wife of the Right Reverend Henry B. Whipple Bishop of Minnesota, U.S.A. An honorary citizen of Bagni di Lucca. Devoted to all good works, beloved by all her friends, loyal and unfaltering in her religious faith. She died 1 September, 1930 in London, England. Blessed are the dead which die in the Lord from henceforth yea, saith the spirit, that they may rest from their labors, and their works do follow them. Rev. XIV 13.

Appendix: Fragments

The following letter fragments, written in Cleveland's handwriting, are preserved in box two of the Whipple-Scandrett papers.[1] Although their labeling suggests that they were written in 1890, their references to Cleveland's property in Dark Harbor, Maine (not purchased until the 1900s), and to London place them between 1897 and 1909. Each fragment is written on a sheet of paper of a different size and color than the others, suggesting they do not belong together. ∾

[*fragment 1*]

. . . extraordinarily set on a long visit from you, set aside the whole month of August if possible and make it possible. Of course you can. There is every reason for it this year. Come to stay with us for August and go to England with me for September. Address answer to Dark Harbor, Maine.

1. Cleveland's correspondence in the MNHS is not a definitive set of love letters. The fragments, along with obvious gaps in the timeline, prove this. The search for additional letters continues, and the editors welcome suggestions from readers.

. . . This time together is due our past, Wingie, and due now. Let other things go and let me have this two months of glorious spree. I have a feeling that now is big with fate. Let it be August and September; we will give you all freedom.

Your C.

[fragment 2]

. . . Buckingham, I conclude you remain there yet awhile—at least long enough to receive them.

Mrs. Crosby's foreign address is
^c/o Brown, Shipley & Co,
Founder's Court
London
I have not heard from Mrs. Johnston (the operator left out the t) for a very long time, but when I last did, her address was still care of Drexel + Harges. If she is still around, she will . . .

. . . arrived here last week, but the first thing I saw on opening it was a package marked as a Xmas present from Brenner, so I discreetly forebore to look further and carefully locked away it and the box, untouched, as I perceived it was a premature investigation; but it was plain to see who the donor was, and when it is polite, the recipients will want to return thanks.

If you return to Boston, before you go South, will you please give me your dates for being there, and your address!

Always, with love,
Rose

[fragment 3]

. . . make those London men my rustic compliments! And your lovely father[2] my warm regards, and stroke (not kiss!) Dainty for me. Hug Motherdie.

2. This fragment was written prior to March 21, 1892, when Whipple's father, Dana F. Marrs, died.

Bibliography

Primary

Photo Coll. 165
Kingsmill Marrs photographs, ca. 1850–1915
Massachusetts Historical Society, Boston, MA

Ms.-N158
Kingsmill Marrs papers, 1836–1914
Massachusetts Historical Society, Boston, MA

III.40
Bishop Henry B. Whipple Indian photograph collection, 1860–1930
Audiovisual Collection, Minnesota Historical Society, St. Paul, MN

P789
Whipple-Scandrett Family papers, 1829–1959
Manuscript Collection, Minnesota Historical Society, St. Paul, MN

P823
Henry B. Whipple papers, 1833–1934
Manuscript Collection, Minnesota Historical Society, St. Paul, MN

M316
Allyn Kellogg Ford Collection of Historical Manuscripts
Minnesota Historical Society, St. Paul, MN

Church records and archives
Cathedral of Our Merciful Saviour, Faribault, MN

Whipple collection
Rice County Historical Society, Faribault, MN

Whipple collection
School archives, Shattuck–St. Mary's School, Faribault, MN

Bishop Henry Whipple collection
Church archives, St. Mark's Cathedral, Minneapolis, MN

Lucas, Lydia, and Duane Swanson (the former collections management supervisor and the manuscripts curator, respectively, of the Minnesota Historical Society). Interview with Lizzie Ehrenhalt, July 17, 2017.

Minnesota Historical Society. Internal memos, December 23, 1969, and March 24, 1978. Manuscripts accession file 10,990.

Sims, Terri (clerk of the Church of the Good Shepherd, Maitland, FL). Personal communication with Tilly Laskey, June 28, 2018.

Secondary

Africa, J. Simpson. *History of Huntingdon and Blair Counties, Pennsylvania.* Philadelphia: J. B. Lippincott & Co., 1883.

Allen, Anne Beiser. *And the Wilderness Shall Blossom: Henry Benjamin Whipple, Churchman, Educator, Advocate for the Indians,* Afton, MN: Afton Historical Society, 2008.

Altman, Janet Gurkin. *Epistolarity: Approaches to a Form.* Columbus: Ohio State University Press, 1982.

Anderson, Marcia. *A Bag Worth a Pony: The Art of the Ojibwe Bandolier Bag.* St. Paul: Minnesota Historical Society Press, 2017.

Anderson, Marcia, and Tilly Laskey. In Honor of the People, a collaboration between the Minnesota Historical Society and the

Science Museum of Minnesota, 2011. http://www.inhonorofthe people.org.

Andreadis, Harriette. *Sappho in Early Modern England: Female Same-Sex Literary Erotics, 1550–1714.* Chicago: University of Chicago Press, 2001.

Ayers, R. Wayne. *Florida's Grand Hotels from the Gilded Age.* Charleston, SC: Arcadia, 2005.

Barrows, Isabel C. *Proceedings of the Thirteenth Annual Meeting of the Mohonk Conference of Friends of the Indian, 1895.* New Paltz, NY: Lake Mohonk Conference, 1896.

Berch, Bettina. *The Woman Behind the Lens: The Life and Work of Frances Benjamin Johnston, 1864–1952.* Charlottesville: University of Virginia Press, 2000.

Brewer, Celeste. "Processing LGBTQ Collections Then and Now: The Ben Duncan and Dick Chapman Papers Come Out." *Archival Outlook* (May/June 2018): 4–5.

Bronski, Michael. "Dangerous Purity." In *A Queer History of the United States*, 83–103. Boston: Beacon Press, 2011.

Buick, Kirsten. *Child of the Fire: Mary Edmonia Lewis and the Problem of Art History's Black and Indian Subject.* Durham and London: Duke University Press, 2010.

Carter, Julian. "Introduction: Theory, Methods, Praxis: The History of Sexuality and the Question of Evidence." *Journal of the History of Sexuality* 14, nos. 1–2 (January-April 2005): 1–9.

Cleves, Rachel Hope. *Charity and Sylvia: A Same-Sex Marriage in Early America.* Oxford, UK: Oxford University Press, 2014.

Cocks, Catherine. "Rethinking Sexuality in the Gilded Age and Progressive Era." *Journal of the Gilded Age and Progressive Era* 5, no. 2 (April 2006): 93–118.

Coe, Alexis. *Alice + Freda Forever: A Murder in Memphis.* San Francisco: Pulp, 2014.

Cusick, Dennis Charles. "Gentleman of the Press: The Life and Times of Walter Newman Haldeman." Master's thesis, University of Louisville, 1987.

Cutler, Harry Gardner. *History of Florida: Past and Present, Historical and Biographical.* Vol. 2. Chicago and New York: Lewis Publishing Co., 1923.

D'Emilio, John, and Estelle Freedman. *Intimate Matters: A History of Sexuality in America.* New York: Harper & Row, 1988.

Dever, Maryanne. "Papered Over, or Some Observations on Materiality and Archival Method." In *Out of the Closet, Into the Archives: Researching Sexual Histories*, edited by Amy L. Stone and Jaime Cantrell, 65–95. Albany: State University of New York, 2015.

Donoghue, Emma. "Doing Lesbian History, Then and Now." *Historical Reflections / Réflexions Historique* 33, no. 1 (Spring 2007): 15–22.

Duggan, Lisa. *Sapphic Slashers: Sex, Violence, and American Modernity*. Durham, NC: Duke University Press, 2000.

Eaton, Harriet. *This Birth Place of Souls: The Civil War Nursing Diary of Harriet Eaton*. Edited by Jane E. Schultz. Oxford and New York: Oxford University Press, 2011.

Emery, Helen Fitch. *The Puritan Village Evolves: A History of Wayland, Massachusetts*. Canaan, NH: Phoenix Publishing, 1981.

Erichsen, Nelly. "Debris of the War." *Anglo-Italian Review* 1 (1918): 166–73.

Eskridge, William N. Jr. *Dishonorable Passions: Sodomy Laws in America, 1861–2003*. New York: Penguin, 2008.

Faderman, Lillian. *Odd Girls and Twilight Lovers: A History of Lesbian Life in Twentieth-Century America*. New York: Penguin, 1991.

———. *Surpassing the Love of Men: Romantic Friendship and Love Between Women from the Renaissance to the Present*. New York: William Morrow and Co., 1981.

———. *To Believe in Women: What Lesbians Have Done for America—A History*. Boston and New York: Houghton Mifflin, 1999.

Flint, Kate. "Unspeakable Desires: We Other Victorians." In *The Oxford Handbook of Victorian Literary Culture*, edited by Juliet John, 193–209. Oxford, UK: Oxford University Press, 2016.

Foucault, Michel. *The History of Sexuality: An Introduction, Volume 1*. New York: Vintage Books edition, 1990.

Freedman, Estelle B. "'The Burning of Letters Continues': Elusive Identities and the Historical Construction of Sexuality." *Journal of Women's History* 9, no. 4 (Winter 1998): 181–200.

Giambastiani, Laura. "Considerazioni Storiche Sul Cimitero Anglicano al Bagni di Lucca." *L'Aldila, Rivista di Storia della Tanatologia* Anno IX, nos. 1–2 (2004): 46–77.

Goldhill, Simon. *A Very Queer Family Indeed: Sex, Religion, and the Bensons in Victorian Britain*. Chicago and London: University of Chicago Press, 2016.

Hall, Elton Wayland, and Frederick Garrison Hall. *Etchings, Bookplates, Designs.* Boston: Boston Public Library, 1972.

Hall, Lesley A. "Scientific Sex, Unspeakable Oscar, and Insurgent Women in the 'Naughty Nineties.'" In *Sex, Gender, and Social Change in Britain Since 1880,* 43–56. Basingstoke, UK: Palgrave Macmillan, 2013.

Hardy, Rob. "The Passion of Rose Elizabeth Cleveland." *New England Review* 28, no. 1 (2007): 180–93.

———. "Rose and Evangeline." Northfield Patch, May 16, 2012. https://patch.com/minnesota/northfield/bp--rose-and-evangeline.

Harkness, Sarah. *Nelly Erichsen: A Hidden Life.* Cheltenham, UK: Encanta Publishing, 2018.

Herring, Stephen W. *Framingham: An American Town.* Framingham, MA: Framingham Historical Society, 2000.

Hewitt, Elizabeth. "Prologue: Networks of Nineteenth-Century Letter-Writing." In *The Edinburgh Companion to Nineteenth-Century American Letters and Letter-Writing,* edited by Celeste-Marie Bernier, Judie Newman, and Matthew Pethers, 1–10. Edinburgh: Edinburgh University Press, 2016.

Horowitz, Helen Lefkowitz. *The Power and Passion of M. Carey Thomas.* New York: Alfred A. Knopf, 1994.

———. *Rereading Sex: Battles Over Sexual Knowledge and Suppression in Nineteenth-Century America.* New York: Vintage Books, 2003.

Hull, Gloria T. "Angelina Weld Grimké (1880–1958)." In *Color, Sex, and Poetry: Three Women Writers of the Harlem Renaissance,* 107–54. Bloomington: Indiana University Press, 1987.

Hunter, Jane. H. *How Young Ladies Became Girls: The Victorian Origins of American Girlhood.* New Haven and London: Yale University Press, 2002.

Hurd, Duane Hamilton. *History of Essex County, Massachusetts, With Biographical Sketches of Many of Its Pioneers and Prominent Men.* Vol. 2. Philadelphia: J. W. Lewis, 1888.

Inness, Sherrie A. "Mashes, Smashes, Crushes, and Raves: Woman-to-Woman Relationships in Popular Women's College Fiction, 1895–1915." *National Women's Studies Association Journal* 6, no. 1 (1994): 48–68.

Katz, Jonathan Ned. "The President's Sister and the Bishop's Wife:

An *Advocate* Inauguration Special." *Advocate* 517 (January 31, 1989): 34–35.

Keim, De Benneville Randolph. *Society in Washington: Its Noted Men, Accomplished Women, Established Customs, and Notable Events.* Washington, DC: Harrisburg Publishing Co., 1887.

Kleber, John E. *Encyclopedia of Louisville.* Louisville: University Press of Kentucky, 2015.

Lachman, Charles. *A Secret Life: The Lies and Scandals of President Grover Cleveland.* New York: Skyhorse Publishing, 2012.

Laskey, Tilly. "A Famous Corner of Tuscany: Evangeline Whipple's Community Development and Philanthropic Efforts in Bagni di Lucca, Italy, Based on Work with Minnesota Indian Nations." *Anglistica Pisana* 10, nos. 1–2 (2013): 35–47.

Lewis, Alfred Allan. *Ladies and Not-So-Gentle Women: Elisabeth Marbury, Anne Morgan, Elsie de Wolfe, Anne Vanderbilt, and Their Times.* New York: Penguin Books, 2001.

Lewis, Susan Ingalls, and Morgan Gwenwald. "Year of the British Blondes." *New York Archives* 13, no. 2 (Fall 2013): 18–22.

Madden, Etta, and Sarah Harkness. "Nelly Erichsen: Writing and Sketching for the House of Dent." *Anglistica Pisana* 10, nos. 1–2 (2013): 49–59.

Marcus, Sharon. *Between Women: Friendship, Desire, and Marriage in Victorian England.* Princeton, NJ: Princeton University Press, 2007.

Marshall, Gail, ed. *The Cambridge Companion to the Fin de Siècle.* Cambridge, UK: Cambridge University Press, 2007.

Martin, Sylvia. "'These Walls of Flesh': The Problem of the Body in the Romantic Friendship/Lesbianism Debate." *Historical Reflections/ Réflexions Historiques* 20, no. 2 (Summer 1994): 243–66.

Maynard, Steven. "'The Burning, Wilful Evidence': Lesbian/Gay History and Archival Research." *Archivaria* 33 (Winter 1991–92): 195–201.

McGuire, Riley. "The Victorian Unspeakable: Stammering and Same-Sex Intimacy Between Men." *DiGeSt: Journal of Diversity and Gender Studies* 3, no. 2 (2016): 43–57.

Moore, Lisa. "'Something More Tender Still Than Friendship': Romantic Friendship in Early-Nineteenth-Century England." *Feminist Studies* 18, no. 3 (Fall 1992): 499–520.

Neslund, Robert. *For a Life of Learning and Service: How Shattuck–*

St. Mary's Came to Be. Faribault, MN: Shattuck–St. Mary's School, 2008.

Newman, Sally. "The Archival Traces of Desire: Vernon Lee's Failed Sexuality and the Interpretation of Letters in Lesbian History." *Journal of the History of Sexuality* 14, nos. 1–2 (January–April 2005): 51–75.

Newton, Esther. "The Mythic Mannish Lesbian: Radclyffe Hall and the New Woman." *Signs* 9, no. 4 (Summer 1984): 557–75.

Novotny, Ann. *Alice's World: The Life and Photography of an American Original, Alice Austen, 1866–1952*. Old Greenwich, CT: Chatham Press, 1976.

Petrik, Paula. "Into the Open: Lesbianism at the Turn of the Century; Rose Elizabeth Cleveland and Evangeline Marrs Simpson Whipple." Unpublished paper, 1978. Lesbian Herstory Archives, New York.

Poole, Leslie Kemp. "The Women of the Early Florida Audubon Society: Agents of History in the Fight to Save State Birds." *Florida Historical Quarterly* 85, no. 3 (Winter 2007): 297–323.

Putzi, Jennifer. "Two *Single* Married Women: The Correspondence of Elizabeth Stoddard and Margaret Sweat, 1851–1854." In *Letters and Cultural Transformation in the United States, 1760–1860*, edited by Theresa Strouth Gaul and Sharon M. Harris, 117–35. London: Routledge, 2009.

Robar, Stephen F. *Frances Clara Folsom Cleveland*. New York: Nova Science Publishers, 2004.

Rodriguez, Suzanne. *Wild Heart: A Life: Natalie Clifford Barney's Journey from Victorian America to the Literary Salons of Paris*. New York: Harper Collins, 2002.

Romiti, Antonio, ed. "Il Cimitero Anglicano di Bagni di Lucca." In *L'Aldilà: Rivista di Storia della Tanatologia*. Lucca, Italy: Istituto Storico Lucchese, 2003.

Rupp, Leila J. *Sapphistries: A Global History of Love Between Women*. New York: New York University Press, 2009.

Rutherford, Mildred Lewis. *The South in History and Literature: A Hand-book of Southern Authors, from the Settlement of Jamestown, 1607, to Living Writers*. [Atlanta]: [Franklin-Turner], 1906.

Salenius, Sirpa. *Rose Elizabeth Cleveland: First Lady and Literary Scholar*. Basingstoke, UK: Palgrave MacMillan, 2014.

Scannell, John James, and William Edgar Sackett. *Scannell's New*

Jersey's First Citizens and State Guide, 1919–1920. Vol. 2. Paterson, NJ: J. J. Scannell, 1919.

Schwartz, Judith. "The Archivists' Balancing Act: Helping Researchers While Protecting Individual Privacy." *Journal of American History* 79, no. 1 (June 1992): 179–89.

Scott, Benjamin Ives, and Robert Neslund. *The First Cathedral, an Episcopal Community for Mission.* Faribault, MN: The Cathedral of Our Merciful Saviour, 1987.

Shettleworth, Earl G. Jr. *Summer Cottages of Islesboro, 1890–1930.* Islesboro, ME: Islesboro Historical Society, 1989.

Sibley, Katherine A. S. *A Companion to First Ladies.* New York: John Wiley & Sons, 2016.

Skidmore, Emily. "The Last Female Husband: New Boundaries of Identity in the Late Nineteenth Century." In *True Sex: The Lives of Trans Men at the Turn of the Twentieth Century,* 15–42. New York: New York University Press, 2017.

Slattery, Charles Lewis. *Rose Elizabeth Cleveland: A Sermon Preached to the Colonial Dames of the State of New York in Grace Church in New York on Sunday, January 26, 1919.* [New York]: N.p., 1919.

Smith, Jane S. *Elsie de Wolfe: A Life in the High Style.* New York: Atheneum, 1982.

Smith-Rosenberg, Carroll. "The Female World of Love and Ritual: Relations Between Women in Nineteenth-Century America." *Signs* 1, no. 1 (1975): 1–29.

Stanley, Liz. "The Epistolarium: On Theorizing Letters and Correspondences." *Auto/Biography* 12, no. 3 (September 2004): 201–35.

———. "Romantic Friendship? Some Issues in Researching Lesbian History and Biography." *Women's History Review* 1, no. 2 (1992): 193–216.

Stanley, Liz, Andrea Salter, and Helen Dampier. "The Epistolary Pact, Letterness, and the Schreiner Epistolarium." *a/b: Auto/Biography Studies* 27, no. 2 (June 7, 2012): 262–93.

Stevens, Lewis Townsend. *The History of Cape May County, New Jersey: From the Aboriginal Times to Present Day.* Cape May City, NJ: Lewis T. Stevens, 1897.

Tawa, Nicholas E. *From Psalm to Symphony: A History of Music in New England.* Boston: Northeastern University Press, 2001.

Trefusis, Violet. *Violet to Vita: The Letters of Violet Trefusis to Vita Sackville-West, 1910–1921.* London: Penguin, 1991.

Vicinus, Martha. "The History of Lesbian History." *Feminist Studies* 38, no. 3 (Fall 2012): 566–96.

———. *Independent Women: Work and Community for Single Women, 1850–1920*. Chicago: University of Chicago Press, 1988.

———. *Intimate Friends: Women Who Loved Women, 1778–1928*. Chicago: University of Chicago Press, 2004.

———. "Lesbian History: All Theory and No Facts or All Facts and No Theory?" *Radical History Review* 60 (1994): 57–75.

Wheeler, Leigh Anne. "Inventing Sexuality: Ideologies, Identities, and Practices in the Gilded Age and Progressive Era." In *A Companion to the Gilded Age and Progressive Era*, edited by Christopher McKnight Nichols and Nancy C. Unger, 102–15. Somerset, UK: John Wiley & Sons, 2017.

Whipple, Henry Benjamin. *Lights and Shadows of a Long Episcopate.* New York: MacMillan & Co., 1899.

Wrathall, John D. "Provenance As Text: Reading the Silences Around Sexuality in Manuscript Collections." *Journal of American History* 79, no. 1 (June 1992): 165–78.

Rose Cleveland's Published Works

"The Dilemma of the Nineteenth Century." *Lippincott's Monthly Magazine* 39, no. 1 (January–June 1887): 140.

George Eliot's Poetry, and Other Studies. New York: Funk & Wagnalls, 1885.

"The Highest, the Best." *Warsaw Daily Times,* March 15, 1887.

"Introduction." In *How to Win: A Book for Girls,* by Frances Willard, 5th ed. New York: Funk & Wagnalls, 1888. https://archive.org /details/howtowinabookfooowillgoog.

"Introduction." In *Our Society: A Complete Treatise of the Usages That Govern the Most Refined Homes and Social Circles. Our Moral, Social, Physical and Business Culture,* 9–16. Detroit: Darling Publishing, 1893.

"Introduction." In *The Social Mirror: A Complete Treatise on the Laws, Rules, and Usages That Govern Our Most Refined Homes and Social Circles,* 9–16. St. Louis, MO: F. B. Dickerson, 1888. https://play .google.com/store/books/details?id=tF8EAAAAYAAJ].

"Introduction." In *You and I, or Moral, Intellectual and Social Culture,*

9–18. Detroit: F. B. Dickerson, 1886. http://babel.hathitrust.org
/cgi/pt?id=mdp.39015071584588;view=1up;seq=11.

The Long Run. Detroit: F. B. Dickerson, 1886.

"My Florida." *Lippincott's Monthly Magazine* 46, no. 4 (October 1890):
521–28.

"Robin Adair." *Godey's Lady's Book* (January–February 1887): 26–32,
136–40.

The Soliloquies of St. Augustine. Translator. Boston: Little, Brown and
Co., 1910.

"Woman in the Home." *Chautauquan*, January 1887.

Evangeline Whipple's Published Works

Simpson, Evangeline Marrs [Van Saxon, pseud.]. *Marplot Cupid.* Boston: W. B. Clarke & Carruth, 1883.

Whipple, Evangeline. *A Famous Corner of Tuscany.* London: Jarrolds,
1928.

Index

Page numbers in *italics* indicate illustrations.
REC is used in the index for Rose Elizabeth Cleveland.
EMW is used in the index for Evangeline Marrs Simpson Whipple.